W9-BSZ-149

How to Plan for a Secure Retirement

HOW TO PLAN FOR A SECURE RETIREMENT

Barry Dickman
Trudy Lieberman

and the Editors of
Consumer Reports Books

CONSUMER REPORTS BOOKS
A Division of Consumers Union
Yonkers, New York

Library of Congress Cataloging-in-Publication Data

Dickman, Barry.
How to plan for a secure retirement / Barry Dickman, Trudy Lieberman, and the editors of Consumer Reports Books.
p. cm.
Includes index.
ISBN 0-89043-338-0
1. Retirement—United States—Planning. 2. Retirement income—United States—Planning. I. Lieberman, Trudy. II. Consumer Reports Books. III. Title.
HG1063.2.U6D55 1992 92-8733
646.7′9—dc20 CIP

Certain portions of the tax information contained in this book have been drawn from Consumer Reports Books *Guide to Income Tax Preparation* by Warren H. Esanu, Barry Dickman, Elias H. Zuckerman, Michael N. Pollet, and the Editors of Consumer Reports Books, who with the law firm of Esanu, Katsky, Korins & Siger, Inc., have given their permission to use this material.

Annuity tables on pages 85 and 86 courtesy of
Jackson National Life Insurance Company.

Design by GDS / Jeffrey L. Ward
Fourth printing, October 1994
Manufactured in the United States of America

How to Plan for a Secure Retirement is a Consumer Reports Book published by Consumers Union, the nonprofit organization that publishes *Consumer Reports*, the monthly magazine of test reports, product Ratings, and buying guidance. Established in 1936, Consumers Union is chartered under the Not-for-Profit Corporation Law of the State of New York.

The purposes of Consumers Union, as stated in its charter, are to provide consumers with information and counsel on consumer goods and services, to give information on all matters relating to the expenditure of the family income, and to initiate and to cooperate with individual and group efforts seeking to create and maintain decent living standards.

Consumers Union derives its income solely from the sale of *Consumer Reports* and other publications. In addition, expenses of occasional public service efforts may be met, in part, by nonrestrictive, noncommercial contributions, grants, and fees. Consumers Union accepts no advertising or product samples and is not beholden in any way to any commercial interest. Its Ratings and reports are solely for the use of the readers of its publications. Neither the Ratings, nor the reports, nor any Consumers Union publications, including this book, may be used in advertising or for any commercial purpose. Consumers Union will take all steps open to it to prevent such uses of its material, its name, or the name of *Consumer Reports*.

To my wife, Carol, whose support means more than words can say, and to the other writers in my family, my children, Steve and Sue

—Barry Dickman

To my parents, Belle and Abe Lieberman, with love

—Trudy Lieberman

Contents

Acknowledgments

Thanks to my partner Elias M. Zuckerman for his help with the tax aspects of retirement; to my associate Beverly Au for her research assistance; to my assistants, Judi Murphy and Carla Tiller, for their diligence in typing and revising the manuscript; and to my colleagues at Esanu, Katsky, Korins & Siger for their patience during the lengthy drafting process.

—Barry Dickman

Thanks to Richard Foster, F.S.A., deputy chief actuary of the Social Security Administration, and to Roy Ferguson, F.S.A., actuary of the Social Security Administration, for their careful and thorough reading of the Social Security chapter; to Donald Grubbs, F.S.A., of Grubbs and Company, both for the many hours spent in explaining the finer points of pensions and retirement income, and for his invaluable suggestions for improving several chapters of this book; to Bonnie Burns of the California Health Insurance Counseling & Advocacy Program for her reading of the health insurance chapters and her tutelage in matters of importance to retirees; to Katie Sloan of the American Association of Retired Persons for her help with the chapter on home equity financing; to Ray Gill and Letty Carpenter of the Health Care Financing Administration, for their help in explaining two complicated programs for the elderly—Medicare and Medicaid; to Marge Frohne of Consumers Union for her assistance and moral support during the preparation of the manuscript; to my editor at Consumer Reports Books, Julie Henderson, for her patience and help in making this a better book. Above all, I owe much to the understanding and love of my husband and daughter, Andrew and Kirsten Eiler, who gave up many a family outing so I could complete this project.

—Trudy Lieberman

HOW TO PLAN FOR A SECURE RETIREMENT

Introduction

Fifty years ago when a man or woman retired, he or she probably had no pension and little savings. Social Security was in its infancy, and the monthly checks from the government barely covered the essentials of retired life. Of course, the average retiree could not expect to live too many more years either.

Today when a man or woman retires, he or she may have both a pension and a savings account, mutual fund, IRA, or a 401(k) plan. Social Security now keeps pace with inflation, and today's 65-year-old man (if he doesn't smoke) can expect to live another 18 years; a woman can expect another 21 years.

Improved Social Security benefits and, to a lesser extent, the growth of private pensions have made many retirees fairly well off financially. Once one of the poorest groups in the United States, the elderly are now among the more affluent. Years of unparalleled postwar prosperity and pension benefits that earlier generations never expected or received have given many retirees respectable incomes and a sizable array of assets. For men over 65, the median income has climbed to nearly $12,000; for women it's almost $8,000. And thanks to the appreciation of their homes, households where the head is 65 or older have an average net worth of more than $60,000.

But increased wealth and longevity mean that retiring is no longer a simple matter. Along with learning how to apply for Social Security and submit Medicare forms, today's retiree must decide:

- Which pension options are best for me?
- Should I convert my savings to an annuity?
- Does it make sense to set up a trust?
- Should I buy an insurance policy to pay for nursing home care?
- What about cashing in old life insurance policies?

Financial services companies have responded to this growing market by offering a profusion of products and plans they claim will answer these questions. Amid their frequent warnings that prospective retirees will not have enough income in retirement to maintain their current life-styles, older Americans are urged to save money and invest in various financial plans, funds, and insurance policies. Whether retirees really need the amount of money recommended by these financial sages is questionable. It is clear, however, that the so-called graying of America, the increasing interest in early retirement, and today's economic uncertainties have resulted in a proliferation of financial products that makes life for retirees and prospective retirees complicated indeed.

This book is intended for those in their sixties or seventies who have already retired, for those in their fifties who are contemplating retirement, and for those under 50 who must cope with the concerns of aging parents or who are beginning to think about their future retirement.

The book covers only the financial aspects of leaving the work force. It will not, for example, help you buy a condominium in Florida or an Airstream trailer for cross-country travel. But it will help you understand life-care communities, the pitfalls of reverse mortgages, and the way your pension will be paid.

Part One, Income, tells you what to expect from Social Security, the pension from your employer, and any savings you have accumulated through IRA, Keogh, and 401(k) accounts. It shows you how to use annuities to produce a steady income and how large your tax bill will be after you retire. There are also pointers on managing your assets should you become incapacitated.

Part Two, Health Care, explains Medicare, the federal government's insurance plan for those 65 and over; health coverage provided by your employer; Medicare-supplement insurance policies, which fill gaps in coverage left by Medicare; long-term-care insurance, which pays for nursing home stays; and Medicaid, which picks up the bill for nursing home care when you are unable to pay. This section also shows you how much to budget for health-insurance premiums and discusses special health-care decisions, such as writing a living will or making organ donations.

Part Three, Housing, describes how reverse mortgages work, notes their pros and cons, and discusses the tax consequences if you opt for one. This part details special tax provisions that apply to elderly homeowners, as well as the financial underpinnings of life-care communities, an increasingly popular form of housing for senior citizens.

Part Four, Estate Planning, discusses wills, trusts, gifts, taxes, and other aspects of organizing your estate.

The appendixes describe where to find your state agency on aging and whether or not your state has a high-risk insurance pool or counseling services for people who need help with insurance problems; identify those states that allow living wills and/or health-care proxies as well as those states with property tax relief programs; and furnish a list of organ donor organizations, Department of Housing and Urban Development field offices, and national senior citizens organizations.

The appendixes also contain worksheets and checklists to help you make financial decisions and detailed plans for your retirement. Many of the decisions you will be making involve trade-offs of one sort or another—it's rarely possible to have everything you want, or think you want, during your retirement years. But this book will make the business of preparing for a future outside of the work force less complex and should speed you on your way to a long, secure, and comfortable retirement.

PART ONE

Income

1

Getting Ready to Retire

WILL YOU HAVE ENOUGH MONEY?

The overriding question facing you as you prepare to retire is whether you will have enough money to live comfortably. Ideally, you should begin planning for retirement the day you take your first job, and saving for your future should continue throughout your entire working life. But in actual practice, putting aside money for a far-off retirement is not always possible—taking vacations, paying school tuitions, and balancing credit card payments often get in the way of building up an adequate retirement fund. Often families come up short on the eve of retirement; many people must continue working, whether or not they want to, because their living costs are greater than their income.

HOW MUCH YOU NEED

Conventional wisdom says that you need less income in retirement than during your working years. How much less depends on your situation and your expectations. The rule of thumb is that you need between 70 and 80 percent of your preretirement monthly income to maintain a comparable standard of living in retirement, but some people need more and some less. Many pension plans are designed so that you receive, along with Social Security benefits, a certain percentage of preretirement income, usually 50 to 80 percent.

The amount of retirement income you need also depends on whether your spouse continues to work. If he or she remains in the work force for several more years after you retire, your immediate need for income may be less important. In that case, keep your nest egg invested for growth as long as possible. Housing costs are another consideration. If your home is already paid for, you may need less income than if you have a hefty mortgage or pay rent each month.

When you retire, some of your monthly expenditures will go down. For example, you won't be paying Medicare taxes, union dues, or even Social Security taxes (unless you continue to work part-time or have a lot of income from investments). You may also spend less for commuting and clothing. However, other costs will increase.

One of the biggest increases you are likely to face in your retirement expenditures is health-insurance premiums. This is certainly the case if your employer pays for your health coverage and you currently have no significant out-of-pocket medical expenses. If you retire at age 65, you will have to pay for Medicare Part B premiums, scheduled to rise to over $500 a year by 1995 and sure to increase after that. In addition, a good Medicare-supplement policy costs between $1,000 and $2,000 a year, and good long-term-care coverage adds another $1,500 to $2,000. If your spouse also needs coverage, double those amounts. What all this means is your postretirement health-insurance bill can easily total $6,000 to $8,000 a year unless your spouse continues to work and you can obtain coverage under his or her policy.

Automobile insurance premiums are likely to remain the same, although many companies give discounts to retirees, who they consider to be better risks than younger drivers. Inquire about these discounts from your current insurer. Expenditures for life insurance should also go down unless you have a specific need to continue your policy. Most older people don't.

You may find yourself spending more money on leisure activities and hobbies. If you spend more time at home, utility bills may increase too. If you decide to begin a new business, you'll face start-up expenses.

If your housing costs are substantial and you're worried about paying for maintenance and repairs later on, you may want to move to smaller, less expensive, and easier-to-maintain quarters. Check out the benefits of any tax breaks from the sale of your home (see chapter 15).

Worksheets: Adding Up Your Assets and Expenses

At least 10 years before you retire, you should have a good idea of what your monthly and yearly expenses are and what you need in the way of income to sustain your current lifestyle. Complete Worksheet 1, Preretirement Income and Expenses, in Appendix A. By listing your monthly income and monthly expenses, you will get a sense of your cash flow and how it supports your current standard of living. For example, if you are taking money out of savings or using credit card debt to pay bills each month, then your expenses exceed your income. If you are adding to savings every month, then your income is sufficient to cover your bills. Obviously, in the years prior to retirement, add as much as you can to your savings. If expenses regularly exceed your income, reexamine your spending and try to increase your savings cushion as you approach your retirement years.

Worksheet 2, Your Savings and Investments, in Appendix A helps you categorize your savings and tells you at a glance where your money is accumulating. The worksheet also helps you decide whether it's wiser to invest your money in other types of instruments or investments that may net a larger return.

As the retirement date draws closer, complete Worksheet 3, Postretirement Expenses, in Appendix A. Unless your spouse is still working or you plan to work part-time, your income will come mainly from Social Security, employer pensions, IRA and Keogh plans, 401(k) plans, and any savings that you have converted to annuity income. If you have worked for several employers and have earned a pension from each, contact the benefits administrator from each employer and ask for an estimate of what your pension will be worth. (Use total pension income in completing the worksheet.)

Once you have completed the preretirement and postretirement worksheets, you can fill in Worksheet 4, Will You Have Enough Money?, in Appendix A. (We recommend that you complete this worksheet every few years to find out whether your projected income will match projected expenses.) If your expenses exceed income and other resources, you have to make some changes. For example, you may have to postpone your retirement date, change plans about selling your home and buying a new one, work part-time to supplement your income, or increase your savings.

Note: All items in the worksheets are measured in present dollars. Items not expected to grow at the rate of inflation are adjusted for the difference between their rate of growth and the assumed 5 percent rate of inflation. Investments are assumed to earn 4 percent more than inflation. If the worksheets show that your projected resources will meet your needs measured in present dollars, then you can expect the growth in your resources to keep up with inflation *if* you follow some of our guidelines in this chapter.

Make several copies of the worksheets so that you can reuse them as your circumstances change.

STRATEGIES FOR MATCHING INCOME AND EXPENSES

Three or four years before retirement—ideally much earlier—consider your options for getting the most retirement income possible in your situation. Carefully weigh the various annuity payouts versus lump-sum payments, investment vehicles that may supply you with other spare cash, and ways that your money can continue to grow after you leave the work force. Too often people fail to look beyond the first couple of years of retirement. You should look at least 10 to 20 years into the future and make sure your income will be sufficient to match increasing expenses resulting from inflation in later years.

Let's look at the facts. At an inflation rate of 5 percent a year, prices will double in 14 years and quadruple in 28 years. For this reason, you should continue to invest a portion of your retirement savings for steady growth. Even if you choose an annuity option that provides a fixed monthly payment, keep some of your cash free and prudently invested so that your money will grow and help cover higher expenses in your later years. But be careful—don't go overboard, especially with stocks. If you decide to invest all your spare cash for growth, you could take a loss if you are forced to sell an investment when the stock market is down. Be sure you are comfortable with this risk before investing.

INVESTING FOR THE FUTURE

No one knows what may happen to change the current financial scene, but your money has the best chance of growing if you put part of it into a diversified portfolio of stocks or stock mutual funds. Over a 65-year period, from 1926 to 1990, the average annual return on common stocks was 10.1 percent, compared to 3.7 percent for U.S. Treasury bills, 4.5 percent for long-term government bonds, and 5.2 percent for long-term corporate bonds. Small-company stocks returned an average of 11.6 percent. In general, stocks of small companies returned more than those of larger companies, although they involve more risk.

If you can't sleep at night worrying about the ups and downs of the stock market, then choose more predictable and conservative investments, such as municipal bonds or bank CDs. But remember, over a long period these investments probably won't keep pace with inflation. And make investments for the long term, not because you expect the market to rise (or fall) over the next year or so. Market values of stocks always rise and fall over time, so don't panic and sell when the value initially falls.

It's also wiser to choose investment vehicles for their return rather than for tax considerations. Differences in investment results generally outweigh any tax savings. Furthermore, tax laws change, and you don't know what the law will be when you decide to cash in your investments. But if two investments appear equal, then tax considerations might tip the balance.

It's important to keep your acquisition expenses as low as possible, and you can do that by buying no-load, that is, without a sales charge, mutual funds. Select funds that have no loads, no redemption charges, and low expense charges. Unless you are an expert who can spend 40 hours a week studying investments, don't try to decide what individual stocks to buy. Stock mutual funds allow you to invest in a diversified portfolio of many stocks, under the management of investment professionals. Be cautious in dealing with stockbrokers and others who get a commission on the investments they sell. They can provide helpful information, but don't expect them to be completely objective about the investments they recommend or too concerned about possible losses.

OTHER SAVINGS STRATEGIES

As you head into retirement, begin to repay any outstanding debts. Once you are living on a fixed income, you don't want to be struggling to pay off loans that you took out years before, especially home equity loans. (However, in your later retirement years, you may have to tap the equity in your home to meet monthly expenses.)

Also repay any outstanding loans on your life insurance policies. This is especially important if you are counting on insurance to provide income for a spouse after your death. Policy loans and the nondeductible interest on them decrease the value of the death benefit as well as the amount of cash value you'll receive if you cash in the policy. If you forget about an old life insurance loan and die suddenly, your spouse or your children will be left with less than you had intended. If you cash in the policy (as most older people should) and haven't paid off the old loan, you'll receive less to invest elsewhere.

CONVERTING SAVINGS TO *RETIREMENT INCOME*

When you retire you have to convert your savings into a monthly income stream. None of the options for doing that is perfect. Each strategy has its advantages and disadvantages.

Purchase a fixed annuity from a life insurance company. An annuity provides an income for you and your spouse for as long as you live. In other words, you can't outlive your income. However, your monthly payment is fixed and won't increase over time. If you live for 20 or more years after buying the annuity, your monthly payment is bound to shrink in value. In 1991, you could buy about $7 of monthly income for each $1,000 put into the annuity. Converting $100,000 of savings yields $700 of monthly income (see chapter 4).

Buy a variable annuity from a life insurance company. Over several years the income keeps pace with inflation, but the income fluctuates each month. For most people, living with this kind of uncertainty is difficult—erratic income levels don't always get the bills paid.

Use your savings over your life expectancy. Few people, however, can predict how long they will live. If you outlive your life expectancy, you could run out of money.

Live off the income from your current investments. If your investments grow with inflation, this strategy may work. But if you have mostly bonds and CDs that produce high income now, they are unlikely to grow much more. On the other hand, if you select only investments for growth, you may have little current income. This strategy requires a careful mix of your investments.

Invest for long-term total growth and use a portion of your investments for monthly expenses. This is the "4 percent strategy." One pension consultant recommends investing with the expectation that your return will average about 4 percent more than inflation. For example, if inflation is running about 5 percent, try to earn an average of 9 percent; if at 3 percent, try for 7 percent, and so forth.

The adviser also suggests using 1⁄12 of 4 percent of your income-producing investments each month for current expenses after you retire. Each year, recalculate the market value of your investments. If the value has risen, increase your monthly amount of savings to one-twelfth of the new amount. If the value has not increased or has decreased, continue to use the amount you started with for another year. If your investments earn 4 percent more than inflation, your monthly retirement income will rise 4 percent each year (this probably won't happen every year). Your actual return will vary substantially from year to year, exceeding the expectation of earning 4 percent in some years and becoming negative in other years. For example, the return on stocks was −26 percent in 1974 and +37 percent in 1975. This strategy gives you less money initially, but if you live a long time after retiring, it is your best chance of maintaining an adequate income for the rest of your life.

Example: Your retirement nest egg amounts to $300,000. During the first year of retirement you withdraw 4 percent—$12,000 annually or $1,000 monthly. If your $300,000 earns 9 percent or $27,000 ($300,000 × .09 = $27,000), at the end of the year you would have $315,000 ($300,000 + $27,000 − $12,000). At the beginning of the second year, you recalculate the amount of your monthly withdrawal. In this case, 1⁄12 of 4 percent of $315,000 is $1,050. This is 5 percent more than you withdrew the first year, enabling you to keep up with a 5 percent increase in the cost of living. In the third year you do a similar calculation and so on.

Investing in stocks that produce this kind of growth can be

risky—your investments are not perfectly safe from the standpoint of preserving your capital. Other "safer" investments are also risky, though, because they are unlikely to keep pace with inflation.

WHICH INVESTMENTS TO SPEND FIRST

You need to decide early which investments to tap first for living expenses. It's probably best to:

- *Spend down one investment completely before tapping income or principal from another.* Start by using money from employer plans with the lowest overall return, generally fixed-income funds.
- *Use investments that are not tax-deferred, if you can afford to do so.* Do not, for example, take money out of IRAs and Keogh and 401(k) plans unless you are at least 70½. (At that point you have to begin withdrawing the money.)
- *Finally, use other assets if necessary.*

If the balance in tax-deferred employer plans and IRAs is subject to tax on an "excess accumulation," you may want to begin withdrawing from these accounts as soon as you can without penalty. Currently this tax does not apply to any lifetime distributions below $150,000, or to a balance at death of less than $600,000, depending on your age. If you think this tax applies to you, consult a tax adviser.

TAKING EARLY RETIREMENT

Do you dream of quitting your job when you turn 55 or 60 and starting your own business? In some cases, your employer may offer what appear to be attractive incentives to make you leave early.

The incentives usually include a higher pension benefit

than is normally available to people your age. Your employer may also add three to five years of service when figuring your benefit. However, these additions usually don't increase your pension to the amount you would ordinarily receive if you had worked up to your employer's normal retirement age.

Your employer may also offer a severance payment of $20,000 or $30,000 or a supplemental payment if you're under 62 and too young to qualify for Social Security benefits. In addition, some health insurance may be added to the package, enabling you to stay on your employer's plan for a longer period. If your employer is very generous, you may be able to retain medical coverage for the rest of your life (such arrangements are rare) or until you're eligible for Medicare.

The decision to leave the work force early depends on whether you really want to retire, your other options for employment or leisure activities, your age, your savings cushion, and what kind of retirement package your employer offers.

If your employer asks you to take early retirement, first consider whether you really want to and whether you have a choice. If you don't want to leave, find out if the retirement package is available to a large number of employees or just to employees over a certain age or in a particular division. If it's offered to only a few people, that could mean the company is planning to eliminate your division or transfer employees elsewhere. If you can't accept a transfer or if you fear you will eventually be laid off, you may have little choice. If you gamble and stay, you could lose your job and end up without the incentives. If you have marketable skills and can easily find another job, that, too, will influence your decision.

Your age also determines how seriously you should consider early retirement. If you're in your mid-fifties, early retirement could be a financial disaster. You are too young for Social Security benefits, too young for Medicare, too young to withdraw money from IRA, Keogh, and 401(k) accounts without penalty, and you will lose several years of service that contribute to a larger pension from your employer as well as sacrifice a larger benefit from Social

Security. All of this means you must have significant savings or a spouse with a secure income to tide you over until you qualify for various benefits. Even if your employer offers an extra year's salary as an inducement to retire, that sum may be paltry when you consider how many years you will have to live on it. Once you've spent that year's pay, what will you live on for the next 3, 5, 10, or 20 years?

If you have relied on term life insurance from your employer for the bulk of your protection, you could lose it unless your employer agrees to continue the coverage for an indefinite time. This may be important if you are relying on that coverage to support a spouse or other dependent who will have no other income after your death.

Health insurance is a major consideration. You will be able to continue coverage under your employer's plan for only 18 months (unless your employer makes a better offer or provides coverage after retirement). After that, you have to find your own policy or take a conversion option. The first option may be impossible if you have health problems. The second is very costly. Your employer's offer to increase your pension by adding three or five years of service may not outweigh the higher costs for health coverage if you retire early. Having to pay for your own health insurance may well be the deciding factor in whether to take early retirement.

On the other hand, suppose you are 62 or 63 when your employer offers a ticket out of the work force. At this point you can qualify for Social Security early retirement benefits, although you shouldn't take them unless it's a necessity (see chapter 2). You may also be able to remain on your employer's health insurance plan until you're eligible for Medicare. You will be able to draw on money in IRA, Keogh, and 401(k) plans, and your savings may be large enough to tide you over until you qualify for full Social Security benefits. If your spouse continues to work and your family can live for a few years on one salary, then you might be able to leave your job early. Remember, though, retiring early means that contributions to your 401(k) plan or other company savings plan will stop and you will be losing the benefit of several years of compounded growth.

In any case, if you are offered such a package, consider it

very carefully. You may be given only 30 to 90 days to make your decision, but if you need more time, ask for it. This could be one of the most important decisions you ever make, and it will have financial ramifications for the rest of your life. If you don't like some part of your employer's package, try negotiating for a better deal. For example, if your company says you can stay on its health plan for three years and you have five years until you're eligible for Medicare, negotiate to see if they can continue your coverage until then.

Then again, you might decide to take early retirement but defer your retirement compensation until normal retirement age. Use Worksheet 4, Will You Have Enough Money?, in Appendix A, and work through all the scenarios: early retirement with the benefit enhancements; early retirement while deferring your compensation until later; waiting until normal retirement age. If delaying your payout nets you more later and you have enough savings to live on in the meantime, or you can get by on a spouse's income or you have other ideas for earning income, then choose that option. However, that course is more realistic if you are only a few years away from normal retirement.

STAYING ON THE JOB

You may want to continue working after you turn 65. If your employer allows that, by all means do so. Besides job satisfaction, you are enhancing your future financial position.

One big advantage is a larger Social Security benefit—you receive "delayed retirement credits" if you don't take your Social Security benefits at age 65. In addition, your pension will probably increase. Most people retire from a company with only about 15 years of service. Obviously, staying a few more years increases the pension benefit. If you've been with your employer a long time, however, check to see whether additional years of service no longer count after some point. Some plans limit the number of years of service that count toward your pension. If, for example, you've already worked for 30 years at your company and you want to continue working past age 65, the additional years of service may not increase your benefit.

If you continue to work and receive raises, your higher salary will go into calculating your pension benefit. Many companies use a "final average salary" plan—the higher your final average salary, the higher your benefit.

Delaying retirement also means that contributions to 401(k) and other company savings plans continue to grow, as do investments you may have in IRAs and Keogh accounts. By April 1, following the year you turn 70½, you have to begin withdrawing money from these accounts. At that point, your retirement planning needs to focus on the best option for withdrawing your money.

Remaining on your employer's health-insurance plan is another plus. If you don't have to pay for health insurance, you might consider using that money to buy a good long-term-care policy whose benefits increase with inflation (see chapter 11). If you continue to work, postpone your Social Security benefits, and remain on your employer's health plan, don't forget to check on the rules for enrolling in Medicare. If you do not sign up when you are first eligible for coverage, that is, at age 65, you have to pay a higher premium for Part B coverage (see chapter 8).

PLANNING FOR YOUR SPOUSE'S WELFARE

If your spouse will have no means of support after your death, any preparation for retirement necessarily involves providing for him or her. Make a rough estimate of your spouse's income needs. Will he or she remain in the family home? Will travel expenses (to visit family members) increase? What expenses are likely to decrease? Obviously food bills and car expenses (if you have more than one car) will decline. (Worksheet 3, Postretirement Expenses, in Appendix A can help you calculate expenses and income for your spouse.)

For many families, survivors' benefits from Social Security are a spouse's main source of income. Table 4 in chapter 2 shows you how large a benefit to expect. But for most people this benefit does not cover expected expenses. You must make up the shortfall from your pension, savings, or life insurance. If your spouse will have no other income, we strongly recommend that you choose a 100 percent joint-and-survivor option (see chapter 3). Most people, however, shouldn't keep life insurance in retirement. The money spent on premiums or the cash value tied up in a policy usually can be better spent or invested elsewhere, even though life insurance salespeople try to convince you otherwise (see chapter 5).

If you have substantial assets, you may also find it advantageous to set up a trust for your spouse (see chapter 18).

REMARRIAGE

Remarriage can cause some of the thorniest problems in retirement planning. If you remarry, give careful consideration to who will get your assets when you die. You may want to provide for children from your first marriage, so prenuptial agreements are one way to specify exactly what your new spouse is entitled to. Chapters 17 and 18 provide help in setting up trusts for children from a first marriage. To avoid problems later on, it's best to make these decisions before remarrying.

2

SOCIAL SECURITY: *The Backbone of Retirement Income*

Retirement income is often compared to a stool with three legs—Social Security is one, pensions from employers the second, and private savings the third. The legs of the stool, however, are not equal. For most people, Social Security provides the bulk of their retirement income.

During the Depression, savings set aside by many of the elderly for retirement were wiped out and younger people, often without jobs, could not afford to care for aged parents. It was under the stress of such conditions that in 1935 President Franklin D. Roosevelt and Congress created the Social Security system.

Social Security is financed by a payroll tax paid equally by employees and employers. Throughout their working years, current workers pay the tax to support current retirees. Thus the money is not an annuity invested at interest to pay for each employee's own future benefits. And contrary to what many think, there is no bank account in Baltimore (where the Social Security Administration [SSA] is located) that has your contributions earmarked for your retirement. Instead, when you reach retirement age, SSA computers determine your benefit by plugging the number of years you have paid payroll taxes and your yearly earnings into complex formulas to determine the amount you receive each month. It then sends payments from the funds the system has on hand.

Over the years, Congress has expanded both the benefits and the categories of workers eligible for them, so the system is now practically universal. Four types of benefits are available: retirement, survivors', disability, and Medicare. (Medicare is discussed in chapter 8.)

RETIREMENT BENEFITS

To qualify for retirement benefits under the Social Security system, you must be "fully insured," that is, you must have accumulated at least 40 "quarters of coverage" under Social Security. In other words, you must have worked for about 10 years in employment covered by the Social Security program. Social Security bases covered quarters on each worker's annual earnings. In 1992, one quarter of coverage is credited for every $570 of earnings during the year, but only four quarters of coverage can be earned in any one year. If you were born after 1928, you need 40 quarters to qualify for retirement benefits. Workers born in 1928 need 39 quarters; in 1927, 38 quarters; in 1926, 37 quarters; in 1925, 36 quarters; and so on.

Figuring your benefit is complicated and you probably won't want to do it yourself (see the following pages for other ways to get the information). However, you should know how the benefit is calculated and understand why you receive the amount you do each month. The benefits you receive are based on a magic number called your *primary insurance amount,* or PIA. Here's how a PIA is figured for most new retirees:

SSA uses a wage-index factor to adjust your earnings for each year before you reach age 60. The adjustment increases your earlier earnings to approximately their current equivalent value. Only earnings up to the "wage base"—the maximum amount of earnings each year on which you must pay

Social Security taxes—are counted. (If you earned more than the wage base in any year, those earnings are not counted.) Earnings after you reach age 60 are not indexed; actual earnings are used instead.

Once your earnings are indexed, SSA determines the number of years needed to calculate the average of your indexed earnings. To arrive at the number of years, subtract 5 from the number of quarters of coverage you must have to be "fully insured." If you need 40 quarters of coverage, you use 35 years in your average. Everyone first eligible to retire in 1991 or later uses 35 years in his or her average.

Next, SSA averages the highest earnings for the number of years you need and divides by 12 to arrive at your *average indexed monthly earnings*, or AIME.

A benefit formula is then applied to the AIME to arrive at your primary insurance amount. For someone first eligible to retire in 1992, the primary insurance amount is figured by adding 90 percent of the first $387 of average indexed monthly earnings, 32 percent of the next $1,946, and 15 percent of the AIME that exceeds $2,333. These dollar amounts, known as *bend points*, change each year.

The weighting in the benefit formula gives workers who earned low wages a greater percentage of their preretirement income than high-wage earners. If your earnings have equaled the U.S. average wage and you retire at the normal retirement age (currently 65, but scheduled to increase), your Social Security check will replace about 42 percent of your pay. If you have always earned the maximum taxable earnings, your benefit will replace about 25 percent of your pay.

The PIA is then adjusted for changes in the cost of living. Changes in the Consumer Price Index (CPI) are applied for each year, beginning in the year a person turns 62. A worker who retires in 1992 at age 65 will have his or her final PIA determined by increasing the amount of the preliminary PIA by 4.7 percent, 5.4 percent, and 3.7 percent. These are the CPI increases for the three preceding years. The result is the final primary insurance amount, which becomes the basis for all benefits paid to you and your dependents. Once you begin to receive retirement benefits, they are increased each January by the percentage increase in the CPI.

There are several ways to estimate your benefits. Table 1 gives you a rough idea if you have been steadily employed and have had average wage increases throughout your career (increases at about the same rate as all workers in the country). *Example:* You have turned 65 and are about to retire. Your current salary is $40,000. Your spouse is also 65 and qualifies for a benefit based on your earnings. According to Social Security rules, your combined monthly benefit totals $1,473. But if you haven't received average wage increases, or were employed intermittently, these estimates are not very accurate.

You can also get an estimate from the SSA and check the information in your records at the same time. SSA will send your earnings record and estimates of retirement, disability, and survivors' benefits to you. The estimate for retirement benefits will be approximate, since it depends on an assumption of your future earnings. Estimates for survivors' and disability benefits will be more accurate, since they are calculated as if you died or became disabled on the day you requested the estimate. (Call 800-772-1213 to request an estimate of your benefits.)

When you receive your statement, check it for errors. Check to see that you have not paid more than the maximum Social Security tax each year. If you have held more than one job in a particular year and have earned more than the maximum earnings for Social Security taxes, you have paid more. In that case, you're entitled to a credit against your federal income tax. If you find any errors, contact your local SSA office. The law requires SSA to go back only about three years to correct mistakes. The agency can try to correct older errors, but it may be unable to do so.

To catch errors in time for corrections, request a statement of your earnings every three years or so.

You can also figure out your benefit with a computer program sold by the Social Security Administration. The software calculates your benefits in a number of different situations. If you have an IBM-compatible personal computer, the program could be a handy tool for retirement planning. To obtain the program, write to Sales, National Technical Information Service, 5285 Port Royal Road, Springfield, VA 22161, or call 703-487-4650. Ask for the Social Security Benefit Estimate Program for personal computers, product number PB91-506519 (for a 5¼-inch disk) or PB91-506527 (for a 3½-inch disk). The cost is $50 plus handling charges.

Normal Retirement Benefits

The *normal retirement age* is the age when you qualify for a full (unreduced) benefit. This age varies, depending on the year in which you were born. If you were born before 1938, the normal retirement age is 65. It gradually increases after that. Table 2 shows how the normal retirement age goes up over the next several years.

If you retire at the normal retirement age, your benefit will equal the primary insurance amount discussed previously.

Getting Less When You Retire Early

You can still receive Social Security benefits if you retire after you turn 62 but before your normal retirement age. The benefit is reduced, however, and the reduction is permanent—that is, your primary insurance amount does not increase when you reach the normal retirement age. This happens because early retirement benefits are "actuarially" reduced to offset the longer time you will be receiving checks. And you also won't have the advantage of three extra years of earnings (probably high earnings at that) to go into your average.

How much your benefit is reduced depends on when you retire. The reduction is 5⁄9 of 1 percent for each month (up to 36 months) that you receive benefits before the normal retirement age, plus another 5⁄12 of 1 percent for any additional month(s) prior to normal retirement age. For example,

TABLE 1
Monthly Retirement Benefits

Worker's Age in 1992	Worker's Family	Retired Worker's Earnings in 1991					
		$10,000	$20,000	$30,000	$40,000	$50,000	Maximum Wage Base or More[1]
25	Retired worker only	$ 672	$ 1,037	$ 1,364	$ 1,535	$ 1,706	$ 1,801
	Worker and spouse[2]	1,008	1,555	2,046	2,302	2,559	2,701
	Final year earnings[3]	13,700	27,400	41,100	54,800	68,500	76,035
	Replacement rate[4]	59%	45%	40%	34%	30%	28%
35	Retired worker only	$ 622	$ 959	$ 1,263	$ 1,421	$ 1,580	$ 1,662
	Worker and spouse[2]	933	1,438	1,894	2,131	2,370	2,493
	Final year earnings[3]	12,700	25,400	38,100	50,800	63,500	70,485
	Replacement rate[4]	59%	45%	40%	34%	30%	28%
45	Retired worker only	$ 570	$ 878	$ 1,159	$ 1,302	$ 1,436	$ 1,491
	Worker and spouse[2]	855	1,317	1,738	1,953	2,154	2,236
	Final year earnings[3]	11,700	23,400	35,100	46,800	58,500	64,935
	Replacement rate[4]	58%	45%	40%	33%	29%	28%

55	Retired worker only	$ 518	$ 796	$ 1,052	$ 1,150	$ 1,231	$ 1,258
	Worker and spouse[2]	777	1,194	1,578	1,725	1,846	1,887
	Final year earnings[3]	10,700	21,400	32,100	42,800	53,500	59,385
	Replacement rate[4]	58%	45%	39%	32%	28%	25%
65	Retired worker only	$ 486	$ 748	$ 977	$ 1,038	$ 1,081	$ 1,088
	Worker and spouse[2]	729	1,122	1,465	1,557	1,621	1,632
	Final year earnings[3]	10,000	20,000	30,000	40,000	50,000	53,400
	Replacement rate[4]	58%	45%	39%	31%	26%	24%

[1]Earnings equal to or greater than the Social Security wage base from age 22 through the year before retirement.
[2]Spouse is assumed to be the same age as the worker. Spouse may qualify for a higher retirement benefit based on his or her own work record.
[3]Worker's earnings in the year before retirement.
[4]Replacement rates are shown for retired worker only.

Source: Social Security Administration, Office of the Actuary

TABLE 2
Normal Retirement Ages

Year of Birth	Normal Retirement Age
1937 or earlier	65
1938	65 and 2 months
1939	65 and 4 months
1940	65 and 6 months
1941	65 and 8 months
1942	65 and 10 months
1943–1954	66
1955	66 and 2 months
1956	66 and 4 months
1957	66 and 6 months
1958	66 and 8 months
1959	66 and 10 months
1960 and later	67

if your normal retirement age is 65, and you retire at 62, your benefit is 80 percent of your primary insurance amount—a reduction of 20 percent, or $\frac{5}{9}$ of 1 percent for each of the 36 months before you're 65. If your PIA is $1,000, your monthly benefit is $800. But if you wait until 64 to retire, you receive 93$\frac{1}{3}$ percent of your primary insurance amount. On the same PIA of $1,000, your benefit is $933. If your normal retirement age is 67, the benefit payable at 62 is 70 percent of the PIA (a reduction of $\frac{5}{9}$ of 1 percent for 36 months and a reduction of $\frac{5}{12}$ of 1 percent for 24 months).

From the standpoint of maximizing your income, it pays to wait until your normal retirement age or later to retire, especially if Social Security will be your primary or only source of retirement funds. Taking a reduced benefit is recommended only if you have other income sources. If you are in poor health, you may have to leave the work force early. Even so, delay taking your benefit as long as possible.

Getting More If You Retire Late

If you work beyond the normal retirement age, you will receive a larger benefit when you do leave the work force. Your primary insurance amount is figured the usual way and then increased by a certain percentage for each month you delay retirement. For those born between 1917 and 1924, the increase is ¼ of 1 percent per month, or 3 percent per year for each month you remain in the work force. For those born after 1924, the percentage by which benefits increase gradually rises, reaching ⅔ of 1 percent per month, or 8 percent per year for people born after 1942. If you turned 65 in January 1992, the annual increase factor is 4 percent. If you wait until 68 to retire, your benefit increases by a total of 12 percent. Table 3 shows your benefit if you delay retirement.

As you can see, delaying retirement offers significant financial advantages. Besides the percentage increase SSA allows,

TABLE 3
Delayed Retirement Credits

Year of Birth	Annual Percentage Increase in Benefits for Delaying Retirement Beyond the Normal Retirement Age
Before 1917	1
1917–1924	3
1925–1926	3½
1927–1928	4
1929–1930	4½
1931–1932	5
1933–1934	5½
1935–1936	6
1937–1938	6½
1939–1940	7
1941–1942	7½
1943 and later	8

your earnings after age 65 may go up, increasing your AIME and, therefore, your benefits. Spouse and other family benefits are also increased to reflect the higher average earnings, but they do not include the increase resulting from the delayed retirement credit. If your spouse outlives you, survivors' benefits based on your earnings are increased by any delayed-retirement increment for which you qualify.

On the other hand, the percentage increase in your delayed retirement benefit is currently too low to compensate fully for the benefits you have forgone by retiring after the normal retirement age. Yes, delayed retirement increases your monthly benefit, but it also reduces the lifetime value of all your benefits. However, once the annual increase percentage rises to 8 percent, this inequity disappears, and the lifetime value of your benefits is approximately the same regardless of when you begin to receive payments.

To see what the delayed retirement credit means in dollars and cents, let's look at your benefits with the assumption that you've always paid maximum Social Security taxes. If you turned 65 and retired in January 1990, your monthly benefit would have been $975. But if you had retired in 1987 at age 62, the benefit would have been $756 in 1990. On the other hand, if you worked until January 1992 when you turned 67, your benefit would have been about $1,075 less any cost-of-living increases. Of the $100 increase, approximately $70 results from the delayed retirement credit, and $30 results from your higher average salary earned during the last years of work. If you continue to work until age 70, the monthly benefit jumps to $1,245 before future cost-of-living adjustments.

Benefits for Spouses

Once you begin to receive monthly retirement checks, your spouse, if he or she is 62 or older, is also eligible for benefits. If your spouse is 65, the benefit equals one-half of your PIA unless your spouse receives a benefit based on his or her own earnings. If your PIA is $700, your spouse's benefit is $350. (As we noted, the benefit increases with cost-of-living adjustments each January.) If your spouse is between 62 and 65 when you retire, he or she can take an early retirement benefit, although it is reduced by $\frac{25}{36}$ of 1 percent for each month before your spouse's sixty-fifth birthday. If your PIA is $700, the benefit for a 62-year-old spouse is $350 reduced by 25 percent, or $263. A spouse younger than 62 is not eligible for a retirement benefit, unless he or she is caring for an eligible child under age 16.

Even if you retire at 62 and your spouse is 62, it's best if he or she waits until age 65 to receive benefits. By waiting until the normal retirement age, your spouse maximizes the family income. However, there is no advantage for a spouse to delay taking a benefit after reaching 65. Spousal benefits taken after 65 don't increase the way your benefits do if you stay in the work force longer. In fact, it may be a financial hardship to wait longer.

Divorced spouses are also eligible for benefits based on a former spouse's PIA. They may receive benefits after turning 62 so long as they were married for at least 10 years and have not remarried. The worker on whose PIA the spousal benefits are based must be at least 62, though not necessarily retired or receiving Social Security disability benefits. If a divorced spouse remarries, monthly checks stop unless his or her new spouse is already receiving benefits.

A spouse of any age who is caring for a child under age 16 is eligible for 50 percent of your primary insurance amount, but he or she must have been married to you for at least one year or be the parent of the child. If your spouse receives this benefit, there is no reduction because you retired early.

As noted, if a spouse has his or her own earnings record, based on his or her own work experience, SSA calculates benefits using that record. The spouse then receives the benefit based on his or her earnings record or one based on the spouse's PIA, whichever is larger. As more women enter and remain in the work force, their benefits will be based on their earnings records.

Children's Benefits

When you retire, your children under age 18 (under age 19 if still in high school) and those who become disabled before age 22 are also eligible for benefits based on your primary insurance amount. Their benefit equals one-half of your PIA.

Maximum Family Benefits

SSA places a cap on the benefit your family gets when you retire. The maximum amount payable depends on the level of your PIA—it varies from 150 to 188 percent of the PIA.

If your family is eligible for benefits, SSA figures the sum of the individual benefits based on your earnings record as well as the maximum family benefit. If the sum of the individual benefits is larger than the maximum benefit, the benefits for each family member (though not yours) are reduced proportionately so the total family benefit does not exceed the maximum.

Working After Retirement

Social Security is meant to replace a portion of your earnings that are lost because of retirement, death, or disability. Nevertheless, you can still collect Social Security benefits and continue working, but if your earnings exceed a specified amount, your benefits are reduced. For 1992, if you're between 65 and 69 and continue to work, your benefit is reduced by $1 for every $3 earned above $10,200. (The earnings limitation also applies to those under 65 who receive benefits. For them, the 1992 reduction is $1 for every $2 in earnings over $7,440.) Any earnings that exceed the allowable amounts affect not only your benefit but also those of your family members. The earnings test also applies to working spouses and children of retired workers. After you reach age 70, the earnings limitation does not apply.

Let's see how the earnings test works. Suppose your monthly benefit is $900 in 1992, but you also earn $12,000 a year doing small jobs for your former employer. If you're between 65 and 69, your excess earnings are $1,800 ($12,000 − $10,200). After the earnings test is applied, your benefits for the year are reduced by $600 ($1,800 ÷ 3 = $600). In effect, you lose about two-thirds of one month's benefits. Sometimes continuing to work wipes out your entire benefit. However, you still receive full Medicare benefits if you otherwise qualify for them.

Self-employed people must also comply with the earnings test. If you own a business, subtract your business deductions from your business income to determine your earnings for the year. If that figure exceeds the earnings limitation, your benefits are reduced. If you work for others and also have your own business on the side, SSA adds your wages and salary plus any net income from the side business to determine whether your total income exceeds the earnings limitation.

Note, however, that during the year you retire, you can continue to work and receive full benefits for the rest of that year regardless of your total annual earnings, so long as you do not perform substantial work as a self-employed person and your wages do not exceed a certain exempt amount each month after you retire. In 1992, the monthly exempt amount is $850 for people between ages 65 and 69 and $620 for those under 65. Therefore, if you earned $50,000 during the first six months of the year, you could still retire and receive benefits during the last six months, so long as your earnings in each month were less than the monthly exempt amount.

What Counts As Income?

In general, only wages and earnings from self-employment count toward the earnings test for Social Security benefits. Income from the following doesn't count: pensions, annuity payments, dividends and interest, capital gains, rental income (unless you are in the real estate business), tips of less than $20 a month, sick pay received more than six months after leaving work, workers' compensation, unemployment benefits, court settlements, gifts, life insurance proceeds, inheritance proceeds, and contest or lottery winnings.

Special Rule for Government Workers

If you worked for federal, state, or local government, were not covered by Social Security when you retired, and are eligible for a Social Security benefit as a spouse, widow, or widower, that benefit is generally reduced by up to two-thirds of the amount of your government pension. The net result: Some government workers don't get Social Security benefits. There are exceptions to this rule, however, and you should check with your local Social Security office to see if they apply to you. If you qualify for Social Security through other nongovernmental employment and you are also eligible for a pension as a government worker, your Social Security benefit may also be reduced. Your local Social Security office can tell you what that reduction will be.

Taxing Your Benefits

If you have substantial total retirement income, you may have to include part of your Social Security benefits in your taxable income when you fill out Form 1040. To see if your benefits are taxable, add together your regular adjusted gross income from Form 1040 (this number includes all taxable investment income), any interest earned on tax-exempt bonds (which is ordinarily not taxable), and 50 percent of your Social Security benefits. If the sum exceeds $25,000 for a single person or $32,000 for married couples filing jointly, then you owe some tax.

To calculate the amount of the tax, determine the excess by which your adjusted gross income, tax-exempt bond interest, and half of your benefits exceed either $25,000 or $32,000, whichever applies. Then take 50 percent of that amount but not more than 50 percent of your Social Security benefits and add it to your adjusted gross income. (The IRS instructions can guide you through this calculation.)

Suppose, for example, you and your spouse receive $10,000 in Social Security benefits and file a joint return. You also have $16,000 of taxable income from your company pension, $5,000 of taxable interest, and $5,000 of taxable dividends. Your adjusted gross income is $26,000 ($16,000 + $5,000 + $5,000). Your adjusted gross income ($26,000) plus half of your Social Security benefit ($5,000) equals $31,000, which is less than the $32,000 threshold for retirees filing joint returns, so your Social Security benefits are not taxable. But if you also had another $2,000 of tax-exempt interest from municipal bonds, your adjusted gross income plus tax-exempt interest plus half of your Social Security benefits would rise to $33,000, which is $1,000 over the threshold. You then include one-half of the $1,000 excess amount (or $500) in your taxable income.

Some states also tax Social Security benefits. Your local Social Security office can tell you if your state is one of them.

BENEFITS FOR SURVIVORS

The eligibility requirements for survivors' benefits differ from those for retirement benefits. In order for your survivors to receive benefits after your death, you must either be fully insured or, in some cases, "currently insured" when you die. SSA determines the required number of quarters by counting the number of years after 1950, or after the year you become age 21 if later, up through the year before death or through the year you turn age 61, whichever occurs earlier. For example, if you were born in 1925 and die in 1992, you need 36 quarters of coverage. Someone born in 1960 needs only 10.

To be currently insured for survivors' benefits, you must have earned at least 6 quarters of coverage during the previous 13 calendar quarters, ending with the quarter in which you die.

What survivors' benefits your family members are eligible for depends on your insured status at the time of your death. If you're fully insured, all types of survivors' benefits are available. If you are currently insured, only some benefits are.

These benefits are available to the following family members:

Surviving spouses who have reached their sixtieth birthday. Your spouse must have been married to you for at least nine months before your death, be the parent of your child, or meet other eligibility requirements. If you die in an accident, this time limit doesn't apply. If your spouse is 65 or older, he or she generally receives 100 percent of your primary insurance amount. For younger spouses, the benefit is reduced. A spouse age 62 receives 82.9 percent of your primary insurance amount; the benefits for a spouse age 60 equal 71.5 percent of your PIA.

If you retire before age 65 (or before the normal retirement age if you were born after 1937) and then die, your surviving spouse also receives the reduced benefit you were receiving, unless it is less than 82.5 percent of your PIA. In that case, his or her benefit equals 82.5 percent of your PIA. For example, suppose you retire at age 64 and your PIA is $700. Your benefit is then $653. Your surviving spouse also receives $653. But if you retire at age 62, your benefit is only $560. Since that's less than 82.5 percent of your PIA, your spouse gets $577. If you retire after age 65, your spouse's survivors' benefit increases by the same delayed retirement credit that you received. As noted in chapter 1, it's important to consider survivors' benefits when you begin planning for retirement.

If your spouse has established his or her own earnings record and is also eligible for retirement benefits, he or she gets only *one* benefit, normally the larger one. An attractive option for widowed spouses under the normal retirement age is to take a reduced benefit based on the deceased partner's earnings record and delay benefits based on his or her own earnings record until he or she reaches normal retirement age. A spouse who takes a survivors' benefit can later switch to his or her own retirement benefit if it is larger. The opposite can also occur. Your spouse can take a retirement benefit at normal retirement age based on his or her own earnings record and later convert to a survivors' benefit based on your work record if the benefit is larger. (A spouse who remarries also continues to receive survivors' benefits.)

Divorced spouses. A divorced spouse age 60 or older receives the same benefits as a married spouse as long as the divorced spouse was married to you for at least 10 years.

Disabled surviving spouses. A spouse between 50 and 59 is eligible for survivors' benefits if he or she is severely mentally or physically impaired and the disability has lasted five months. In this case, the benefit equals 71.5 percent of your primary insurance amount. As with benefits payable to surviving spouses who are not disabled, these benefits continue even if the disabled spouse remarries.

Surviving spouses caring for children. If your youngest child is under 16 or you have a child who was disabled before reaching his or her twenty-second birthday, your spouse is eligible for benefits equaling 75 percent of your PIA. This benefit stops when the youngest child turns 16 (unless a disabled child is in the home) or if the spouse remarries.

Eligible children. Children meeting certain requirements also receive benefits equal to 75 percent of your PIA. The eligibility rules are the same as for children qualifying under a retired worker's benefit. If both parents are dead, the children can qualify for benefits based on the earnings record of either parent, whichever is larger. In such cases, the law also provides for a limited pooling of the family maximum amounts for the two parents.

Maximum family benefit rules and the earnings test also apply to survivors' benefits. *Example:* A 60-year-old widow is eligible for an $800 monthly benefit in 1992, but she continues to work. Her annual benefit is then reduced by $1 for every $2 of earnings in excess of $7,440. If she earns $10,000, a total of $1,280 will be withheld for the year. Thus, she loses about one and a half months of benefits ($10,000 − $7,440 = $2,560 ÷ 2 = $1,280). When she is eligible for her own retirement benefit, that benefit is also subject to the earnings test.

If you die and are only currently insured, Social Security benefits are payable to your so-called young survivors. In other words, the program pays benefits to a surviving or divorced spouse who is caring for either a child under age 16 or a child who was disabled before age 22. Children under age 18 (under age 19 if the child is still in high school) and disabled children are also eligible for their own benefits. Those eligible for survivors' benefits receive the same percentage of the worker's PIA that survivors of fully insured workers receive.

Table 4 will help you estimate your survivors' benefits if you should die in 1992. The table gives you a good estimate only if you have worked steadily and have received average pay raises. If you haven't worked steadily, or want to know what benefits your survivors can expect based on your PIA, contact the Social Security Administration at 800-772-1213 for a Personal Earnings and Benefit Statement.

Lump-Sum Death Benefit

When you die, a payment of $255 is made to a spouse who is still living with you. Your spouse is eligible for this benefit whether you are retired or still working. If no spouse lives with you, the Social Security Administration pays the benefit to any spouse or children who are eligible for monthly benefits based on your earnings record. If you have no eligible survivors, SSA pays no benefit.

DISABILITY BENEFITS

To receive Social Security disability benefits, you must comply with strict rules, and those rules tend to be rigidly enforced.

Qualifying for Benefits

To be eligible for benefits, you must have suffered severe mental or physical impairment. You must be unable to perform any *substantial* gainful work (considering your age, education, and work experience), and your impairment must be expected to continue at least 12 months or result in death. Whether your illness or disability renders you "severely" impaired and unable to perform "substantial" work is occasionally subjective and open to interpretation.

Your state's Disability Determination Service decides whether your disability fits the SSA's definition of a disability. In cases that don't neatly meet the standard criteria, officials tend to deny benefits. As a result, nearly two-thirds of those applying for disability benefits are initially denied. Many of them appeal the decisions, and administrative law judges who work for the Social Security Administration reverse those initial decisions about 60 percent of the time. If you are severely disabled, but Social Security has turned you down, pursue all available appeals and seek guidance from a lawyer, if necessary, to gain your benefits.

To qualify for disability benefits, you must also be fully insured and have *disability insured status.* That means you must have earned at least 20 quarters of coverage in the 40-quarter period ending with the quarter in which you were disabled. Less stringent rules apply for people under age 31. Table 5 shows how many quarters of coverage you need if you become disabled. As you can see, the number of quarters you need is based on your age when you become disabled. The requirements are a bit different for workers born before 1929.

Payment of Benefits

Social Security disability benefits, like those from private insurance carriers, are paid only after a waiting period. You must be disabled for five full calendar months before any benefits are paid, but you won't have to satisfy a second waiting period if you have already received disability benefits that ended less than five years before your current disability began. *Example:* You were injured on the job four years ago and received Social Security disability benefits for one year. You then returned to work. The work proved too arduous, and after eight months you had to stop working. You are

TABLE 4
Monthly Survivors' Benefits

Worker's Age	Worker's Family	Deceased Worker's Earnings in 1991					
		$10,000	$20,000	$30,000	$40,000	$50,000	Maximum Wage Base or More[1]
25	Spouse and one child[2]	$728	$1,122	$1,484	$1,668	$1,852	$1,912
	Spouse and two children[3]	729	1,384	1,731	1,946	2,161	2,231
	One child only	364	561	742	834	926	956
	Spouse at age 60[4]	347	535	707	795	883	911
35	Spouse and one child[2]	$724	$1,112	$1,476	$1,658	$1,840	$1,878
	Spouse and two children[3]	724	1,375	1,722	1,934	2,146	2,190
	One child only	362	556	738	829	920	939
	Spouse at age 60[4]	345	530	703	790	877	895
45	Spouse and one child[2]	$722	$1,110	$1,474	$1,636	$1,752	$1,770
	Spouse and two children[3]	723	1,373	1,721	1,910	2,044	2,064
	One child only	361	555	737	818	876	885
	Spouse at age 60[4]	344	529	703	780	835	843

55	Spouse and one child[2]	$722	$1,108	$1,462	$1,566	$1,640	$1,652
	Spouse and two children[3]	723	1,372	1,705	1,828	1,914	1,927
	One child only	361	554	731	783	820	826
	Spouse at age 60[4]	344	528	696	747	782	787
65	Spouse and one child[2]	$728	$1,122	$1,464	$1,556	$1,622	$1,632
	Spouse and two children[3]	729	1,386	1,711	1,818	1,894	1,906
	One child only	364	561	732	778	811	816
	Spouse at age 60[4]	347	534	698	742	773	778

[1]Earnings equal to or greater than the Social Security wage base from age 22 through 1991.
[2]Amounts shown also equal the benefits paid to two children, if no parent survives or surviving parent has substantial earnings.
[3]Equals the maximum family benefit.
[4]Amounts payable in 1992. Spouses turning 60 in the future would receive higher benefits.

Source: Social Security Administration, Office of the Actuary

TABLE 5
Quarters of Coverage Needed to Qualify for Disability Benefits[1]

Age at Onset of Disability[3]	Number of Quarters of Coverage Required for[2]	
	Fully Insured Status	Disability Insured Status
25	6	8 in 16-quarter period ending with disability
30	8	18 in 36-quarter period ending with disability
35	13	20 in 40-quarter period ending with disability
40	18	20 in 40-quarter period ending with disability
45	23	20 in 40-quarter period ending with disability
50	28	20 in 40-quarter period ending with disability
55	33	20 in 40-quarter period ending with disability
60	38	20 in 40-quarter period ending with disability

[1]For persons disabled in 1989 or later.
[2]Both fully insured status and disability insured status requirements must be met to qualify for benefits.
[3]Worker is assumed to reach the age shown in the same calendar quarter in which he or she becomes disabled. Number of quarters of coverage required can vary by one or two if this assumption is not met.
Note: Special provisions apply to blind persons and persons who were previously disabled.

again eligible for disability benefits and do not have to satisfy another waiting period.

After you have received benefits for nine months, your local Social Security office reviews your case and decides whether your benefits should continue. If they determine that you can work again, the benefits stop. If you return to work and your earnings subsequently drop below the "substantial gainful activity" level, Social Security reinstates benefits without a new application as long as three years have not passed in the interim.

Figuring the Benefit

Your disability benefit equals your primary insurance amount on the day you become disabled and is adjusted according to the Consumer Price Index, the same as normal retirement benefits. Other than cost-of-living increases, your disability benefit does not increase as you get older. When you reach normal retirement age, your disability benefit becomes a retirement benefit, but the monthly check remains the same.

Table 6 shows your disability benefits if you become disabled in 1992. *Example:* You are 55 years old and earn $40,000 a year. You suddenly become disabled and cannot support your spouse and young child. Social Security will pay your family a disability benefit of $1,567 a month. Again, the table assumes you have worked steadily throughout your career and have had average wage increases.

Family Benefits

If you're disabled, your family members are also eligible for benefits based on your PIA. A spouse age 65 receives 50 percent of your primary insurance amount; a spouse age 62, 37½ percent. If your spouse is also caring for children who are disabled or who are under age 16, he or she receives 50 percent of your PIA. Those of your children who meet the eligibility requirements also receive 50 percent of your PIA.

TABLE 6
Monthly Disability Benefits

Worker's Age	Worker's Family	Disabled Worker's Earnings in 1991					
		$10,000	$20,000	$30,000	$40,000	$50,000	Maximum Wage Base or More[1]
25	Disabled worker only	$484	$ 745	$ 987	$1,109	$1,231	$1,266
	Disabled worker, spouse, and child[2]	691	1,118	1,480	1,664	1,847	1,899
35	Disabled worker only	$482	$ 740	$ 984	$1,105	$1,221	$1,240
	Disabled worker, spouse, and child[2]	685	1,111	1,476	1,657	1,831	1,860
45	Disabled worker only	$482	$ 739	$ 983	$1,086	$1,159	$1,170
	Disabled worker, spouse, and child[2]	684	1,109	1,475	1,629	1,738	1,755
55	Disabled worker only	$482	$ 739	$ 974	$1,044	$1,094	$1,101
	Disabled worker, spouse, and child[2]	684	1,109	1,462	1,567	1,641	1,652
64	Disabled worker only	$486	$ 746	$ 975	$1,034	$1,076	$1,082
	Disabled worker, spouse, and child[2]	691	1,119	1,463	1,551	1,614	1,623

[1]Earnings equal to or greater than the Social Security wage base from age 22 through 1991.
[2]Equals the maximum family benefit.

Source: Social Security Administration, Office of the Actuary

The maximum family benefit, however, is lower than the maximum paid for retirement or survivors' benefits.

Example: You become disabled at age 59. Your spouse is 53 and you have a 13-year-old child. If your PIA and thus your benefit is $900, your spouse is eligible for a benefit of $450 because he or she is caring for a child who's eligible for benefits. The child is also eligible to receive $450. Your family's benefit, however, is not $1,800, because the maximum benefit provision applies. Total benefits cannot exceed 85 percent of your AIME or 150 percent of your PIA, whichever is lower. In this example, total family benefits come to $1,350. Your spouse and child receive a total of $450 each month, in addition to your benefit of $900, which is not subject to a reduction.

The earnings test also applies to benefits paid to other family members. If your spouse works, his or her benefit is reduced by $1 for every $2 he or she earns in excess of $7,440. (In this instance, however, the child's benefit increases as the spouse's benefit decreases, and the family benefit stays the same.)

Coordinating Disability Benefits

Disability benefits may be reduced if you receive workers' compensation or other disability benefits from another federal program or a state or local government insurance program. The total benefits from all government sources cannot exceed 80 percent of your earnings before you were disabled. Disability benefits from a private insurance carrier or a company pension don't count for this test.

Disabled Spouses

As noted, disabled widows and widowers between ages 50 and 59 are also eligible for benefits based on your PIA. The benefit equals 71.5 percent of the PIA you would have had at age 65 and does not increase except for cost-of-living increases.

To be eligible, a widow or widower must have been disabled within seven years after a spouse's death or seven years after your last child reaches age 16 (or is no longer disabled). The definition of disability is the same as we described previously.

Disabled Beneficiaries and Medicare

A disabled person receiving Social Security benefits for at least 24 months is also entitled to Medicare benefits. This includes disabled workers, disabled widows and widowers, and disabled children over 18 whose disability occurred before age 22. Medicare may well be the only source of health insurance for disabled persons (see chapter 8).

HOW TO APPLY FOR SOCIAL SECURITY BENEFITS

As soon as you decide when you want your benefits to begin, contact your local Social Security office. Although you can make an appointment to apply in person, you can usually complete the application over the phone. If you plan to retire before you turn 65, be sure to apply for benefits no later than the last day of the month you want benefits to begin. Benefits payable for the months before you turn 65 usually can begin no earlier than the month in which you first apply.

If you apply for benefits after you turn 65, the Social Security Administration may make back payments to you for up to six months before the month in which you apply. We recommend, therefore, that you apply up to three months *before* the month in which you want benefits to begin. It takes about eight weeks for the application to be processed. Keep this in mind as you begin to plan for your income in retirement.

When you apply for benefits, you need your Social Security number, birth certificates for yourself and your children (or other proof of age such as a passport), and a record of your recent earnings, such as last year's W-2 form or last year's self-employment tax return. If you're applying for benefits based on a spouse's earnings, bring a marriage certificate. If your family is applying for survivors' benefits, they must bring a death certificate.

If you want Social Security checks deposited directly in your checking or savings account, bring the numbers of those accounts. Direct deposit is safer and more convenient for most people. But if you want your checks sent in the mail, Social Security will do that too.

If you're applying for disability benefits, the application process can be lengthy. Apply as soon as you become disabled.

3

Your Pension

Currently pension plans provide some retirement income for about 27 percent of those 65 or older. And a number of workers among the remaining 73 percent have previously received a distribution of money from a pension plan, which they then invested on their own for future retirement benefits.

Pension benefits come from all employee plans that defer income or provide payments after retirement, including 401(k), Keogh, profit-sharing, and employee stock ownership plans (ESOPs). IRA accounts—individual pensions funded with your own money over the years—also provide additional retirement funds.

Your employer pension is most likely a *qualified* plan. That means contributions escape taxation, and you have to pay taxes on the money either at the time you retire, or sometime after. You may also have a nonqualified pension, such as a bonus plan, a deferred compensation plan, or a phantom stock plan. If you are to receive benefits from any of these, your employer or a tax adviser can help you with any tax consequences. Obviously, taxes figure prominently into how much you can expect to get from your pension, but besides taxes, the actual number of dollars you receive depends on the type of plan your employer has established, your years of service with the employer, your age, the specific benefit formulas built into the plan, your compensation, and the amount of contributions made by you and your employer. To understand how all these factors interact, it's important to review some pension basics.

HOW PENSIONS WORK

Types of Plans

Your pension plan is either a defined benefit plan or a defined contribution plan. Sometimes you may have both. A *defined benefit* plan is one in which your employer determines in advance what monthly benefits you eventually receive, usually depending on age, years of service, and compensation. Specific formulas, established when the plan was set up, are used to figure your retirement benefits. During your working years, your employer funds the plan so that it can meet this predetermined level of benefits.

This type of plan may use one of the following three formulas. The first is not based on the amount of an employee's pay; the others are.

- *Dollars per year of service.* Under this formula, an employee receives a specified number of dollars per month multiplied by the number of years of service. Therefore, if a plan gives $15 per month per year of service and an employee works for 20 years, the pension would be $300 per month or $3,600 a year.
- *Career-average salary plan.* This type of plan credits a percentage of salary for each year of service. For example, your plan might credit a pension of 1 percent of your salary for each year. The annual credits are added to determine your total pension. Employers using this method sometimes adjust the early years' salaries to bring them into line with inflation.

- *Final average salary plan.* This method is similar to the career-average salary plan except the benefit is based upon an employee's *average* salary for the last 3 or 5 years with the employer. In some plans, the highest 5 consecutive years out of the last 10 are used. Employers using this plan sometimes credit a smaller percentage of employees' salaries than they would if they used the career-average salary plan.

The other type of pension arrangement you may have participated in is a *defined contribution* plan. Under most of these plans, contributions are fixed, but the actual benefit you receive is not known until you retire. For example, a plan might require an employer to contribute 7 percent of each employee's salary each year to the fund. Profit-sharing plans, 401(k) plans, thrift plans, money purchase plans, and ESOPs are all types of defined contribution pension arrangements. Some profit-sharing plans and ESOPs leave the contribution up to the employer's discretion and give guidelines on how contributions are to be allocated among all the participants. Under most 401(k) plans, employees elect to defer part of their salary and have it contributed to the plan, along with the employer's matching contributions, which are equal to some percentage of the employee's deferrals.

Each individual's account receives, at least annually, his or her share of the plan's investment income plus any appreciation in the market values of the underlying investments. Thus the actual benefits you receive depend on the amount that has accumulated in your account.

Unlike defined benefit plans, there are generally no benefit formulas associated with defined contribution plans. Whatever is in your account when you retire becomes your benefit. Your plan may use the money to buy an annuity, or it may give you the money as a lump sum.

A summary of your pension plan, given to you by your plan administrator when you first begin employment, outlines the type of plan you have and the benefit formulas that are applicable (if you are in a defined benefit plan). We suggest that you consult this document, known as the *summary plan description,* a few years before you begin to contemplate retirement. Because you may not have access to all your salary records for each year you worked, your plan administrator can probably estimate the amount of pension you will receive.

Under the Employee Retirement Income Security Act (ERISA), the law that governs many pension plans, you are entitled to a statement of your pension benefits once a year. If your plan doesn't provide this information automatically, request it. The law requires that you make your request in writing. If you have any trouble with your plan or employer, you can seek help from: Division of Technical Assistance and Inquiries, Pension and Welfare Benefits Administration, U.S. Department of Labor, 200 Constitution Avenue, N.W., Washington, DC 20210.

Vesting. To be eligible for a benefit funded by employer contributions, you must be *vested;* that is, you must have worked a certain number of years for the same employer.

At one time 10-year "cliff" vesting was the norm for most pension plans, which meant employees had to work at the same company for at least 10 years. However, the 1986 tax law liberalized the rules. Now employees who work for a single employer earn the right to a pension after they have been on the job for only 5 years. The 10-year rule still applies to multiemployer plans—those collectively bargained plans to which two or more employers contribute.

Instead of cliff vesting, your company may use graded vesting, which means 20 percent of your pension is vested after three years of service. Under this arrangement, an additional 20 percent of your pension is vested each year until 100 percent is vested after seven years. Other plans allow benefits to vest more rapidly, some even providing for 100 percent vesting immediately, as soon as an employee joins the plan.

As you prepare to retire, review all the companies you have worked for during your career that maintained a pension plan. Check to see whether you're eligible for a pension from any of them. If you worked for one employer less than 10 years, or if you previously received your benefit as a lump-sum distribution, you probably won't be eligible. But if the plan provided for more rapid vesting, you might qualify for a small benefit. If you've worked fewer than five years in any one job, you probably won't get anything. Because of the vesting rules and the fact that many employers do not maintain pension plans, it's possible to work for many employers and walk away with nothing at retirement. If you're not sure, check with the pension administrators at your former employers.

The vesting rules apply only to plans funded by employer contributions. In plans that are funded with your own contributions, such as 401(k) plans, your pension is vested immediately.

Years of service. Generally, under defined benefit plans, the more years you have worked, the larger your pension. But not every year you work is necessarily counted as a year of service for purposes of figuring your benefit. For example, you earn a full year of credit if you belong to the plan for an entire year, and partial credit if you work half time or for half of the year. If you worked fewer than 1,000 hours during the year, you may have earned no pension credits for that year. Or if you worked for an employer that did not have a pension plan for some of the years you were employed, your plan may or may not count the years before the plan started.

In calculating your pension, your employer also considers any breaks of service in your years with the company. A break in service is a year in which you did not work more than a minimum amount, usually 500 hours. For example, you work for an employer for four years and leave the company for a period of five years. When you eventually come back to work, you may have lost the credit for the four years you worked there previously.

There are exceptions to this rule, however. If you left because of pregnancy or to take care of a child, up to 501 hours of your leave does not count as a break in service. If you serve in the armed forces during a war or in a national emergency, that time away from your job is not considered a break in service. But if you had a break in service before 1976 for reasons other than military service, your employer may not give you credit for some of those years.

SOCIAL SECURITY BENEFITS AND YOUR PENSION

Some pension plans, especially those defined benefit plans that use benefit formulas based on an employee's salary, are likely to be integrated with Social Security. That means your employer has considered the amount of your Social Security benefit in designing its pension plan, so that the combination of both will provide a certain percentage of your preretirement income.

Some employers also use integrated plans to give more pension benefits to its higher-paid employees. As noted in chapter 2, Social Security is designed to replace a larger percentage of pay for lower-paid workers. Partially to make up for this, many integrated pension plans provide higher-paid workers with a larger percentage of their preretirement earnings than is the case with lower-paid workers. The following table shows how three employees with different earnings might fare under a typical integrated defined benefit pension plan. (The table assumes that a 65-year-old employee retired with 35 years of service on January 1, 1991.)

TABLE 7
Annual Retirement Income

		Percent of Compensation from		
Employee	**Compensation in 1990**	**Social Security**	**Employer Pension**	**Total**
A	$200,000	6	50	56
B	51,300	24	42	66
C	20,000	43	27	70

To mesh pension benefits with Social Security, a plan may subtract part of an employee's Social Security benefit from his or her pension benefit, or it may provide more pension benefits for earnings above a certain level. That level is usually the amount of earnings on which your employer has paid your Social Security taxes.

In the past, integration rules often resulted in lower-paid workers receiving a very small company pension or none at all. However, new rules now require plans to leave you with at least one-half of your pension benefit after accounting for Social Security. But the rule applies only for the years worked after 1988. If your plan subtracts Social Security benefits, you may still find yourself without a pension for those early working years. Because the integration rules are complicated, you should consult your plan administrator to find out how they affect your benefits.

WHEN CAN YOU TAKE YOUR BENEFITS?

Under most defined contribution plans, you may choose to receive your pension account balance whenever you terminate your employment. You can get it in a single sum or leave it invested in the plan. (For account balances of less than $3,500, you may have to take your money in a lump sum.)

All defined benefit plans pay out pensions when you retire on or after your normal retirement age, usually 65. Most defined benefit plans also provide benefits to those taking early retirement. (ERISA doesn't require all plans to offer early retirement benefits, however.) Your plan may also allow you to take a reduced benefit at 55 or 60 instead of a full pension beginning at normal retirement age. Your pension is smaller because you have fewer years of service and you do not have the benefit of the salary increases you might have received if you had continued working until you were 65.

In addition, if your benefits begin before the normal retirement age, there is a reduction for early retirement that varies from plan to plan. It reflects the fact that the pension begins sooner and is expected to be paid for more years. Usually count on losing up to 7 percent of your benefit for each year you are under 65 when payments begin. *Example:* If you ordinarily receive a monthly pension of $1,000 at 65 but choose to take your benefit at 60, you could lose about one-third of your monthly benefit and only receive $667. If you begin to collect your pension at age 55, it may be reduced by half or even more than half. In this example, you'd receive $500. But you do have the advantages of receiving the benefit sooner and receiving it for more years.

A few plans offer early retirement benefits without the usual reduction to employees who have been with the company for 20 or 25 years. Even if you are in one of these plans, you may still have to meet further eligibility requirements. For example, you must only be doing work covered by the plan when you reach early retirement age. Similarly the plan may allow employees with 20 years of service to receive a pension at age 60 without any reduction, but the employee must actually be working in order to collect benefits. Someone who quits at 58 will not receive the unreduced pension even if he or she has worked the required 20 years.

Taking Early Retirement

Should you take your pension early? It depends on your continued satisfaction with your job, whether or not you can afford to leave the work force, and your employer's plans for keeping you on in the company. If your employer forces you to take early retirement, you have little choice. In that case you must decide whether or not to take an unreduced deferred pension or a reduced pension that begins immediately.

Employers often increase your pension benefits as an added inducement to take early retirement. If your employer is not offering improved benefits and still wants you to leave, try to negotiate better terms. Try at least to obtain an unreduced immediate pension.

If you leave your employer but intend to collect your pension later, consider whether those benefits will continue to grow indefinitely. If you are a member of a defined benefit plan, your pension, payable at the normal retirement age, is generally fixed. The main advantage to delaying your pension payout in this case is to get an unreduced benefit instead of the reduced early retirement pension. If you are in a defined contribution plan, the money in your account will continue to earn interest.

Delaying Retirement

Under the Age Discrimination in Employment Act (ADEA), an employer cannot force most employees to retire because of age. As a result, you may be able to postpone retirement past your employer's normal retirement age, which is usually 65. However, pension laws require that you begin withdrawing your money according to a prescribed schedule by April 1 following the year you turn 70½. As we point out in chapter 1, you may or may not get credit for the additional years of service you work past age 65. If you do, and you're in good health and want to continue working, your pension obviously will be larger.

PENSION PAYMENT OPTIONS

One of the most difficult and important decisions you face at the time of retirement is how to take your pension benefits. This decision will affect your financial well-being for the rest of your life.

Most defined contribution plans make the money available as a lump sum, and many such plans also allow payment in installments or in various forms of annuities. You may be able to choose among a lump-sum payment and several annuity options. (If your benefits have a value of $3,500 or less, the plan may require you to take a lump-sum payment.) Each option has its advantages and disadvantages, and tax considerations may also affect your decision.

ERISA says that defined benefit plans must pay your pension as some form of an annuity unless you elect otherwise. Most plans first determine the amount of your pension as a monthly annuity payable for your lifetime, with no benefits payable after your death. This is called a *life annuity* and is the plan's normal form. However, most plans offer other options. They must offer married participants a *qualified joint-and-survivor annuity,* which provides an annuity for as long as the retired employee lives. This annuity also provides the retiree's surviving spouse with a benefit at least equal to 50 percent of the benefit the retiree received; payments to the surviving spouse must continue for the rest of his or her life. This arrangement is called a *50 percent joint-and-survivor annuity.* Some plans also offer married participants a *100 percent joint-and-survivor annuity,* which provides the surviving spouse with the same payments the retiree received.

For married participants, the plan must pay the pension in the form of a joint-and-survivor annuity unless the employee elects otherwise with the consent of his or her spouse. The consent form that follows is typical of those provided by most pension plans. If you're the spouse of a retiree, be sure you understand what you are doing if you are asked to sign such a form. You may be giving up a valuable benefit that will affect your financial well-being for the rest of your life, assuming your spouse dies before you do.

There are differences between the 50 percent joint-and-survivor annuities offered through pension plans and those offered by life insurance companies (see chapter 4). Pension annuities pay benefits to a retired participant for his lifetime and pay 50 percent of that amount to the survivor when the retiree dies (assuming a 50 percent joint-and-survivor arrangement). Insurance company annuities usually pay benefits to both persons jointly and then reduce the monthly benefit to the survivor when either of the parties to the annuity dies.

There are other kinds of annuities. Your plan, for example, may offer a *life annuity with a 10-year period certain.* Under this arrangement, the retiree receives payments for the rest of his or her life. But if the retiree dies before receiving 120 payments (in other words, within 10 years of retirement), his or her beneficiary continues to receive the payments until a total of 120 payments has been made, to either the retiree or to the surviving spouse or to another named beneficiary. Payments then stop, and the surviving spouse receives nothing

RETIREMENT BENEFIT PLAN

Spouse Election to Waive Qualified Joint-and-Survivor Annuity

Name of Participant ______________________________

I, ______________________________, certify that I am the
(print name of Participant's spouse)

spouse of the Participant named above. I hereby elect to waive the qualified joint-and-survivor annuity form of benefit under the Retirement Benefit Plan. I acknowledge that this election may cause me to forfeit part or all of the benefits that would otherwise be payable to me if I am still living after the death of my spouse.

______________________ ______________________________
Date Signature of Participant's spouse

WITNESS BY *EITHER* PLAN REPRESENTATIVE OR NOTARY PUBLIC

WITNESS BY PLAN ADMINISTRATOR

______________________ ______________________________
Date Signature of Plan Representative

WITNESS BY NOTARY PUBLIC

On this ________ day of ________________, 19 ____, personally appeared before me the above-named Participant's spouse, known to me (or satisfactorily proven) to be the person whose name is subscribed to the above instrument, and in my presence signed and sealed the same, and acknowledged that he (she) executed the same for the purposes therein contained and acknowledged the same to be his (her) act.

IN WITNESS WHEREOF, I hereunto set my hand and official seal.

____
Notary Public

more. Sometimes you may find a plan that offers an annuity with a 5-year period certain. In this case, payments to a surviving spouse continue for only 5 years. If you choose a form of annuity other than a life annuity, your monthly payments are lower to reflect the payments that will be made to your survivors.

Many plans also allow you to take your pension as a lump-sum payment that is equal to the value of the annuity payments you would have received if you had chosen that option. The plan determines the amount of your lump-sum distribution by calculating a number of factors that are spelled out in your plan document. These factors differ from plan to plan and often change when interest rates change. Consult your plan document to see how a lump-sum distribution is calculated under your pension plan.

The following table shows what you and your surviving spouse can expect to receive from different pension options. In this example, we have assumed that both husband and wife are 65 and the retiree is entitled to a $1,000 monthly payment under his or her plan's normal form.

TABLE 8
Pension Options

	Monthly Benefit	
	Retiree	**Survivor (if payable)**
Life annuity (normal form)	$1,000	0
100% joint-and-survivor annuity	$820	$820
50% joint-and-survivor annuity	$900	$450
Life annuity with 120 payments guaranteed (life annuity with a 10-year period certain)	$910	$910
Lump-sum distribution (single payment)	$100,000	0

SURVIVORS' BENEFITS

ERISA requires that pension plans offering retirement benefits in the form of annuities also offer survivors' benefits. There are two kinds of survivors' benefits—those available after you have retired and those available before. After you have begun collecting your pension, your surviving spouse is eligible for a portion of your benefits so long as you have selected a joint-and-survivor annuity.

Under defined contribution plans, your full account balance is usually provided as a death benefit when you die, regardless of whether or not you are vested. Under a defined benefit plan, if you have not retired and your benefit is vested, the amount your surviving spouse would receive—called a *preretirement survivor annuity*—depends on whether you died after becoming eligible for early retirement benefits or before. *Example:* You die at 57, two years after you first become eligible for early retirement. You have accrued a monthly pension benefit of $1,000 payable at 65. The plan calculates the survivors' benefits as if you had retired and received an early retirement benefit under a qualified joint-and-survivor annuity on the day before you died, and then death immediately followed. Your early retirement benefit, payable as a single life annuity, would have been $500. The plan then assumes you had selected a qualified joint-and-survivor annuity (ordinarily a 50 percent joint-and-survivor annuity) and reduces the $500 by approximately 10 percent. Your monthly pension is now $450, and is further reduced by half to reach the amount that your spouse is entitled to under a 50 percent joint-and-survivor option. In this example, your surviving spouse would receive $225 each month for life as a preretirement survivor annuity. As you can see, if you die very soon after reaching your plan's early retirement age, your spouse cannot expect a very large benefit from your pension plan. The benefit becomes larger the closer you are to the plan's normal retirement age, usually 65.

If you have a vested benefit but die before you reach early retirement age, your spouse's benefit is even lower. In calculating this benefit, the plan assumes you had: (1) terminated employment immediately prior to your death; (2) lived to your early retirement age, typically 55 or 60; (3) elected to receive early retirement under the plan's qualified joint-and-survivor annuity; and (4) immediately died. Many plans also will not pay a benefit to a survivor until the date when the deceased spouse would have reached the plan's early retirement age. Thus if you die at 50, your spouse may have to wait until you would have been 55 or 60 to collect a benefit.

Preretirement survivors' annuities are not likely to provide much income for widowed spouses unless the employee died when he or she was close to retirement. In planning for a spouse's income after your death, be sure to consider the amount of the benefit and when your spouse is eligible for it. For most people, it's wise not to count too much on your defined benefit plan alone. A combination of Social Security, a defined contribution plan, and group life insurance often provides substantial benefits.

If you are working somewhere else when you die and have a fully vested pension from another employer, your spouse is still eligible for a preretirement survivor annuity from your first employer. However, these benefits are usually not available to people who have left pension plans before 1985 (or before 1987 in some collectively bargained plans). Check with the plan administrators at your former employers to see if your spouse is eligible.

If you are not vested, your spouse ordinarily receives nothing from the defined benefit plan when you die.

DISABILITY BENEFITS

Defined contribution plans usually pay the balance of the employee's account when he or she becomes disabled. Defined benefit plans, on the other hand, handle disability benefits in one of three ways, assuming that the employer maintains a separate long-term disability insurance program.

First, the pension plan may provide no disability benefit

until the employee is 65, when the insurance benefit stops. At that point, the pension plan may pay the pension earned up to the time of disability, or it may pay the pension the employee would have received if he or she had continued working to age 65. Second, the pension plan may pay a disabled worker an immediate pension equal to the benefit that he or she has accrued to date, with or without a reduction for early retirement. (These benefits tend to be very small.) Third, a plan may pay an immediate pension benefit that's larger than the worker's accrued benefit, assuming the disabled worker had worked until 65. Obviously a person would do better under the latter arrangement.

Pension plans generally specify no minimum age for receiving disability benefits. Payments may continue as long as the employee is disabled, or they may stop when a worker turns 65, when the plan begins paying regular retirement benefits. Survivors' benefits are usually available to spouses of workers who had been receiving disability benefits.

Each pension plan has its own rules for determining eligibility benefits for disabled workers. Some, for example, may use the same standard that the SSA uses for determining disability benefits (see chapter 2). Others may use more liberal or even stricter tests.

COST-OF-LIVING INCREASES

Most pension plans don't provide for cost-of-living increases once monthly payments start. That means the monthly benefit you receive at retirement remains the same until your death. This lack of adjustment for inflation is a significant drawback of private pensions. *Example:* You receive a monthly pension of $100 at age 65. Inflation runs 4 percent a year, so your pension is worth only $68 by the time you are 75. If you're lucky enough to have cost-of-living increases, be sure to consider them when you complete the worksheets discussed in chapter 1.

Some pension plans occasionally do give ad hoc increases to retirees. Check to see whether employees who have retired before you have received any such increases, although there's no guarantee that the plan will continue to give cost-of-living adjustments when you retire.

HOW PENSION PLANS ARE TAXED

Payments from pension plans are generally taxable in the year you receive them. With certain exceptions, they are added to your income in determining your federal and state income taxes. But any part of your pension payments that represents amounts on which you have already paid taxes (your after-tax contributions) is not subject to additional taxes. Various payment options are taxed in the following manner.

Lump-Sum Payments

If you receive a lump-sum payment, you are probably able to reduce your tax by electing forward averaging. Under five-year averaging, the balance of your pension payment is taxed (1) as if you were single, (2) you received one-fifth of the amount each year for five years, and (3) you had no other income. *Example:* You receive a pension of $100,000 and choose five-year averaging. The amount is taxed as if you were a single taxpayer, had received payments of $20,000 a year for five years, and had no other income.

If you were born before 1936, you are also eligible to elect 10-year averaging, which is similar to 5-year averaging except that 10 years instead of 5 are used in the calculation. The tax rates required for 10-year averaging are the higher rates that were in effect in 1986, the date of the last tax reform act.

Five- or 10-year forward averaging almost always results in your paying less tax than if you take a lump sum and pay all the taxes that are due the year you receive the money.

To use either averaging method, you will, however, have to meet a few requirements:

- You must take all of your pension from a particular plan in a lump sum.

- Your payment must result from your death, retirement, or other separation from service of your employer, or because you are disabled.
- The payment must be made after you reach 59½, and you may elect averaging only once in your lifetime.

Example: You retire after 20 years with the police force, take your pension as a lump sum, and choose five-year averaging. Then you go to work as a security guard for a department store and are also covered by a pension plan. When you leave that plan and take a lump sum, you are not eligible for any type of forward averaging.

If you were born before 1936 and were a member of a pension plan before 1974, a portion of the benefits you earned before 1974 may be taxed at the old capital gains rates. This may lower your tax. (To calculate your tax on a lump-sum distribution using either 5- or 10-year averaging or capital gains rates, use IRS Form 4972.) Compute your tax using each method you are eligible to use to see which way is best.

If your company has funded your pension plan over the years with its own stocks or bonds, your lump-sum payment may be eligible for favorable tax treatment. This means if you take a lump sum in the form of employee securities, an amount equal to the employer's cost for the securities is treated as ordinary income. But you usually don't have to pay tax on the appreciation until you sell the securities, when that appreciation is taxed as a capital gain. If your distribution of employer securities doesn't qualify for this special treatment, you'll have to pay taxes on the securities' value when you receive the money, just as if you had received the distribution in cash.

Annuities

Taxation of pensions taken as annuities can be complicated. It depends largely on whether the money has been taxed before it went into the pension plan. All annuity payments are taxable unless you made contributions to the plan that were not deductible, or unless your employer previously reported taxable income for you. In those cases, the portion of each annuity payment that represents a return of those amounts that you already paid tax on will escape further taxation.

If your pension plan was noncontributory, that is, your employer funded the plan and you contributed nothing, all of your annuity payments are usually taxed as ordinary income. If your plan was contributory—you contributed some of your salary to the plan—the taxation is less straightforward.

In many plans only the employer makes contributions. Some workers are covered by plans in which they make all the contributions, or by plans where both employer and employee contribute. All of your employer's contribution as well as the earnings from contributions made by both you and your employer are taxable. But if you made some contributions with money that was already taxed, then the portion of your payments that represents the return of your own contributions will come back tax-free. If you previously had taxable income on the cost of insurance protection provided by the plan, these previously taxed amounts are treated as if they were nondeductible employee contributions.

Note: If your employer provides a 401(k) or other salary reduction plan, the salary reductions put into the plan are treated the same way as your employer's contribution, and you have to pay taxes on the amount when you begin to withdraw it.

If you must pay taxes, at least they are spread out over several years. Each year your plan administrator will provide you with IRS Form 1099-R that states how much you received from the plan and how much of that amount is taxable income.

Taxes After Death

Benefits payable to your beneficiaries or to your estate after your death are generally taxable in a manner similar to the taxation of your own benefits while you are alive. If you die with a relatively large estate, your estate may be subject to estate tax as well. Your taxable estate also includes your vested account balance in a defined contribution plan and the value of future payments under a joint-and-survivor annuity or other annuity that began, or could have begun, prior to your death. However, most estates do not have to pay any tax (see chapter 17).

In addition to the regular estate tax, your estate may have to pay a tax on excess accumulations described later in this chapter.

Additional Taxes

Pension distributions are subject to various additional taxes in certain circumstances. These additional taxes can cut deeply into your pension accumulations and affect your financial well-being. Keep them in mind as you begin planning for retirement.

Taking payments too early. If you take money out of a qualified plan, including IRA and Keogh accounts, before you're 59½ and do not roll them over into another qualified plan or IRA, you may have to pay a penalty of 10 percent of the amount withdrawn. However, no penalty tax applies to: (1) amounts paid as an annuity over your lifetime or your life expectancy, (2) amounts paid from a qualified plan upon separation from service after age 55, (3) distributions upon death or disability, (4) payments under a qualified domestic relations order, or (5) amounts withdrawn to pay certain medical expenses.

Besides the tax penalty, you'll have to pay ordinary income taxes on all the payments made to you. If you're in this situation, you may want to minimize the tax bite by taking a life annuity that avoids the penalty tax and spreads out the ordinary income tax over your lifetime. Or you might want to roll over the money into an IRA and defer taxes until you're 70½. But the IRA option is feasible only if you have other money to live on until you can begin collecting Social Security benefits. If you need the money from your pension, your choices may be between a life annuity, installments over your life expectancy, or a lump-sum payment with the attendant tax penalty. Unfortunately, none of these options may be ideal.

Taking too little. When you turn 70½, you *must* begin taking money from a qualified plan. (The IRS specifies a minimum amount that must be withdrawn.) If you fail to take out the required amount, you may have to pay a stiff 50 percent penalty on the amount of the shortfall on every payment. *Example:* The minimum withdrawal is $1,250 and you take out only $750. You have to pay a tax of $250 on the shortfall of $500, in addition to the regular tax. Bear in mind that this tax is not deductible. You must take your first payment by April 1 of the following year and subsequent payments by December 31 of every year.

The minimum distribution requirement is satisfied if you receive your entire benefit in a lump-sum distribution by the required starting date, or if you begin to receive your entire benefit by that date in the form of a life annuity payable over your lifetime or the combined lifetimes of you and your spouse.

Otherwise, the minimum payment you must take is calculated by dividing the balance in your plan at the beginning of the year when you reach 70½ by your life expectancy (or the life expectancy of you and your spouse combined), according to the IRS regulations and tables. *Example:* You are unmarried and turn 70½ on September 6, 1992. The balance in your qualified plan on December 31, 1991, is $100,000. You decide not to take a lump-sum distribution or a life annuity. According to the IRS regulations and tables, your life expectancy is 15.3 years. Dividing $100,000 by 15.3 years results in a minimum payment for 1992 of about $6,536, which must be paid to you by April 1, 1993. On December 31, 1992, your account balance is $110,000 and your life expectancy is 14.6 years. Reducing this by the $6,536 required to be distributed for 1992 on the following April 1, only $103,464 must be considered in determining the required distribution for 1993. The amount you must withdraw for 1993 is $103,464 divided by 14.6 years, or $7,086. You must make this withdrawal of $7,086 by December 31, 1993, in addition to the $6,536 withdrawal required by April 1, 1993.

Thus two minimum withdrawal amounts are required in 1993, the first year of required withdrawals. Each year thereafter a new minimum withdrawal amount must be calculated and withdrawn by December 31.

As you can see, the rules for determining life expectancy as described in the IRS regulations are complex. You may need assistance from a professional tax adviser to determine the correct amount.

Receiving excess distributions. Those few pension recipients who receive a very large payout will find that the IRS wants its share. If you withdraw more than $150,000 a year or take a lump sum greater than $750,000 (these numbers will be adjusted in future years for inflation), you may pay a 15 percent tax.

Excess retirement accumulations at death. If your estate includes large amounts of benefits payable from your pension plan, the estate may have to pay an additional 15 percent estate tax on the excess retirement accumulation. The amount that is subject to this tax depends on your age at death and other factors. For example, it may apply to amounts in excess of $1,350,000 if you die at 45, or amounts in excess of $1,050,000 if you die at 65. The amount subject to tax is not eligible for the marital deduction. Thus your estate may be liable for this tax even though it may escape all other death taxes. We suggest seeking guidance from a tax attorney if you think this tax applies to your estate.

HOW DO YOU WANT YOUR MONEY?

In choosing a payment option, you have to consider both the nontax and the tax aspects of each payment method.

Nontax Aspects

If your plan gives automatic cost-of-living adjustments to retirees, or has given ad hoc adjustments in the last five years, you probably should not take a lump-sum distribution. If you do, you would lose out on any future increases, which could be vital to your financial well-being. If you don't expect any benefit increases, consider the following points.

1. If you are married and your plan offers a 100 percent joint-and-survivor annuity that provides an income to your spouse after your death, we recommend that you take it. It is important to provide a continuous income for your spouse after your death. As we pointed out before, your plan may automatically give you a joint-and-survivor annuity unless your spouse elects in writing to give up the benefit. Be careful, though, the plan may give you a 50 percent joint-and-survivor annuity rather than a 100 percent joint-and-survivor. Though two people can live together more cheaply than each alone, the reduction in living expenses is not 50 percent.
2. Compare the annual pension you receive under a 100 percent joint-and-survivor plan with the annual income you receive by investing a lump-sum distribution. Determine what you can earn on the lump sum and choose that option if it will give you a larger income.
3. Don't choose a joint-and-survivor annuity if your spouse is in ill health and has only a short time to live.
4. Don't be tempted to give up a joint-and-survivor annuity in favor of a life insurance policy. In chapter 5, we point out that life insurance agents often try to persuade prospective retirees to give up a joint-and-survivor annuity and buy life insurance instead. That's usually not a good idea.
5. Consider taking a lump-sum payout if your plan offers only a 50 percent joint-and-survivor annuity. The 50 percent plan may give your spouse too little to live on, and you may do better investing the lump sum and allowing your spouse to live off the income. Work through several calculations to make sure that your spouse will do better under the lump-sum option.
6. Consider your personality and possible propensity to spend a lump sum. If you feel you may quickly use up your pension distribution, then an annuity is a better option for you. With most annuity options, you will have money coming in on a regular basis for the rest of your life.

Tax Aspects

You also must give some thought to the tax treatment of various payment options.

If you choose a lump sum, you may roll it over into an IRA and defer taxes until you reach age 70½, when you must begin withdrawing a minimum amount each year. If you choose the rollover option, you have only 60 days from the time you get your distribution to complete the rollover process. After 60 days, any pension proceeds you have failed to roll over are fully taxable.

Starting January 1, 1993, if you receive a lump-sum payment from a qualified plan, a federal withholding tax of 20 percent will be deducted from the distribution *unless* it is rolled over directly to an IRA (or other qualified plan). Once you choose a rollover, then, have the money transferred directly from the plan to the IRA, instead of receiving a check and depositing it in an IRA within 60 days. Consult the plan administrator or your tax adviser.

If you choose a lump sum and elect not to roll it over into an IRA, consider the various tax treatments described previously in this chapter. Remember, you can use forward averaging only once in your lifetime. If, for example, you decide to take your lump sum and pay the taxes using five-year forward averaging, you cannot use it again when you withdraw funds in your IRA a few years later. Similarly, it makes no sense to roll your pension money into an IRA and then withdraw the money as a lump sum—you'll no longer be able to use forward averaging.

We recommend that you figure the present value of a stream of income after tax under each arrangement and see which way you come out best. If you can't make the calculations yourself, get help from your employer's benefits administrator or a tax adviser. The following illustrates some tax comparisons among various options:

1. You retire on January 1, 1993, when you turn 65. You receive a lump-sum distribution of $125,000. You are considering either taking the lump sum and paying all the taxes

that are due using 10-year forward averaging or taking the money and rolling it over into an IRA.

If you choose to take a lump sum and pay the taxes, 10-year forward averaging will reduce the tax on the amount you receive as if you had earned the $125,000 over a period of 10 years. After you make the calculation using IRS Form 4972, the taxes on your distribution amount to $19,183. Subtracting this sum from the $125,000 lump sum results in $105,817, the present value of your distribution after taxes. (We have not considered state income taxes in this calculation.)

Now consider the IRA rollover option. Assuming you don't need the pension money for living expenses, you can let it earn interest inside an IRA for another five years and three months—until April 1 following 1998, the year when you turn 70½. If you earn 7 percent on your IRA by 1998, it grows to about $188,000. At that point you must begin withdrawing your money, although the withdrawal for the first year, 1998, is not due until the following April 1. Assuming the remainder of your funds continue to earn 7 percent and you withdraw money in level annual installments over your life expectancy of 15 years (15.3 years according to the IRS tables), you have an annuity of $19,249. Assuming you are in the 28 percent tax bracket (again ignoring state taxes), your annual income after taxes comes to $13,859. The present value on your retirement date of this stream of income that begins in 1999 is about $99,000.

As you can see in this example, you are better off taking the lump sum, as far as taxes are concerned. However, whether or not you come out best taxwise depends on the amount of your pension, tax bracket, life expectancy, and your assumptions of how much your money can earn inside the IRA.

2. Now compare a lump-sum payment of $125,000 with an immediate life annuity from your company pension plan. Again, choosing a lump sum with 10-year forward averaging, you'll have $105,817 after paying taxes. If you choose the life annuity, the monthly amount you receive will be based upon factors specified in the plan document. Whether this option is better or worse than a lump sum depends on what

those factors are, and how long you actually live.

Another alternative is to choose the lump sum if you think you can invest it profitably at a higher rate. You could also receive a lump-sum distribution and roll it over into an individual retirement annuity providing a lifetime income. There is no tax on the rollover, but the monthly annuity payments are taxable as they are received, and this may give a higher monthly life annuity than your company's plan (see chapter 4).

HOW SAFE IS YOUR PENSION?

In recent years, some financially strapped companies have discarded a number of financial benefits for their workers, including pension plans. If a company decides to terminate its pension arrangements and has enough assets to pay the benefits promised, the federal government allows the company to end the plan. The company then provides for the benefits by giving employees a lump-sum payment upon retirement or by buying annuities from life insurance companies equal in value to the employee's accrued benefit.

If your employer is in this group, you and your fellow workers should investigate the insurance company that your employer is using. It may have chosen a carrier that is financially unstable or one that puts its money in high-risk investments, such as junk bonds. You may, in the end, have little say in your employer's decision. But you should at least check the insurance company's ratings from Moody's, Standard & Poor's, and A. M. Best and make your feelings known to your plan administrator.

If your employer terminates a pension plan and has insufficient assets to pay all the promised benefits, then it's up to the federal government to make sure workers get their benefits. The government also gets involved if your employer goes into liquidation or bankruptcy reorganization. Sometimes the government's pension agency, the Pension Benefit Guaranty Corporation (PBGC), makes its own determination that an employer and its pension plan are in bad financial shape. Sometimes the PBGC even initiates a plan termination.

Most tax-qualified defined benefit plans set up by private corporations are insured by the Pension Benefit Guaranty Corporation, which was set up in 1974 to protect workers' pensions. Your money in defined contribution plans, and money in some defined benefit plans established by state and local governments, church and fraternal organizations, and professional organizations, is *not* protected by the PBGC.

If a pension plan insured by the PBGC cannot pay vested benefits to workers, the agency becomes the trustee of the plan and continues to pay pension benefits up to a maximum specified by the law. In 1991, the agency was allowed to pay up to $2,250 each month to a worker in a single-employer plan who retired at the plan's normal retirement age. For workers in multiemployer plans the maximum limit is lower. The maximum limit, is smaller still for benefits to workers who retired early or who took their benefits in a form other than a life annuity.

The agency also pays survivors' benefits. If a surviving spouse is receiving benefits before a pension plan is terminated, the PBGC will continue to pay them. If a plan ends before a worker has reached the plan's normal retirement age, and the worker dies, the agency will pay the surviving spouse's benefits.

If your pension plan terminates, your plan administrator must notify you in writing at least 60 days beforehand. If your employer is terminating the plan and has enough assets to pay benefits, you will receive a second notice that tells you the amount of the benefit, how it has been valued, and the assumptions used in the calculation. If the company has purchased an annuity from a life insurance company, be sure you receive a certificate from the carrier.

If your plan has insufficient assets to pay benefits, and the PBGC takes over the plan, it must notify you of this action. The PBGC keeps records of plan participants and their benefits. If you are about to receive retirement benefits, the PBGC pays them directly to you.

4

Annuities

Annuities serve many purposes. They can act as investment vehicles allowing you to continue saving money and taxes at the same time. Or they can provide you with a guaranteed income each month for the rest of your life. You might even have an annuity that does both. Some annuities are deferred; others give you immediate payment.

An *immediate* annuity begins to pay off as soon as you invest in it. You can set up such an annuity at retirement either by investing your accumulated savings or by electing to have your company's pension benefits paid to you as a lifetime stream of income.

A *deferred* annuity is one that you invest in now and draw on later. You can buy a deferred annuity by investing a lump-sum payment or by making periodic payments. Later you can convert that money into an income stream. Deferred annuities have two phases—an *accumulation* phase, during which you save money at a stated rate of interest, and a *payout* phase, when the insurance company where you have invested your money returns your accumulation in the form of monthly or yearly payments.

THE ACCUMULATION PHASE

The main factors affecting the value of an annuity between the time you pay the premium and the time you start getting something back are (1) the interest rate, (2) the terms governing your ability to cash in the policy, and (3) administrative charges.

Interest rate. Each month or so an insurance company declares the interest rate it will credit on new annuity contracts, a rate determined primarily by the investment opportunities the company has for new money coming in. This rate is called the *current rate*. In late 1991, these rates were in the 7 percent range.

The current rate is usually good for an initial *guarantee period*. Some policies let you choose one of several guarantee periods, ranging from 1 to as many as 10 years. Some annuities offer higher rates if you choose a longer guarantee period. Once a guarantee period is over, companies offer a new current rate good for the next period, which may be shorter or longer than the period you first selected.

Although you don't know at the start of one period what rate will be declared for the next period, there is a contractual minimum rate, which may also vary over the life of the annuity. An annuity contract might specify, for example, a current rate of 8 percent guaranteed for 1 year as well as a minimum of 6 percent for the first 10 years and a minimum of 4 percent after that.

A few companies credit your money with a certain interest rate during the accumulation phase but actually pay those rates only if you convert to the payout phase of the contract. If you take your money in a lump sum rather than annuitize or take your money in regular monthly payouts at the end of the accumulation phase, the company recomputes your earnings using a lower rate.

In recent years, insurance companies have promoted annuities by touting a high current rate. Don't buy merely on the basis of that high rate and don't ignore the other elements of the contract.

Cashing in your policy. Sellers promote annuities by emphasizing their total accumulated value to prospective buyers after 5, 10, 15, and 20 years. But, in many cases, you can't cash in your annuity and receive that particular sum. You receive instead the *cash surrender value,* your total accumulation after the insurance company deducts surrender charges.

The surrender charge, designed to discourage you from cashing in your contract before the company has recouped its expenses, is usually expressed as a percentage of the accumulation value. A few annuities express surrender charges as a percentage of the premium. That's a more favorable arrangement, since policyholders who cash in the annuity pay a penalty only on the original investment, not on the interest earnings.

Usually, surrender charges are high if you cash in early, but they decline over time and disappear after seven or eight years. Typical surrender charges start at 6 percent of the accumulation value and disappear by the seventh year. Some charges may be much higher and last much longer. Surrender charges can be important if you have recently bought an annuity but sudden poor health forces you to take early retirement and you need the money for immediate living expenses.

Obviously, a surrender charge that's glued to an annuity for the entire accumulation phase is more onerous than one that decreases after seven or eight years. For example, one that remains level at 7 percent for seven years is less desirable than one that starts out at 7 percent, tapers off, and disappears in the eighth year.

Some plans guarantee that you won't lose any principal if you cash in early. In effect, they promise that the surrender charge will not exceed the interest you've earned. That's helpful to those who must cash in soon after investing in an annuity.

All companies waive surrender charges if the annuitant dies. Beneficiaries receive the entire accumulation value. (If the person actually owning the annuity is different from the person named as the annuitant, surrender charges are not waived.)

Administrative charges. Some companies deduct annual administrative charges, usually $12 to $30, from your accumulation value. These charges often apply only to small accounts, such as those less than $10,000, and effectively reduce the accumulation value. A $25 charge equals a one-quarter of one percentage point reduction in the interest rate on a $10,000 accumulation. Other companies forgo an administrative charge but offer lower rates on small accounts, which has a similar effect.

Reading the Fine Print

A number of other contract clauses can affect the size of your accumulation.

Bailout clause. This clause allows you, under certain conditions, to cash in your annuity without paying surrender charges. It usually specifies that if the current interest rate at the time of surrender is lower than the initial rate by some specified amount, the company will waive any surrender charge that would otherwise apply.

Some companies explicitly charge for their bailout clause; others do not. A few contracts let you choose between a bailout clause or getting up to one-half of one percentage point more without it. Generally, a bailout clause is not worth that price and can offer a false sense of security.

Some bailout clauses are so restrictive that they're unlikely to be used. For example, a company may allow you to surrender early only if the rate it currently credits is both two percentage points below your annuity's initial rate and more than one percentage point below the rate on one-year Treasury bills—an unlikely pair of contingencies. Or a bailout clause may work only if the current rate is *three* percentage points below the rate for the previous year. In less restrictive policies, bailout clauses are triggered if the current rate is only one percentage point below the initial rate.

Market-value adjustment. When interest rates fall, the market value of the insurance company's assets (usually bonds) rises. If you cash in during a guarantee period when interest rates are down, the company increases your accumulation value; in effect, it shares the gain on its assets with you. Even though you would have to pay applicable surrender charges, the market-value adjustment in this case produces a higher cash surrender value. Conversely, when interest rates rise, the value of the company's assets goes down, and you share in the loss.

In theory, a market-value adjustment should give an insurance company more flexibility to invest for higher returns, and thus credit higher rates to policyholders, producing higher accumulations over the years. In practice, other factors have a greater influence on an annuity's performance.

Persistency bonus. If you keep your annuity for a certain number of years, the company adds a specified amount to the annuity's accumulation value. This might be 5 percent or 10 percent of the premium. That percentage might increase as the years go on. Some companies entice you to stay by offering higher rates at the beginning of each new guarantee period. These rates are higher than those companies offer new customers.

Partial Withdrawals

Annuities are not meant to be sources of ready cash. For that reason, you can't borrow against your accumulation value if your annuity is "nonqualified" (an annuity on which you have already paid taxes on your contributions). Contributions to a qualified annuity, such as a tax-sheltered annuity (TSA), have not been taxed, and you may borrow against your accumulation in these types of accounts.

Most companies do allow "free" partial withdrawals from nonqualified annuities—that is, you can take part of your money without paying a surrender charge. The free-withdrawal provision doesn't mean you can use an annuity as a checking account, though. Insurance companies limit either the number of withdrawals or the minimum size of a withdrawal. Some companies also impose a charge, usually $25, on partial withdrawals. Most contracts allow you to withdraw up to 10 percent of your accumulated value without incurring a surrender charge.

Sometimes the free-withdrawal provision applies only to the first withdrawal you make in any year. A company might apply a surrender charge to a second withdrawal, even though the total for the year does not equal 10 percent of the accumulation value.

THE PAYOUT PHASE

For people about to retire, the *payout phase* is the most important aspect of a deferred annuity.

When you're ready to cash in your annuity, usually at age 65 or 70, you can withdraw the accumulated value in a lump sum or in monthly payments as lifetime income. The lump sum is yours to invest, spend, or pass on to your heirs. But monthly annuity payments are usually higher than the income you could earn by investing a lump sum yourself. They may even be higher than the amounts you could receive if you arranged your investment so that you drew both interest and some principal in the expectation you won't live very long (see Table 11, How Long Will the Money Last?, on page 87).

By turning all or a portion of the accumulated value into monthly payments for life, or *annuitizing,* you strike an irrevocable bargain with the insurance company. You no longer have the money to do with as you please, but you also have the security of knowing that you cannot outlive the payments.

You can annuitize your accumulation from a deferred annuity into a lifetime income stream from the same company, or you can take your accumulation in a lump sum and go to another company and buy an immediate annuity. In either case, insurance actuaries compute the size of the monthly annuity payment by applying a *settlement-option rate,* expressed as dollars of monthly income per thousand dollars of accumulated value. Settlement-option rates depend on how long the actuary believes the company will be making payments to you and on the company's forecast of how well it can invest the money during that period.

The actuary figures two settlement-option rates. One, called the *guaranteed settlement-option rate*, is spelled out in every deferred-annuity contract and represents a minimum. The other, called the *current settlement-option rate*, is not written into the contract, but it will apply when the time comes to annuitize your accumulation if it's higher than the guaranteed rate written into the contract. In recent years, companies' current settlement-option rates have been much higher than the guaranteed rates.

The difference between the current and the guaranteed settlement-option rates can be substantial. In recent years, a typical current settlement-option rate for a 65-year-old man who took a life annuity was about $9 a month per $1,000 of accumulated value. A typical guaranteed rate found in many newly issued deferred-annuity contracts was about $6.50 a month per $1,000. On a $100,000 accumulation, that works out to a lifetime income of $10,800 a year at current rates, compared with $7,800 annually at guaranteed rates.

Just as the typical current and guaranteed settlement rates vary widely, so do the rates offered on any given day vary from one company to the next. Obviously, it pays to shop carefully for settlement-option rates. Note, however, that companies usually offer a better settlement rate to policyholders converting from the accumulation phase of a contract than to people buying an immediate annuity with money that they've saved elsewhere. That's meant to discourage shopping. Nevertheless, some companies specialize in immediate annuities and offer high monthly payments on your accumulation.

The longer a company figures it must pay benefits, the lower each payment is. Thus, for the same accumulated value, the payments for a 60-year-old just beginning to annuitize are lower than for a 70-year-old. Payments to a woman beginning to receive an income stream are lower than for a man of the same age, since women live longer. For example, one company recently offered 65-year-old men an annuity rate of $9.20 for each $1,000 of accumulated value.

It offered women the same age a rate of only $8.41. Some companies have unisex rates; that is, the settlement-option rates for men and women are the same. If you're annuitizing from a qualified plan, the company must use unisex rates. If the plan is nonqualified, the company usually uses sex-distinct rates.

Payout Options

When it comes time to annuitize your accumulation, you are in effect placing a bet with an insurance company. You are betting that you'll live long enough to receive the value of your accumulation in the form of monthly or yearly payments. The insurance company is betting that you won't.

These are your payout options.

Life annuity. With a life annuity, you receive payments for the rest of your life. When you die, the payments stop and your heirs receive nothing. A life annuity provides you with the most monthly income. *Example:* A 65-year-old man annuitizing $100,000 would receive around $930 a month, or $11,160 a year, if the company paid an interest rate of about 8.5 percent.

Life annuity with periods certain. Under this arrangement, the company agrees to make your monthly payments for the rest of your life. But if you die within a certain period, usually in 5 or 10 years, your heirs continue to receive your payments until the specified period ends. Monthly payments for a life annuity with a 10-year period certain, for example, are generally 5 to 10 percent lower than for a life annuity. *Example:* The same man converting a $100,000 accumulation into an annuity with a 10-year period certain from the same company at the same interest rate would receive around $880 each month. If he died within 10 years of taking the annuity, his beneficiary would receive the balance of the payments through the tenth year. If he chose a life annuity with a 5-year period certain, his monthly payment would be around $915.

Joint-and-survivor annuity. This annuity is written on both your life and the life of another person, such as your spouse. Full payments are made so long as you and the joint annuitant are alive. When one annuitant dies, the insurance company reduces the amount of the payments by one-third or one-half (depending on the option you choose) and continues to make reduced payments to the survivor until he or she dies. You can also elect a 100 percent joint-and-survivor option in which your survivor receives your full benefit. As noted in chapter 3, this type of joint-and-survivor annuity is different from the ones available from your company pension. In those arrangements, payment is made to a survivor when the retiree dies.

The amount of the payment under a joint-and-survivor annuity may be dramatically or only slightly lower than the monthly payment under a life annuity, depending on the ages and sexes of the two annuitants. If the other annuitant is older than you or close to your age, the initial payment may not be much different from the payments under a life annuity on your life alone. If the other annuitant is much younger, the monthly payments will be considerably lower.

Example: A 65-year-old man annuitizes $100,000. If he chooses a two-thirds joint-and-survivor annuity for himself and his 64-year-old wife, his monthly payment will be around $845, if the company pays an interest rate of about 8.5 percent. When either he or his wife dies, the insurance company reduces the monthly payment to around $560. When the second spouse dies, payments stop. With a 50 percent joint-and-survivor annuity, the same man receives $885 a month. When either he or his wife dies, the company lowers the payment to about $440.

The advantages and disadvantages of joint-and-survivor options are obvious. You receive less money while you are alive, but when you die, your spouse has a guaranteed income. If your spouse would otherwise have to live only on income from Social Security, a joint-and-survivor annuity is a desirable option. It's important to calculate carefully how much income you both will need to live and how much your spouse will need after you're gone. The larger the payment to a spouse, the lower your payments during retirement. You might also consider an annuity with a period certain as a way to have more money during retirement but still provide for your spouse if you should die within 10 years. This option is appropriate if both you and your spouse are in the later years of your retirement.

Other Ways to Get Your Money

Systematic withdrawals. In a *systematic withdrawal plan,* the insurance company calculates a monthly payment based on your life expectancy, sex, and the amount of money in your account. This arrangement allows you to obtain the money saved through a deferred annuity without actually annuitizing your accumulation. The money remaining in your account continues to earn income, tax-free, at a rate of interest determined by the insurance company.

Systematic withdrawals have several advantages. Because the annual income from the annuity is less than what it would be under other payout options, you save income taxes (part of your accumulation is taxable when you begin to take monthly payments). Withdrawals are also attractive to people who need a monthly income but still wish to leave money to their children. If you later decide to annuitize the remaining accumulation, most insurance companies let you do that. Many insurers also give you a choice of systematic withdrawal options that allow you to tailor payments to your needs.

Example: A man turning 65 in 1990 began to take systematic withdrawals from his $100,000 accumulation. He could take those payments in one of two ways (see Tables 9 and 10 on pages 85 and 86). Under one arrangement, he would receive a monthly payment of $416.60; under the other, he would receive $811.61 each month. Under the first plan, his monthly payments continue until he is 85, and rise to $1,093. With the second, the payments decline through the years until, when he reaches 85, they have dropped to $583.34 a month. If he takes a life annuity, he'll receive $931 a month and somewhat less if he takes other annuity options (see Table 11 on page 87).

With a life annuity, the monthly payment is fixed until you

die. But with systematic withdrawals, annual payments can increase or decrease depending on how much the fund grows, and on Internal Revenue Service rules. The IRS requires that you withdraw a minimum amount each year based on your life expectancy. For example, if your life expectancy at 65 is 16 years, you must withdraw one-sixteenth of the fund the first year, one-fifteenth the second year, and so on. The size of your accumulation also changes as you withdraw money and earn interest. As a result, your payments may go up or down each year.

Suppose, for example, you want to retire at 55 but must tap your savings for living expenses. You might want systematic withdrawals that let you take larger monthly payments when you first retire and lower ones when you begin receiving Social Security benefits. Or you decide to retire at 70 but don't need the money in your annuity right away. In that case, you might prefer a plan that lets you withdraw smaller amounts in the early years and larger ones later to pay any medical or nursing home expenses.

Systematic withdrawals can also be calculated for joint lives. As with the joint-and-survivor options, monthly payments are lower. When you die, payments continue to your spouse so long as he or she lives. When your spouse dies, money remaining in the account becomes part of his or her estate. If payments are to be made only to you, any money in your account passes to your estate when you die. The following tables show different types of systematic withdrawals. Both tables assume a person retiring at age 65 who has a $100,000 accumulation on which to base withdrawals. Table 9 illustrates lower annual payments in the early years of retirement and higher ones in the later years. Table 10 shows higher payments early and lower ones later. Both arrangements assume the company will credit an 8.5 percent rate on funds remaining in the account.

Lump-sum payments. At the end of the accumulation phase of an annuity contract, you can take the money as a lump sum, invest it, and try to live on the interest alone, leaving the principal to your heirs. You gamble, of course, that

TABLE 9
Systematic Withdrawal with Minimum Payments
DATE OF FIRST WITHDRAWAL: FEBRUARY 21, 1990

		Projected	
Age	Monthly Payment	Cumulative Payment	Accumulation Value
65	$ 416.60	$ 5,000.00	$103,112.26
66	447.53	10,370.43	106,089.91
67	480.48	16,136.19	108,894.67
68	515.60	22,323.39	111,483.72
69	552.99	28,959.33	113,809.80
70	592.76	36,072.41	115,818.40
71	630.82	43,642.24	117,506.11
72	670.70	51,690.60	118,821.63
73	712.36	60,238.92	119,710.25
74	755.75	69,307.88	120,113.38
75	800.76	78,916.95	119,968.78
76	840.12	88,998.36	119,302.92
77	887.67	99,650.41	117,965.58
78	927.40	110,779.24	116,000.81
79	966.67	122,379.32	113,361.24
80	994.40	134,312.08	110,138.82
81	1031.26	146,687.23	106,165.80
82	1053.23	159,326.02	101,571.00
83	1071.42	172,183.11	96,350.41
84	1085.02	185,203.44	90,510.17
85	1093.12	198,320.86	84,068.89

you'll die before the money is used up. If, on the other hand, you choose an annuity payout option, you can never outlive your money.

Table 11 shows a number of ways a 65-year-old man in good health might deal with a $100,000 accumulation. If this man chooses a life annuity, he receives $931 a month for life,

TABLE 10
Systematic Withdrawal with Maximum Payments

DATE OF FIRST WITHDRAWAL: FEBRUARY 21, 1990

Age	Monthly Payment	Projected Cumulative Payment	Projected Accumulation Value
65	$811.61	$ 8,927.71	$98,921.54
66	816.24	18,722.59	97,084.50
67	815.60	28,509.79	95,099.34
68	814.68	38,285.95	92,956.99
69	813.45	48,047.35	90,647.99
70	811.89	57,790.03	88,523.29
71	807.27	67,477.27	85,523.29
72	802.08	77,102.23	82,725.12
73	796.27	86,657.47	79,762.04
74	789.77	96,134.71	76,628.69
75	782.50	105,524.71	73,320.25
76	770.52	114,770.95	69,880.97
77	761.67	123,910.99	66,260.44
78	747.31	132,878.71	62,512.40
79	731.75	141,659.71	58,641.09
80	709.87	150,178.15	54,715.36
81	692.00	158,482.15	50,680.24
82	667.00	166,486.15	46,615.93
83	640.60	174,173.35	42,537.52
84	612.75	181,526.35	38,462.02
85	583.34	188,526.43	34,409.25

but none of the accumulation passes to his heirs. A life annuity with a 10-year period certain provides $883 per month, but leaves something over if he dies before reaching age 75.

If he takes the accumulation and lives on the interest alone, he has only $682 a month for life, assuming an 8.5 percent effective annual interest rate earned on safe investments such

TABLE 11
How Long Will the Money Last?

Monthly Payment	When Money Runs Out	Chance of Outliving the Money[1] (Percent)	Estate Left If Man Dies at Age 67	Age 70	Age 75	Age 80	Age 85	Age 90
The Annuity Options								
$ 931[2]	Never	0	0	0	0	0	0	0
883[3]	Never	0	$62,469	$43,654	0	0	0	0
The Investment Options								
$ 682[4]	Never	0	$100,000	$100,000	$100,000	$100,000	$100,000	$100,000
719[5]	Age 100	3	98,918	96,925	92,302	85,349	74,895	59,176
742[5]	Age 95	11	98,321	95,230	88,057	77,271	61,054	36,668
779[5]	Age 90	26	97,350	92,468	81,142	64,112	38,505	0
842[5]	Age 85	45	95,690	87,752	69,334	41,641	0	0
960[5]	Age 80	65	92,615	79,012	47,453	0	0	0
1,215[5]	Age 75	81	85,945	60,058	0	0	0	0

[1] 1983 Individual Annuity Mortality Table.
[2] Life annuity.
[3] Life annuity with 10-year period certain option.
[4] Interest income at an effective annual rate of 8.5 percent.
[5] Interest income at an effective annual rate of 8.5 percent plus some principal.

as certificates of deposit. But the entire nest egg passes to his heirs.

To increase the monthly payment to himself, he has to draw on the principal. The table shows how long the money lasts at increasingly larger monthly payment amounts, what the chances are of outliving the money under each assumption, and how much of an estate remains as time passes.

If a woman takes a life annuity or a life annuity with a 10-year period certain, her monthly payments are smaller. If she chooses to withdraw only interest and principal, the chances of outliving her money are greater.

Example: A 65-year-old woman buys a life annuity from one company. Her monthly payment is $855. If she buys a life annuity with a 10-year period certain, she has $831 a month. If she "annuitizes" on her own, withdrawing interest and principal, her chances of outliving her money at age 80 are 78 percent. At age 90, her chances are 50 percent.

Split-funding techniques. You can take a sum of money and divide it into two annuities—an immediate annuity to provide an income stream and a deferred annuity that continues to grow at some rate of interest.

This arrangement may be useful for people taking early retirement. *Example:* You decide to retire at age 55, too early for Social Security benefits. But for the next 10 years you need additional income to supplement your company pension. If you have saved $100,000, for example, you can take around $56,000 of that sum and buy an immediate annuity with a 10-year period certain, which will provide about $660 each month or almost $8,000 a year, assuming an 8.75 percent rate. The remaining $44,000 can be invested in a deferred annuity. When you turn 65, you can annuitize the new accumulation to supplement Social Security benefits.

HOW ANNUITIES ARE TAXED

If you annuitize from a qualified annuity, your monthly payments are fully taxable. But if you annuitize from a nonqualified plan, only a part of your payments are taxable. With these plans, the IRS considers part of your monthly payment a return of principal and the other part a return of interest earnings. You pay taxes only on the interest. You don't have to figure the interest yourself—the insurance company sends a statement showing what percentage of each annuity payment can be excluded from income.

Example: A 65-year-old man takes a life annuity. His yearly payment equals $11,160. Of that, $6,160 is taxable and $5,000 is considered a return of principal and is therefore exempt from taxes. If he takes a life annuity with a 10-year period certain, his income is reduced to $10,596 a year, and his tax goes down accordingly. The taxable portion of his yearly income amounts to $5,896.

In estimating your tax bill (see chapter 6), be sure to include the taxable portion of any annuity income. A word of warning: Once you have recovered all of your principal, your entire monthly payment is considered interest and is fully taxable for the rest of your life. When you are shopping for annuities, ask the agent for an estimate of your yearly tax.

If your spouse is the beneficiary of your annuity or will be the new owner of the policy upon your death, the IRS taxes the proceeds the same way as when you were alive. If you have named a child or someone else as the owner or beneficiary, the IRS requires that he or she take the proceeds from the annuity within five years of your death. Otherwise, the amounts not withdrawn are subject to a penalty. At the time of your death, the value of the annuity is usually included in your estate and is subject to federal and state estate taxes.

Penalties

If you withdraw your money before age 59½, the IRS imposes, in addition to income taxes, a 10 percent penalty tax on the amount by which the value of the annuity exceeds the premium that you paid in. This rule assumes that the annuity is nonqualified. For qualified annuities, the entire amount withdrawn is taxed, as we've noted.

There are, however, exceptions for both qualified and nonqualified annuities. If you choose a systematic withdrawal and meet certain conditions, you may be able to avoid IRS penalties. For example, once payments begin, they must continue for at least five years and until you turn 59½. Payments must be based on your age on your birthday nearest the first withdrawal. This rule, which is applicable only to qualified plans, requires the insurance company to recalculate the amount withdrawn every year until you reach 70½. Payments must be based on your account values on December 31 of the year preceding the date of the withdrawal. That means you cannot split the annuity accumulation among several investments unless you plan to take comparable, systematic withdrawals from all investments. If you are annuitizing from a nonqualified plan, your payments can remain level, since there is no requirement that you begin withdrawing money at age 70½.

If you fund your payments with money saved in a qualified plan, the IRS imposes a penalty of 50 percent of the difference between the amount you took and the amount you should have taken if you don't begin withdrawing your money by age 70½. This penalty is similar to the one for failing to withdraw money from an IRA or a Keogh account.

If you take a partial withdrawal from an annuity purchased after 1982, the IRS considers that you withdrew all interest before any principal and taxes you accordingly. If your withdrawal exceeds your total interest earnings, you are taxed only on the interest, not on the principal. *Example:* Your $10,000 annuity has grown to $15,000. If you withdraw $5,000, the IRS treats that $5,000 as interest subject to taxes. But if you withdraw $6,000, you are taxed on only the $5,000 that's considered interest. (Different rules apply to annuities funded before 1982. Check with your tax adviser.)

VARIABLE ANNUITIES

So far we have described only fixed annuities. During the accumulation phase, your money grows at a specified rate of interest determined by the insurance company. During the payout phase, your monthly payment is also fixed; the insurance company calculates the settlement-option rate and your payments never change. This can be a major drawback if inflation increases significantly. With a *variable* annuity, however, neither the rate of interest during the accumulation phase nor the monthly payment during the payout phase is fixed.

During the accumulation phase of a variable annuity, the insurance company usually gives you a choice of one or more stock, bond, or money-market fund in which to invest your money. The amount in your account rises or falls depending on the fortunes of the fund you select. Many annuities also offer a fixed-account option, which provides about the same rates as a fixed-dollar annuity. You can divide your money among the various investment options, and you can usually switch investments every 30 days.

Investing in a variable annuity is very much like investing in mutual funds outside an annuity. You assume the same market risks as any investor. But there are important differences. Because the investments are inside an annuity "wrapper," there is no tax on any dividends, interest, or capital gains until you withdraw your funds. As with any annuity, there's a 10 percent penalty tax on any withdrawal made before age 59½. This tax advantage is partly offset by fees that range anywhere from 1.5 to 2.5 percent of your fund's assets each year and by surrender charges discussed previously.

Though you have the flexibility to allocate your money among several types of investments inside the annuity, the number of funds may be limited. When investing outside an annuity, you may choose among hundreds of stock, bond, and money-market funds, some with no sales fees.

At the end of the accumulation phase of a variable annuity, you have the same options as with a fixed-dollar arrangement. You may withdraw the accumulated value or convert to a guaranteed monthly pension for life. You may also opt for a variable payout—a monthly pension whose size can vary from month to month according to investment results.

With variable monthly payments you cannot predict your income. Some months your income will go up; other months it may go down, depending on the performance of the funds you select. Therefore, choosing a variable payment is a gamble. If you do decide to play the odds, it helps to know how a variable payment is figured.

With a fixed annuity, you receive a certain number of dollars each month. With a variable annuity, you receive the value of a fixed number of annuity units. The value of those units fluctuates according to the performance of the underlying investments. To calculate the number of units you will receive, the insurance company uses what is known as the assumed interest rate, or AIR. Using the assumed interest rate and a mortality table, the company computes a net single premium for an annuity that would be paid if the underlying funds earned exactly the AIR. The company then divides your account value on the day you annuitize your accumulation by the net single premium. The result is the number of annuity units you will have during your retirement.

The value of those annuity units fluctuates monthly as the investments in the funds you selected change. If the net earnings of those funds is greater than the AIR, the value of each unit rises to reflect the excess earnings. If the funds earn at a rate less than the AIR, the value of your annuity units goes down.

Shop carefully for a variable annuity payout. Don't automatically take the plan from the company offering the highest AIR. *Example:* One company is offering an AIR of 6 percent and another offers an AIR of 4 percent. At the beginning, the higher AIR will pay higher monthly payments. But if you live a long time, the 4 percent AIR will produce higher payments in the end. That's because changes in the annuity unit values reflect the differences between the interest rate the funds assumed and the rate they actually earned. Since there's no way to know when you'll die, your choice is between smaller payments in the early years, when you may have other sources of income, or smaller payments in the later years, when you may have high medical expenses.

In choosing an immediate annuity with a variable payout, be sure to compare annuities at the same AIR. Ask the agents to show you illustrations using the same assumed interest rate. Of course, your monthly payments will be smaller from companies with higher mortality and expense charges.

HOW SAFE IS YOUR ANNUITY?

In recent years, several large insurance companies have experienced severe financial trouble. Thus it is important to check the insurance company's rating in a resource such as Best's Insurance Reports, available in most public libraries. Best rates the financial stability of insurance companies on a scale from C (fair) to A+ (superior) and lists only companies that have been under the current owner at least five years. If a company is a wholly owned subsidiary of a parent company that has a rating, Best assigns the parent company's rating until the subsidiary has the required experience. Best's ratings are far from perfect, however, and should be used only as a rough guide.

You might also check to see how the insurance company invests its money. If it is promising very high rates—perhaps much higher than other companies—it may be putting its funds in risky investments, such as junk bonds.

Most states have guaranty associations that make good on the promises of an insolvent life insurance company. In most cases, when a court liquidates a company, the guaranty association in each state where the company did business collects money from other companies that write policies in that state. The guaranty funds then pay the claims made by policyholders from the troubled company. (Policyholders must usually collect from the guaranty association in the state where they live.) Guaranty associations do have their limitations, however. Policyholders may not recover their entire investment, and there may be long delays in receiving payment.

All states now have life insurance guaranty associations.

5

Life Insurance

Life insurance has two purposes in retirement planning. It can provide income for your surviving spouse or other dependents and it can be an estate planning tool. In this chapter we explore the use of life insurance for income protection. In chapter 17 we discuss life insurance in estate planning.

Insurance agents try to make a compelling case for maintaining or even buying a life insurance policy in the retirement years. On the surface, their arguments sound sensible. After all, when you die, your spouse has the proceeds from the policy to supplement his or her income. But if you analyze this argument, you will see why holding on to a life insurance policy in your later years may not always be wise.

Life insurance is a way to provide income for dependents if the family breadwinner dies. For that reason, we recommend that families with young children carry large amounts of life insurance on the adult family members. But as children grow up, a family's needs for protection diminish. By the time you reach retirement, for example, your children are probably through with college and on their own. In that case, does it make sense to keep your life insurance in force?

For most people, keeping a life insurance policy during retirement years doesn't make economic sense. If you have a term policy, it probably isn't renewable once you reach age 65 or 70. Even if it is, the premiums are high. *Example:* A 47-year-old man who buys a $75,000 term policy from New York Savings Bank Life Insurance (SBLI), a company offering low-cost insurance, will pay $1,916 a year for his coverage by the time he is 65.

If you have a term policy, the insurance carrier may encourage you to convert it to a cash-value form of insurance when you are near retirement. We don't recommend that option for most people. If you own a cash-value policy, the premiums are also high. Paying high premiums for life insurance could mean your family has less money for more pressing immediate needs, such as health insurance or rising fuel or medical bills. If you keep the policy, you're gambling that one spouse will die early enough so the proceeds from the policy will supplement what may be a meager income for the other.

In deciding whether to keep a life insurance policy, consider your total annual outlay for all your insurance needs. Premiums for Medicare, a good Medicare-supplement policy, and a good long-term-care policy may take a very large chunk of your income.

If you own term insurance, you can invest or put into a savings account the money you would otherwise pay in premiums for cash-value forms of insurance. If you have a cash-value policy, you should cash it in and invest the cash in a high-yielding certificate of deposit or money-market fund. Remember, if you do cash in a policy, the amount you receive is net of any outstanding policy loans. Check to see if you have an old loan you have forgotten about. If you do, the loan, plus any unpaid interest, is subtracted from the policy's face amount so that your surviving spouse receives less than the face value if you die while the policy is still in force.

If you have a paid-up cash-value policy and are no longer paying premiums, it might make sense to keep the policy, especially if the company is paying high dividends. Some people who own small paid-up policies like to leave the proceeds to their children. In that case, be sure to name your children as the policy's beneficiaries (see chapter 17). You also may want to keep one or more policies in force if your estate is illiquid—tied up in real estate or a family business, for example—and there won't be enough in it to pay the taxes.

You may also want to retain a policy if cashing it in results in high tax bills for a particular year. The interest that builds up inside a cash-value policy is tax-deferred until the day you withdraw it, and then only a portion of it is taxed. The IRS collects tax on the amount by which the cash value exceeds the sum of the premiums you paid over the years, minus any dividends you received. That portion is called your *gain,* on which you pay ordinary income taxes. The gain may not be trivial if your company has consistently paid high dividends through the years. *Example:* If your gain is $12,000 after owning the policy for 20 years, your tax bill could be well over $3,000 (assuming a 28 percent marginal tax rate). If you want to cash in a life insurance policy, and doing so will result in a large tax bill, you might consider cashing in the policy in a year when you have a smaller tax liability. For example, it may be unwise to cash in a policy the same year that you take a lump-sum withdrawal from your IRA or pension plan.

LIFE INSURANCE OR A JOINT-AND-SURVIVOR ANNUITY?

Your employer will probably offer you several options for taking a pension. These options include a life annuity, which gives you payments so long as you live but your spouse receives nothing after your death, or a joint-and-survivor annuity with lower payments but monthly checks for your spouse after you die. You can choose a 50 percent joint-and-survivor annuity, which provides your surviving spouse with half the monthly income you receive when you are alive, or a 100 percent joint-and-survivor annuity, which gives your spouse the same monthly payments you receive during your lifetime. The latter option, however, gives you the lowest monthly payment of all.

In recent years, life insurance agents have developed a new argument for selling policies to people about to retire. If you are married and expect a sizable pension from your employer, an agent may try to persuade you that buying a life insurance policy is a better option than the joint-and-survivor annuity offered by your company. Why should you take a reduction in your monthly income when you can buy a life insurance policy? But unless your spouse is terminally ill when you retire, you're almost always better off taking a joint-and-survivor annuity.

In the long run, buying a life insurance policy is far more costly. For one thing, the insurance company must pay its usual expenses to put the policy on the books. These expenses, which include the agent's commission, can run as high as 100 percent of the first year's premium. Usually there are no similar expenses with the annuity.

Insurance companies also charge higher premiums to people who have health problems. By the time you retire, your health may have deteriorated, perhaps to the point where the company classifies you as a "substandard" risk and charges a very high premium for coverage. If the insurance company charges you "substandard" rates, you're better off choosing the annuity option, which provides your spouse with the most income until he or she dies. Insurance companies also charge higher premiums to older people, whatever their health, so you may be unable to afford much coverage. The smaller the policy, the less money your spouse has to live on after your death.

To determine which is the better option, fill out Worksheet 5, Life Insurance Versus a Joint-and-Survivor Annuity, in Appendix A. Our example uses an employee eligible for a $1,000 monthly pension taken as a life annuity or a $900 monthly pension taken as a 50 percent joint-and-survivor annuity. The employee is 65 years old and the spouse is 62. The rates are from a major life insurance company that does not pay dividends. If you're offered a lower-cost whole life policy than the one used here, the resulting calculation may be slightly more favorable for life insurance. But it's still doubtful that life insurance will turn out to be better in the long run than a joint-and-survivor annuity. In the example, the joint-and-survivor annuity pays $450 a month; the annuity bought with the life insurance proceeds pays $200 a month. If the insurance buys less monthly income than the joint-and-survivor annuity, which is often the case, the annuity is the better deal.

ACCELERATED DEATH BENEFIT LIFE POLICIES

Accelerated death benefit life policies are usually marketed to people approaching retirement who are starting to think about their potential need for long-term care and the devastating financial effects of a catastrophic illness.

These policies work the same way as other cash-value policies such as whole life and universal life except that part of the death benefit is paid when a specific event, other than death, occurs. That event might be a serious illness such as cancer, a heart attack, kidney failure, or a stroke. Or part of the death benefit might be paid if you are confined to a nursing home.

Policies specify how much of the death benefit is payable when a specific triggering event occurs. For example, a policy might pay 25 percent of the death benefit in the case of a heart attack or stroke. If the policy carries a $100,000 death benefit, the company pays $25,000. At the same time, the company reduces all the elements of the policy by 25 percent. Thus the new face amount becomes $75,000, and the cash value and premium are similarly reduced by 25 percent. Once part of the death benefit is paid, you can cash in the policy and take the remaining cash value, or you can keep the policy in force and allow the cash value to continue to accumulate. Remember, though, that your death benefit has been permanently reduced, so your beneficiary will no longer receive the original face amount of the policy.

Policies that call for the death benefit to be paid when you enter a nursing home work a little differently. Such policies usually pay 2 percent of the death benefit per month, subject to a maximum amount. The benefits may change from year to year, depending on how the policy is structured. For example, a policy with a face amount of $120,000 sold by one company in 1991 paid a monthly benefit of $2,400 for 25 months if a policyholder was confined to a nursing home during the first year the policy was in force. If he or she enters a nursing home in the fifth year of the policy, the monthly benefit may be larger or smaller, depending on the interest rate the company credits to the accumulating cash values and on the amount it deducts each year for a "mortality" charge. (These charges help pay the death benefit.) It's possible that you could stay in a nursing home long enough to exhaust all of the policy's nursing home benefits. In that case, there would be no death benefit payable to your survivors.

These policies specify whether benefits are paid for skilled, intermediate, custodial, or home care. Home care benefits may be lower, however (see chapter 11). Policies also specify when benefits are payable. Some require policyholders to be in a nursing home for six months or longer before they begin to pay benefits. Others pay benefits after the policyholder has been in a nursing home for 30 days. The policy fine print also notes what kind of care is not covered. For example, a policy may not pay benefits if care is performed by family members or if care is given by a doctor who is the owner, operator, or employee of the facility providing the care.

As with those that provide benefits for acute illness, with these policies the death benefit, the cash-value accumulation, and the guaranteed cash surrender value are all reduced if the policyholder uses the money to pay for long-term care. If the policy is structured as a universal life contract, the policyholder might be able to pay extra premiums to increase benefits, but if partial withdrawals have been made, the benefits are reduced. Outstanding policy loans also lower the benefits.

Like other cash-value insurance, accelerated death benefit policies carry a high price tag, especially if you buy them when you're older. For example, a 55-year-old man would pay around $3,550 for an accelerated death benefit policy from one company; a 55-year-old woman would pay about $2,780. A regular whole life policy without the acceleration feature would cost a few hundred dollars less. You may also be able to buy an accelerated death benefit policy that combines term insurance with whole life or universal life as a way of lowering premiums. Sometimes companies let you buy a policy with a single, large premium.

Deciding whether to buy a policy that accelerates the death benefit should hinge solely on whether you need life insurance at all. As we've noted, people approaching retirement or those already retired rarely need life insurance coverage. Therefore, we don't recommend that you buy an accelerated death benefit policy on the gamble that a misfortune listed in the policy will befall you. Instead, spend your money on good health insurance that provides benefits for more illnesses or on a good Medicare-supplement policy.

If you decide to buy long-term-care insurance, look carefully at some of the accelerated death benefit policies on the market and compare them to regular long-term-care insurance described in chapter 11. Compare the same features outlined in Worksheet 7, Long-Term-Care Policy Checklist, in Appendix A. These features include waiting or elimination periods, home-care benefits, gatekeepers, restrictions on facilities, preexisting conditions clauses, maximum benefits, and, of course, price.

Premiums for an accelerated death benefit policy, whether it is structured as whole life or universal life, remain level for your life—they don't increase as you get older. However, the mortality charge that comes out of your accumulating cash values may increase if the insurance company has paid substantial nursing home claims and finds that the mortality charge has been too low. If that happens, your cash values build more slowly. Companies that sell regular long-term-care policies also have a way to adjust for increases in the cost of nursing home care and bad claims experience. They simply raise the premiums.

GUARANTEED ACCEPTANCE POLICIES

Some companies specialize in small life insurance policies for older people, arguing that anyone can buy a policy regardless of health conditions. "As long as you're between 45 and 79 years of age, your acceptance is guaranteed regardless of past or present health conditions," reads one advertisement. While the annual premiums may be low, perhaps $400 or $500 a year, death benefits are similarly low—$2,000, $3,000, or $5,000. At some companies you may have no coverage the first two years the policy is in force. At others, the benefits may decline as you get older.

This coverage is akin to that offered by hospital-indemnity policies that we discuss in chapter 12. In fact, they may even be sold by the same companies or their subsidiaries. We don't recommend these policies.

6

Taxes

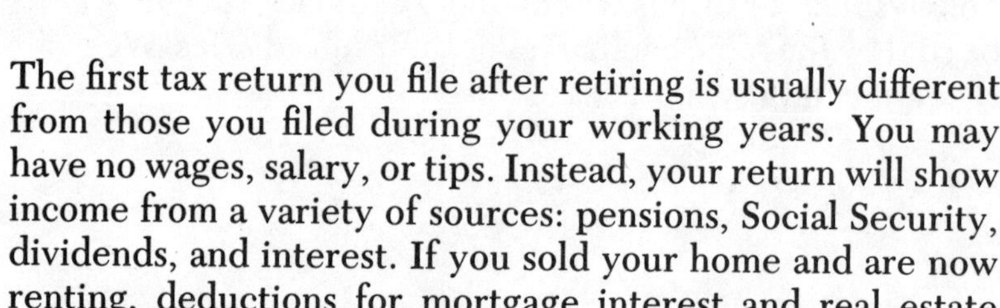

The first tax return you file after retiring is usually different from those you filed during your working years. You may have no wages, salary, or tips. Instead, your return will show income from a variety of sources: pensions, Social Security, dividends, and interest. If you sold your home and are now renting, deductions for mortgage interest and real estate taxes will disappear. If you bought a smaller home, those deductions may be lower. And if you have moved from a state that has an income tax to one that doesn't, it may not pay to itemize deductions.

In addition, there will be no taxes withheld by your employer, and you may have to pay estimated taxes each quarter. These payments are due on January 15, April 15, June 15, and September 15, and you need to file Form 1040-ES when you pay them. If you don't pay estimated taxes, the IRS can impose a tax penalty equal to the current interest rate it charges for underpayments. (That rate varies every quarter.)

HOW YOUR INCOME IS TAXED

After retirement, there is no change in the way your income from interest and dividends is taxed. But special rules apply to payments from Social Security, disability insurance, and pensions.

Social Security Benefits

If your only source of income is Social Security, your benefits probably won't be taxable. But if you have other income, be prepared to pay taxes on as much as half of it. (In some states, you have to pay state income taxes as well.)

As explained in chapter 2, to determine whether you owe any taxes on your benefits, add your regular adjusted gross income from Form 1040, any interest earned on tax-exempt bonds (which is ordinarily not taxable), and half of your Social Security benefits. If the sum exceeds $25,000 for a single person or $32,000 for married couples filing jointly, tax is due. To calculate the tax, determine the excess by which your adjusted gross income, bond interest, and half of your benefits exceed either $25,000 or $32,000. Then add 50 percent of that amount, but not more than 50 percent of your benefits, to your adjusted gross income.

The tax described above applies to Social Security retirement, disability, survivors' benefits, and to Tier 1 Railroad Retirement payments. It does *not* apply to Supplemental Security Income (SSI) or the lump-sum death benefit paid to a surviving spouse.

If it turns out that your Social Security benefits are taxable, restructuring your investments may be in order. For example, interest earned on municipal bonds, though normally tax-free, is counted in figuring the tax on Social Security benefits. If you earn substantial interest from these bonds, you might consider selling them and putting your money into taxable but higher-yielding investments. You may end up with a higher income even after paying taxes. But remember, if you sell the bonds at a profit, the capital gains tax reduces the amount available to reinvest. Likewise, selling at a loss could wipe out part of your investment if the value of the bond is down when you have to sell. If you are in a high tax bracket, switching to taxable investments could leave you with less money than keeping your investment in municipal bonds and paying some tax on your Social Security benefits. Deciding which way is best requires some careful planning.

Example: You are a single taxpayer over age 65, receiving $10,000 from Social Security, $11,000 in taxable pension benefits, $4,000 of taxable interest from a bank CD, and $6,000 of tax-free interest from a municipal bond. You include only half of your Social Security benefits in estimating your modified adjusted income. So including the interest from the bond, your modified adjusted gross income is $26,000 ($5,000 of Social Security plus $11,000 plus $4,000 plus $6,000 of other income), which exceeds the $25,000 base amount. If you claim a standard deduction ($3,600 plus the extra $750 for those over 65), your taxes come to $1,995. Since the interest from the bond results in a tax on your Social Security benefits, you decide to sell it and buy another fully taxable corporate bond yielding $9,000 per year. Your adjusted gross income is now $24,000 ($11,000 plus $4,000 plus $9,000). This amount, plus $5,000 or half of your Social Security benefits, equals $29,000. Your federal tax has now risen to $3,598, about $1,600 more than you would have paid if your money had stayed in the municipal bond. Your after-tax income has risen by about $1,400. If you sell at a loss and have to pay state income taxes as well, you haven't gained much by switching.

Another strategy to avoid paying taxes on Social Security benefits is to defer the income from some of your investments. You might, for example, consider investing in a deferred annuity (see chapter 4) or in Series EE savings bonds. You do not have to pay current income taxes on earnings from these investments. Be sure, however, to check the yields on Series EE bonds. They may be too low to justify giving up some of the income you would otherwise earn from municipal bonds.

If you continue to work while receiving Social Security benefits, carefully consider the impact on your tax bill. Until you turn 70, you pay Social Security taxes on your earnings, and the income from your job may push your Social Security benefits into the taxable range. If your earnings are high enough, you could even lose part of those benefits. As explained in chapter 2, if you're between 65 and 69 and continue to work in 1992, you lose $1 in benefits for every $3 of earnings above $10,200. If you're under age 65 and receive Social Security benefits, you lose $1 for every $2 in earnings that exceed $7,440. After you reach age 70, your benefits are no longer reduced if you keep working.

Disability Payments

Most of the time disability payments are not taxable. However, in some cases they are.

If you are receiving workers' compensation because you were injured at work, your benefits receive the same tax treatment as damages awarded in a lawsuit to compensate injured victims; that is, they are not usually taxable. But sometimes they are. *Example:* You're over 70, still working, and collect $800 in monthly Social Security benefits. You're injured on the job and receive workers' compensation payments of $200 a month for three months. Because of that payment, Social Security reduces your monthly benefit by $200. When tax time comes, the $600 paid in workers' compensation benefits are treated as if they were the Social Security payments they replaced and are subject to the same rules as all Social Security benefits. Depending on your other income, you may or may not pay taxes on the $600. If you are well enough to go back to work but still receive workers' compensation, those payments are considered income, and the IRS takes its share.

If you have purchased a disability income policy and paid the premiums yourself, you do not have to pay taxes on any benefits you receive. But if you and your employer split the cost of a disability policy, only part of your benefits are taxed. (The insurance company will send Form W-2 showing the taxable portion.) If your employer has paid the full premiums, payments made under the policy to pay medical expenses and to compensate for a permanent disability or the loss of use of any part of your body are not considered income and thus aren't taxed. But benefits paid to replace lost wages are.

If you receive disability payments from your employer's qualified pension plan, the government usually taxes those payments as income. However, the credit for the elderly and disabled may partly offset any taxes (see following section). Any payments you or your family receive from the Veterans Administration as disability compensation or as pension payments for disabilities are not taxed.

Pension Income

How income from your pension is taxed depends on whether you take your money in a lump sum or as an annuity, and on whether any money you put into the plan was previously taxed. The rules are complex. How these rules work and strategies for taking your pension are explained in chapter 3.

YOUR TAX DEDUCTIONS AFTER RETIREMENT

The Standard Deduction

The standard deduction, an amount you subtract to arrive at your taxable income, is available at retirement to almost everyone. But if someone else claims you as a dependent on his or her tax form—your child, for example—your deduction is reduced. In that case, you may deduct the amount of the regular standard deduction that applies in your situation, or $500, whichever is less.

The amount of the standard deduction varies according to your filing status, your age, and whether you're blind (see Table 12). For 1992, the basic deduction for single people is $3,600, for a head of household $5,250, and for a married couple filing jointly $6,000. You can deduct more if you're over 65, blind, or a qualifying widow or widower. These extra amounts, however, are available only to senior citizens who don't itemize their deductions. You can, of course, itemize your deductions if you have enough to make it worthwhile.

TABLE 12
Maximum Standard Deductions in 1992 for Taxpayers over Age 65

Filing Status	Standard Deduction	Increase in Standard Deduction Due to Age	Increase in Standard Deduction Due to Blindness
Single	$3,600	$900	$900
Married filing jointly	6,000	700	700
Married filing separately	3,000	700	700
Head of household	5,250	700	700
Qualifying widow(er)	6,000	700	700

Medical Expenses

Medical expenses are deductible only if they exceed 7.5 percent of your adjusted gross income and if they and all of your itemized deductions are greater than the standard deduction. If you have an adjusted gross income of $25,000, for example, you can deduct any medical expenses above $1,875 if you are single, have other itemized deductions of at least $2,625, and your standard and extra deductions amount to $4,500.

You may deduct any medical expenses you have paid for yourself and your dependents. You cannot, of course, deduct amounts reimbursed by an insurance company. In general, you may deduct expenses for the diagnosis, cure, treatment, or prevention of disease, and the cost of transportation to and from the place of treatment. You can also deduct the amount you pay for health-insurance premiums so long as the policy is the type that reimburses you for actual expenses. You cannot deduct the premiums for hospital-indemnity policies that pay a fixed amount per day. (See chapter 10 for a description of these kinds of policies.)

These are some expenses you can deduct: hospital charges; doctor bills, including those from dentists, chiropractors, and Christian Science practitioners; guide dogs for the blind; Medicare Part B premiums and Part A premiums if you must pay them yourself; premiums to health maintenance organizations; special equipment such as wheelchairs, braces, and oxygen; special items such as false teeth, hearing aids, and eyeglasses; nursing services; and prescription drugs. Experimental or unorthodox procedures are usually deductible so long as they fit the general definition of "medical expenses."

You cannot take deductions for expenses that enhance your general well-being. For example, the IRS doesn't allow a deduction for health club dues, but if your doctor prescribes daily whirlpool treatments to relieve an arthritic condition, that expense is acceptable. You can't usually deduct these expenses: general household help, illegal operations or treatment, cosmetic treatments, life insurance premiums, nonprescription drugs even if your doctor recommends them, toiletries and cosmetics, trips that are supposed to improve your overall health, and weight loss programs.

The following items are deductible, except for the caveats mentioned.

Transportation. If you travel by car, taxi, public transportation, or ambulance to obtain medical treatment, you can deduct transportation costs. If you use your car, the deduction equals actual expenses or nine cents per mile. If you travel to another city for medical care, you can deduct up to $50 per night for lodging costs. If someone else travels with you, the government lets you deduct another $50 per night.

But to claim lodging expenses, you must receive treatment at a nearby medical facility or the treatment must be for a specific medical condition. If you and your spouse spend the winter in the Caribbean because the warm weather helps your arthritis, you can deduct the cost of your transportation but not your spouse's. You cannot deduct food and lodging expenses for either yourself or your spouse. If your trip has nothing to do with a specific medical problem—you go to Florida to avoid the cold and flu season in Maine—you can deduct no expenses whatsoever.

Nursing homes. Expenses incurred for care in a nursing home can be deducted so long as the care you receive is skilled and not intermediate or custodial in nature (see chapter 11). If you need help with activities of daily living, such as eating, bathing, and dressing, or your condition is not likely to improve with medical treatment (for example, you're blind or have arthritis), nursing home expenses usually aren't deductible. If you receive skilled care at least part of the time you're in a nursing home, those costs can be deducted. You need to get an itemized bill from the facility showing what portion of the total expense is actually for skilled care.

If you move into a continuing-care retirement community (CCRC) that provides nursing care and you prepay for that care as part of a nonrefundable entrance fee, you can deduct the portion of the payment that prefunds the care. Part of your monthly fee is also deductible. The CCRC will tell you how much to deduct (see chapter 16).

Home improvements needed for medical conditions. Part of the cost of renovations to your house or apartment can be deducted as a medical expense so long as they are prescribed by a doctor to remedy a specific condition, they are not lavish or extravagant, and they have not been made primarily for personal convenience or enjoyment. Moreover, if the renovation increases the value of your home, that increase must be subtracted from the deduction. *Example:* You live in a two-story house, but a heart condition prevents you from climbing stairs. You need to install a new bathroom on the first floor. The bathroom costs $5,000 and increases the value of your home by $3,000. You must subtract the value of the increase, or $3,000, leaving you with a deduction of $2,000.

Many types of improvements don't increase the value of

TABLE 13
Income Limits for Tax Credits for the Elderly or Permanently and Totally Disabled

You may be able to claim a credit for the elderly or the permanently and totally disabled if you are		And receive nontaxable Social Security or other nontaxable pensions or disability benefits of less than	And the amount on Line 31, adjusted gross income, Form 1040, is less than
Single, an unmarried head of household, or a qualifying widow or widower and	65 or older	$5,000	$17,500
	Under 65 and retired on permanent and total disability	5,000	17,500
Married filing a joint return and	Both of you are 65 or older	7,500	25,000
	Both of you are under 65 and one of you retired on permanent and total disability	5,000	20,000
	Both of you are under 65 and both of you retired on permanent and total disability	7,500	25,000

	One of you is 65 or older, and the other is under 65 and retired on permanent and total disability	7,500	25,000
	One of you is 65 or older, and the other is under 65 and not retired on permanent and total disability	5,000	20,000
Married filing a separate return and did not live with your spouse at any time during the year and	65 or older	3,750	12,500
	Under 65 and retired on permanent and total disability	3,750	12,500

If your base amount is limited to your disability income, the amount of income that will keep you from taking the credit will be less than the amounts shown in this table.

your home, so you can deduct their full cost. These include adding exit and entrance ramps, widening doorways, and modifying stairways; installing railings or support bars in bathrooms; modifying kitchen cabinets and other equipment; relocating or modifying electrical outlets or fixtures; and installing lifts (but not elevators, which do raise your home's value). In the case of elevators, operating costs may be deductible.

Nursing services. Payments for nursing services are deductible so long as they are medically necessary. They need not be performed by a registered nurse. Payments to a practical nurse or to an attendant (even a relative) are deductible if he or she changes bandages, bathes you, gives medication, or renders other medically necessary nursing services. Besides the nurse's salary, you may deduct expenses for the attendant's food and lodging. If you move to a larger apartment to provide space for a live-in helper, the extra rent and utility costs are deductible. If your attendant also does household chores, you cannot claim those costs as medical deductions.

SPECIAL TAX CREDITS

If you meet certain criteria, you may qualify for tax credits (extra deductions) on your income taxes. If you are at least 65, are permanently or totally disabled, and have a relatively low income, you may qualify for a special tax credit of up to $1,125. If you are a single taxpayer, your adjusted gross income cannot exceed $17,500; if you're married filing a joint return, your adjusted gross income cannot be more than either $20,000 or $25,000 depending on your age, your spouse's age, and whether one of you is permanently and totally disabled. Table 13 shows you if you're eligible. If you are, file Schedule R. The IRS will help you fill it out.

To figure the credit, first determine your "base amount." For instance, if you file a joint return and both you and your spouse are over 65, your base amount is $7,500. That means any nontaxable Social Security benefits, nontaxable pensions, or disability benefits cannot exceed $7,500. After figuring the base, reduce it by the total of your nontaxable Social Security benefits, nontaxable pensions, disability benefits, and one-half of your "excess" adjusted gross income. The excess is the amount by which your adjusted gross income exceeds:

- $10,000 if you are married filing a joint return.
- $5,000 if you are married, filing a separate return, and you and your spouse didn't live in the same household anytime during the year.

If the answer is zero or less, you can't claim the credit. If the result is greater than zero, multiply it by 15 percent to arrive at the amount of your credit.

See Table 14 to help you calculate the credit. It assumes you and your spouse are both over 65 and file a joint return.

TABLE 14
Calculating the Credit

Income		
Taxable interest		$ 6,000
Part-time wages		5,500
Adjusted gross income		$11,500
Nontaxable Social Security benefits		$ 2,500
Credit		
Base amount		$ 7,500
Subtract total of:	Social Security	2,500
	One-half excess adjusted gross income ($11,500 − $10,000 ÷ 2)	750
		3,250
Result:	($7,500 − $3,250)	4,250
Credit:	$4,250 × 15% =	$ 638

7

Who Manages Your Money When You Can't?

Sooner or later we all have to think about the unthinkable—who will handle my financial affairs if I'm incapacitated?

Deciding who will manage your finances is as much a part of retirement planning as learning where to get a Medicare card. The tools for accomplishing this task include: joint accounts, powers of attorney, living trusts, and conservatorships and guardianships.

JOINT ACCOUNTS

Joint Tenants with Right of Survivorship

Establishing a joint account at a bank or brokerage firm is an easy way to enable someone to share in managing your money. When you set up a joint account by signing an authorization card, you give one or more joint owners the right to withdraw or deposit funds from the account. If the account has two owners, either can withdraw all the assets in the account for any reason, although in general, an owner who didn't contribute to the account can't keep more than half. In any case, when one owner dies, the remainder of the account immediately belongs to the other. In some states, however, the new owner may need tax waivers to use the money if the account is large. The new owner may also have to pay applicable estate taxes, depending on who contributed to the account.

Setting up a joint account allows your spouse or your children to make deposits and write checks to pay your bills if you can't. If, for example, you're confined to a nursing home, the joint owner can tap your account to pay for your care. Joint accounts also provide a way to transfer money to someone without having the account go through probate at your death. If a husband and wife establish a joint account, the surviving spouse has the money right away. That is a significant advantage if your spouse has no other immediate funds to live on.

These accounts do have a few drawbacks:

The person you choose as joint owner can raid the account at any time and take all your money. It's a good idea to have some money in another account that's all yours. Put only enough money in the joint account to cover the bills you will have to pay if you become incapacitated, or the expenses your spouse will have immediately upon your death. Put the rest of your assets in a separate account no one can touch—but remember, that account goes into your estate at your death and goes through probate.

By setting up a joint account you could unwittingly circumvent your will. Suppose your will gives equal shares of your estate to all your children, but most of your estate is in bank certificates of deposit that are held jointly with only one of your children. Since your will governs property that goes into probate, that is, property in your name only, the money in the CDs passes to the child who is the joint owner and not to the other children you thought you provided for in your will. You can avoid a family fight by making sure a substantial portion of your assets are outside the joint account or by setting up a power of attorney.

Setting up a joint account does not protect your money from Medicaid. Fifty percent of the assets belong to you, and Medicaid can count them in determining your eligibility for benefits. Whether the other 50 percent is safe depends on *when* you created the joint account. If you set up the account at least 2½ years before you enter a nursing home, then Medicaid probably can't touch the money.

Joint tenancy should not be confused with *tenancy in common,* another device for transferring assets. Under this arrangement, each person owns half of the assets, but at the death of one owner, the survivor is entitled only to his or her half. The other half of the money goes into the estate of the deceased. This device is often used in situations where property, such as real estate, is difficult to divide.

Joint accounts are not the same as accounts that are held "in trust for" someone else. With these accounts, you retain control over the money while you are alive. At your death, the person you are holding the money in trust for becomes the owner of the account. That person cannot touch it during your lifetime. Thus "in trust for" accounts are not useful devices for managing your money.

POWERS OF ATTORNEY

A power of attorney is a legal tool under which you give another person the power to act for you. The person you invest with this power is called an "agent" or an "attorney-in-fact" but does not have to be a lawyer.

To set up a power of attorney, you simply sign a prepared form obtained from a bank or brokerage house, a legal supply store, or your attorney, and list the powers you want your agent to have. A power of attorney may be limited or extensive. For example, you may want someone to sign papers for you only at a real estate closing, or manage your finances while you are on vacation. Or you can give someone broader powers—to sign checks, to deal with your broker, or to get into your safe-deposit box.

Powers of attorney cannot be used after your death. Nor can they be used if you become disabled unless you specifically say so. If you give your agent the power to act on your behalf when you're incapacitated, you are establishing a *durable power of attorney.*

Powers of attorney are easy to set up and can be especially useful if you include the durability feature. They are most suitable if you have only a few assets, such as bank certificates of deposit or perhaps a mutual fund or two. They are not necessarily permanent documents, however. If you change your mind, you can prevent your agent from using it by simply tearing up the piece of paper assigning the powers. Your bank or brokerage firm may then ask you to assign a new power of attorney to someone else.

Powers of attorney have some pitfalls. Your agent can act while you are alive and make decisions for you even though you can make your own decisions and don't want any interference. Although an agent is required to make decisions for your benefit, there are few safeguards to prevent him or her from misusing your funds. If that happens, your only recourse may be an expensive lawsuit that may come too late to recover your money. Because powers of attorney are easy to use, financial institutions in some states may not accept standard-form documents. In that case, use a form provided by the institution.

Be sure someone such as your lawyer or a trusted family member knows where you have stored your powers of attorney. They should be accessible if you become disabled.

LIVING TRUSTS

The most complicated way of assigning someone the task of managing your money is to set up a living trust. These trusts, which are explained in greater detail in chapter 18, provide for a trustee or trustees to sign checks, give instructions to brokers, and otherwise manage the assets you put into the trust. Under some arrangements, you may also be one of the trustees.

You need a lawyer to set up a trust and the cost can run several hundred dollars or more. But if you have several types of investments, or assets in real estate or a business, a living trust is much more practical than a durable power of attorney.

GUARDIANS, CONSERVATORS, AND COMMITTEES

If you don't arrange for someone to take care of your financial affairs and you become incapacitated, the state may have to appoint someone to do it. States are also empowered to appoint someone to supervise personally people who are unable to care for themselves. States have different names for those who perform these tasks—guardians, conservators, committees, curators—but their duties are similar.

They may collect all or part of your assets, manage them, pay your bills, collect income from your property and accounts, including Social Security, and periodically report to the court on how they are carrying out these functions. Each time a report is filed, the court awards them a commission, usually a percentage of the current value of your property or income. If a guardian is called on to perform particularly difficult jobs, such as running your business or managing investment real estate, the judge may increase the commission. Some states require guardians to post a bond, which is paid out of your funds.

How Guardians Are Appointed

If a guardian is to be appointed, a family member or another person acting for you files papers with the court requesting a hearing. The papers usually specify the relevant facts about your mental and physical condition and your assets and liabilities. An application for guardianship may also set out a plan for managing your money and caring for you. Your doctor may be asked to testify about your mental and physical condition and provide evidence that you are incapable of handling your own affairs. In some states, the appointment of a guardian amounts to a legal declaration of insanity. In other states it does not.

In some states, like California, you must give permission before a guardian is appointed; in others, you have little say in the matter. Nevertheless, there are legal procedures in place to protect you and your money. For instance, you have the right to be represented by a lawyer. If you don't have one, the court will appoint one to act on your behalf. He or she is called a "guardian ad litem" or a "special guardian."

Who Can Be a Guardian?

Anyone can be a guardian. Most states allow you to choose your own guardian or at least recommend someone to the court. If you have not made any other arrangements and feel that at some time in the future a guardian may be appointed, see your lawyer and make your preferences known while you are still able to do so. Some states allow you to designate a committee to act on your behalf. Check with your lawyer to see if this option is available to you.

If you do not tell the court whom you want as a guardian, most state laws leave the choice up to the judge, who usually appoints a family member following this order: spouse, adult children, parents, brothers and sisters, and other blood relatives, especially those you have been living with for some time. Some states require the guardian to reside in your state. Even so, in some circumstances the judge may have to choose a blood relative who lives far away.

Appointing a guardian is a complicated and costly procedure that often involves emotional pain. It's best to avoid the need for it. If possible, establish a joint account, power of attorney, or living trust instead.

PART TWO

Health Care

8

MEDICARE: *What the Government Pays*

When Lyndon Johnson signed the Medicare Act in the summer of 1965, he promised that older Americans would never be denied "the healing miracle of modern medicine," nor would "illness crush and destroy the savings they had so carefully put away." For the last quarter century the federal government has struggled to keep that promise, spending ever-increasing sums on health care for the elderly. In 1967, the first year benefits were paid, the government spent $3.2 billion on Medicare. By 1990, the bill amounted to over $90 billion. For elderly patients, the cost of medical services not fully covered by Medicare has also risen dramatically, now threatening to "destroy the savings they had so carefully put away."

The seeds of Medicare's cost explosion, as well as the explosion in all health-care costs, were sown the day Congress embraced fee-for-service reimbursement plans as the model for Medicare. For years Medicare paid whatever health-care providers demanded.

But in the early 1980s Medicare stopped payment on the blank checks it had given hospitals. Now Medicare tells hospitals what it will pay for an inpatient diagnosis and care. Almost all hospital services today fall into 1 of 490 diagnostic-related groups (DRGs). Hospitals are reimbursed according to the diagnostic group for which you are admitted. A hospital usually receives a fixed dollar amount for a given diagnosis, no matter how long you stay or what treatment is given.

To some extent, the DRG schedule (sometimes called the prospective payment system) has slowed the growth in expenditures for hospital claims. Hospitals have become somewhat more efficient since they can no longer automatically pass on their costs to Medicare. But Medicare has been unable to cut costs for physicians' services to the same degree. In the last five years, Medicare's costs for physicians' services alone have doubled, growing 40 percent faster than the economy as a whole. While Medicare has tried to limit what hospitals and doctors can charge Medicare patients, it has not cut benefits for the elderly, except for a return to the more limited hospital benefits after Congress repealed the Catastrophic Coverage Act in late 1989.

The fact is that Medicare was never meant to cover all the hospital and medical bills for the elderly. Medicare beneficiaries pay their share of the costs through premiums, deductibles, coinsurance, and excess charges.

MEDICARE BASICS

Medicare's prospective payments for hospital inpatient care are designed to cover 100 percent of the costs of medically necessary services for Medicare beneficiaries. (Patients do pay a hospital deductible, however.) For most physicians' services, outpatient hospital services, and supplies, Medicare pays 80 percent of what it determines is the "allowable charge."

The portion of the allowed charge not paid by Medicare is called *coinsurance* and is paid by the beneficiary. Beneficiaries also pay *deductibles,* those amounts that they must pay before Medicare benefits begin. Beneficiaries also may pay *excess charges,* that is, an amount above Medicare's allowed charge that physicians may bill to the beneficiaries. Excess physicians' fees represent one of the biggest gaps in Medicare coverage today.

Part A Coverage: Hospital Services

Acute care. For the first 60 days you are in a hospital in each benefit period, Medicare pays your entire bill except for a deductible. In 1992, the hospital deductible is $652. (Each year it is adjusted to account for rising costs.) If you are hospitalized for 61 to 90 days, you pay coinsurance for each day you are in the hospital. In 1992 that amount is $163 per day. If your stay exceeds 90 days, you can use your lifetime reserve days—each beneficiary gets 60 lifetime reserve days to use for long hospitalizations—and pay a daily copayment of $326 in 1992. Once you have used those days, however, they are gone forever. And if you're unfortunate enough to have a very long hospitalization and you've used up those reserve days, you'll have to pay the entire remaining cost yourself. The hospital automatically uses your reserve days for extended stays unless you request in writing that those days not be used. Medicare pays nothing if you are hospitalized longer than 150 days in any benefit period.

A "benefit period" begins when you enter a hospital and ends when you've been out for 60 consecutive days. If you are hospitalized for, say, 15 days, discharged, then readmitted 20 days later, you are still in the same benefit period.

For Medicare to pay your hospital bills, a doctor must prescribe the care, and the care must be given in a hospital that participates in Medicare. (Almost all hospitals do.) There's no coverage for care in a nonparticipating hospital except in an emergency, and even then, Medicare may not pay the entire bill.

Medicare picks up the tab for most hospital expenses, including the cost of a semiprivate room, lab tests, X rays, nursing services, meals, drugs provided by the hospital, medical supplies, appliances, and the cost of operating and recovery rooms. Telephones and televisions are not covered; neither is the cost of private-duty nurses or private rooms unless they are medically necessary.

If you need blood, Medicare pays the entire cost of replacing the blood (a requirement at some hospitals), but only after you have used three pints. The blood deductible applies for each benefit period (you must pay for the first three pints).

Skilled-nursing care. Medicare imposes strict eligibility requirements for these benefits. It pays only if care is provided in a Medicare-approved facility, if a doctor certifies that such care is needed daily, and you have been in a hospital for at least 3 days prior to needing skilled-nursing care. For the first 20 days in a skilled-nursing facility, Medicare picks up 100 percent of the cost of a semiprivate room, meals, nursing services, medical supplies, and appliances. For stays lasting from 21 to 100 days, you must pay coinsurance. In 1992, that amount is $81.50 a day. If you require skilled-nursing care for longer than 100 days, you must pay out of your own pocket or with the proceeds from a long-term-care policy (see chapter 11). So don't count on Medicare paying much of your bill for skilled-nursing care, especially if you need it for a long time. In fact, Medicare pays only about 2 percent of all skilled-nursing costs nationally.

Home-health care. There are strict eligibility rules for home-health benefits. Medicare pays if care is provided by a Medicare-certified home–health care agency, if you require intermittent skilled-nursing care or physical or speech therapy, if you are homebound, and if a doctor orders and regularly reviews such care. Medicare picks up 100 percent of the charges for occupational and physical therapists, medical supplies, medical social services, and the part-time services of home-health aides. But if you need medical equipment at home (oxygen or a hospital bed, for example), Medicare pays only 80 percent of the allowed charge.

Hospice care. A hospice is a facility that provides inpatient, outpatient, and home care for the terminally ill. Unlike hospitals, hospices don't try to cure patients but focus on counseling, symptom control, and pain reduction. Medicare pays all expenses for nursing and doctor services, supplies, appliances, social services, counseling, and home-health and homemaker services in Medicare-approved hospices. Benefits last 210 days if a physician says you are terminally ill and have elected the hospice benefit instead of regular Part A coverage. As part of the hospice benefit, Medicare also pays 5 percent of the cost of outpatient drugs or five dollars toward each prescription, whichever is less.

Psychiatric care. Medicare pays the entire cost for inpatient care, less the yearly hospital deductible. Coverage is limited to 190 days for your lifetime.

Part B Coverage: Medical Services

For most Part B services, Medicare pays 80 percent of the allowed charge. You pay the remaining 20 percent. You are also responsible for paying the annual deductible, that is, the first $100 of your medical bills each year, before Medicare starts paying for Part B services. You can meet the deductible requirement in one doctor's visit or by using a combination of services.

The allowed charge. Understanding how Medicare figures the allowed charges is central to understanding your coverage under Part B. When a doctor submits a Medicare claim, the claim goes to an insurance company that works under contract with Medicare to process claims. This company, known as the *carrier*, determines the allowed charge for the particular service you needed. The allowed charge is the smaller of the actual charge the doctor bills, or is a set fee determined by Medicare. In 1992, Medicare began paying doctors according to a national fee schedule based on the relative value of the services performed. The effect of this fee schedule is to compensate general practitioners more fairly and reduce fees to more highly paid specialists, such as radiologists and ophthalmologists. (Medicare determines the value of each service by calculating the amount of work, overhead costs, and malpractice insurance expenses needed to provide the service.)

Excess charges. Medicare gives doctors the option of accepting the allowed charge based on the new fee schedule as payment in full or requiring you to pay the difference between the allowed and the actual charge. That gap, as we explained earlier, is called the excess charge. Suppose, for example, a surgeon charges $2,000. Medicare determines that the allowed charge is $1,400. The $600 difference not covered is the excess charge, which you pay. (You must also pay the coinsurance of 20 percent of the $1,400, or $280.)

Many doctors bill excess charges. About one-fourth of all Medicare Part B claims involve some excess charges, and these charges continue to mount. But Congress has taken some steps to reduce them. Today, a physician's excess charge cannot exceed 20 percent of Medicare's allowed charge; in 1993, that figure can't be more than 15 percent.

A doctor who agrees to accept the allowed charge in all cases is called a *participating* physician. In Medicare parlance, such a physician "accepts assignment." (Doctors who don't accept assignments are "nonparticipating.") About half of the doctors serving Medicare beneficiaries are participating physicians. The rest may accept assignment only if they believe you cannot pay the extra charges. In effect, doctors are free to provide their own "means test," accepting the allowed fee for some patients and billing others a higher fee.

The likelihood of your doctor accepting assignment depends on where you live, the doctor's specialty, and your age. Massachusetts requires all medical doctors to accept the Medicare allowed charge as payment in full. But in Wyoming, which has no such requirement, only 39 percent of the state's physicians are participating doctors. Surgeons and nephrologists are more likely to accept assignment than are anesthesiologists and general practitioners. And doctors are more apt to take assignment from patients who are 85 than from those who are 65. Doctors who do not take assignment for elective surgery must give you a written estimate of your out-of-pocket costs if the charge is likely to total more than $500. If a doctor fails to give you this estimate, you are entitled to a refund of any amount you paid over Medicare's allowed charge.

To find a participating doctor, consult the *Medicare-Participating Physician/Supplier Directory,* which you can find at your local Social Security Administration office. You can also obtain the directory free of charge from the insurance company that handles Medicare claims for your area. Your local Social Security office or Area Agency on Aging can tell you the name of your carrier. The carrier is also listed in *The Medicare Handbook* you receive when you sign up for the program.

Part B Benefits

Doctors' fees. Part B benefits cover services furnished in a doctor's office or in your home as well as those provided in an inpatient or outpatient hospital setting. Services include anesthesia, radiology, pathology, surgery, some podiatric treatment, second-opinion consultations, dental care if it involves jaw surgery or setting broken facial bones, and chiropractic treatment to correct an out-of-place vertebra shown on an X ray.

Outpatient hospital coverage. These benefits cover outpatient hospital services, including those required in an emergency room or outpatient clinic. Blood transfusions are also covered under Part B, but the deductible is different from the one under Part A. If you use three pints and have paid the $100 annual deductible, Medicare picks up 80 percent of the allowed charge. You pay the 20 percent coinsurance plus replacement costs for the first three pints of blood you use.

Physical and occupational therapy. For you to be eligible for this coverage, your doctor must prescribe a treatment plan for you and periodically review it. If therapy is provided in an outpatient-hospital facility or skilled-nursing facility or by a home–health care agency, clinic, or Medicare-approved rehabilitation agency, the usual cost-sharing arrangement applies. But if a Medicare-certified therapist who practices independently provides your treatment, Medicare limits its payment to $500 a year.

Psychiatric care. Medicare pays for care in either a doctor's office or outpatient hospital facility, but the benefits are different, depending on where the service is performed. If care is given in an outpatient facility, Medicare pays 80 percent and you pay 20 percent, but if it's given in a doctor's office, Medicare pays about 50 percent of the allowable charge, up to a maximum annual benefit of $1,100.

Laboratory fees. Medicare pays 100 percent of the allowed charge for clinical diagnostic tests (such as for blood and urine) performed in independent laboratories certified by Medicare. If tests are done in a noncertified lab, you must pay for them yourself. Neither laboratories nor doctors who perform clinical lab tests in their offices can bill you for excess charges. For other diagnostic tests such as X rays, EKGs, and tissue biopsies, Medicare's usual cost-sharing applies and nonparticipating physicians can bill more than the allowed charge.

Ambulance services. If the following conditions are met, Medicare pays 80 percent of the allowed charge: You must have a medical need for an ambulance; the ambulance and its equipment must meet Medicare's standards; and the use of an alternative vehicle could endanger your life.

Drugs. Medicare does not cover prescription drugs you purchase from a pharmacy. There is an exception, however, for immunosuppressive drugs that are taken within one year after an organ transplant that Medicare has covered. Medicare does pay for drugs while you are in a hospital or skilled-nursing facility. It also covers certain injections in physicians' offices.

To sum up, most Part B services require you to pay 20 percent of the allowed charge. However, for a few services, you pay neither coinsurance nor the deductible. These include pneumococcal vaccines and the charge for administering them, second opinions that Medicare requests for certain surgical procedures, and outpatient clinical diagnostic laboratory tests performed by physicians who take assignment and by Medicare-certified hospitals and laboratories.

WHAT MEDICARE DOES NOT COVER

Medicare does not pay for in-hospital private-duty nurses or for private rooms in hospitals or skilled-nursing facilities unless a doctor says your condition is so serious that you need such services. Nor does it pay for televisions, telephones, and other personal items such as hearing aids, eyeglasses, or orthopedic shoes.

In general, it pays only for services that are reasonable and necessary to help you recover from an illness. You can't submit a claim for setting a broken arm and then bill Medicare for a routine chest X ray, too. Nor does the program pay for preventive care such as routine annual physicals. However, for women 65 and older, the program does cover mammograms every two years. With few exceptions, it does not pay for immunizations or for insulin injections that patients can administer themselves. It doesn't pay for ordinary foot or dental care, almost all chiropractic services, or cosmetic surgery.

There are no benefits for skilled care in nursing homes that you need for more than 100 days or for intermediate or custodial nursing care. The latter helps you cope with daily activities such as eating and bathing. And Medicare doesn't pay for meals delivered to your home. If you become sick while visiting or living in a foreign country, Medicare won't cover your expenses. The program pays for treatment only in some Canadian and Mexican hospitals and then only in certain situations.

FILING A CLAIM

The federal government does not pay your medical bills directly. It contracts with private insurance companies to process claims and pay health-care providers. The companies that pay claims for Part A coverage are called intermediaries; those that pay Part B claims are called carriers. After you are dismissed from a hospital, the facility bills Medicare directly. You receive a *Medicare Benefit Notice* that tells you what services are covered. For services covered under Part B, your doctor or medical supply company must submit your claim to the carrier even if they don't accept assignment. Neither a doctor nor a medical supply company can charge extra for preparing your claim form. If your doctor refuses to prepare your claim form, contact the carrier. If the doctor or supplier accepts Medicare's payment as payment in full, the carrier pays the doctor directly. If the doctor refuses to accept assignment on your claim, Medicare pays you, and you pay the doctor. Medicare will send you an *Explanation of Medicare Benefits* or EOMB, which shows the services that were covered, the charges Medicare approved, how much was credited toward your $100 deductible, and the amount Medicare paid.

If you disagree with the amount that Medicare pays or dispute coverage for certain services, you can appeal the decision. Your EOMB can tell you how to do that, or consult *The Medicare Handbook.*

WHAT YOU PAY FOR MEDICARE

Part A is financed through Social Security taxes. Most beneficiaries pay no additional premiums for their Part A coverage. However, some people must pay monthly premiums for hospital coverage, including disabled persons who have gone back to work but are still disabled and people who have not worked the required 10 years to obtain Social Security benefits. If you do not have the required work history, you may still be eligible for Part A benefits based on your spouse's work record. However, if you and your spouse divorce before being married 10 years, you have to pay the Part A premiums to continue your coverage. The Part A premium in 1992 is $192 per month.

Part B, which is optional, is financed through general tax revenues and premiums paid by beneficiaries. The U.S. Treasury pays about 75 percent of the cost of the program; beneficiaries pay the rest. In 1992, beneficiaries pay $31.80 a month; in 1993, the premium will be $36.60; in 1994, $41.10; and in 1995, $46.10. Premiums are deducted from your Social Security checks. If you don't sign up for Part B during the initial enrollment period, you'll pay more.

SIGNING UP FOR MEDICARE

If you elect early retirement benefits from Social Security, you automatically receive a Medicare card in the mail when you turn 65. If you sign up for Social Security benefits when you are 65, you receive your Medicare card at the same time. However, if you have turned 65 and want to delay your Social Security benefits, you have to apply for Medicare. In that case, do so during the first three months of your initial enrollment period, which is the seven-month period that begins three months before the month you are first eligible for Medicare. *Example:* You turn 65 on October 1 and become eligible for Medicare on that date. Your initial enrollment period begins on July 1 and lasts through January of the following year. If you don't enroll during the three months before your eligibility date, your benefits may be delayed from one to three months. If you don't enroll during the seven-month initial enrollment period, the delay could be as long as 16 months.

Furthermore, if you do not enroll in Part B during your initial enrollment period, but later decide you want benefits, you can sign up during the general enrollment period held each year from January 1 through March 31. If you delay enrolling, however, your monthly premium goes up by 10 percent for each 12-month period you are not enrolled in the program.

VETERANS BENEFITS

If you have served in the armed forces, you may be eligible for a variety of veterans benefits. The ones of most interest to retirees are usually medical and burial.

Medical. Most veterans can receive care for a non-service-related medical condition in a Department of Veterans Affairs facility. Admittance depends on your income level, and if space is available in the veterans' hospital. Medical benefits are sometimes extended to spouses as well.

Burial. Any person who has completed the required period of service and has been discharged under other than dishonorable conditions can be buried in any of the 113 national cemeteries operated by the Veterans Department.

For more information about benefits or the location of the nearest VA facility, contact the regional VA office in your state.

MEDICARE AND COVERAGE FROM YOUR EMPLOYER

Special rules apply if you work past age 65 and your employer continues to provide health insurance for you and your spouse. You can continue coverage under your employer's plan and enroll in Medicare. However, Medicare pays only after the employer's plan does. In other words, Medicare is the second payer.

If you are covered under your employer's plan when you become eligible for Medicare, you may be able to delay Medicare coverage without paying a penalty and without waiting for a general enrollment period when you finally decide to take the coverage. Your company may offer a monetary incentive to opt out of its group health plan in an effort to shift its own health care costs to Medicare. If that's the case, be sure your company offers the same deal to all those who are eligible for Medicare. If the company doesn't, it may be fined $5,000, and you may be at a disadvantage. Carefully weigh such offers. If your employer picks up most of the cost for your health care, it may be cheaper to stay in the plan rather than pay the Medicare Part B premium and the premium for a supplemental policy.

IF YOU ARE DISABLED

Medicare pays the health-care bills for disabled persons under age 65 who qualify for Social Security disability benefits and have been disabled for at least two years. However, if you have been receiving Medicare benefits as a disabled person and then go back to work before you turn 65, you can continue to receive Medicare benefits only if you are still disabled. After you start working, Part A benefits continue for at least 48 months and Part B benefits continue for the same time as long as you pay the Part B premium. Once your hospital benefits run out, you can continue buying both Part A and Part B benefits so long as you're disabled.

MEDICARE AND HMOs

You can enroll in a health maintenance organization (HMO) or a competitive medical plan (CMP) and receive Medicare benefits. Joining such a plan may offer you some advantages. Most HMOs and CMPs must provide certain benefits not available to Medicare beneficiaries who choose fee-for-service doctors. For example, they may cover extended hospital and skilled-nursing stays, expanded home-health benefits, and drugs.

HMOs usually charge set monthly premiums and require small coinsurance payments, and they cover preventive care that Medicare does not pay for.

So if you cannot afford to pay premiums for a Medicare-supplement policy, consider joining an HMO if there is one in your area that accepts new members who are not part of an employer group. The monthly premiums are likely to be less than those for a traditional supplemental policy. Keep in mind, too, that you can join an HMO and later decide to return to your fee-for-service physician. You can drop a prepaid health plan in any month and begin to receive fee-for-service benefits at the beginning of the following month.

But in order to get optimum benefits, you must be aware of the HMO's arrangement with Medicare.

Medicare/HMO Plans

It is very important that you know what kind of plan an HMO is offering because it affects the benefits you receive and how you receive them. Medicare has three different arrangements with HMOs:

Risk contracts. In this type of arrangement, Medicare pays the HMO a monthly sum to provide all of the coverage for beneficiaries who join the plan. In a plan involving a risk contract, you may or may not pay an additional premium to the HMO (you must pay the Part B premium to Medicare). In some parts of the country, HMOs offer coverage for no premium at all. Most of the time, no copayments are required for any of the traditional Medicare benefits furnished by the HMO plan. There may be copayments, though, for prescription drugs and any preventive services that Medicare normally does not cover. Once you sign up for such an HMO plan, you are obligated to receive all your care from the HMO except in emergencies; this is known as the lock-in feature. If you do seek medical care outside of the plan, you will have to pay the entire cost yourself.

Cost contracts. Here Medicare pays the HMO for the actual cost of providing Medicare services to its beneficiaries. You pay a monthly premium to the HMO for the basic Medicare package, plus any additional services the HMO provides. (You must also pay the Medicare Part B premium.) There are also copayments for services not usually covered by Medicare. You can receive all your care from the HMO, or go outside the plan for medical services. If you choose to go outside the plan, Medicare will make its usual reimbursement of 80 percent of the allowed charge for medical care. You must pay the remaining 20 percent, along with the $100 annual deductible and any excess charges billed by the doctor.

Health care prepayment plans. In this type of plan, an HMO arranges with Medicare to provide some or all of the Part B services. The monthly premium covers the cost of Part B coinsurance and the deductible for services obtained through the HMO. For Part A and Part B services obtained outside the HMO, you have to pay the normal coinsurance and deductibles that are required by Medicare. This plan can be confusing, because some of your care is provided by the HMO and a portion is provided by outside sources. If you receive much of your care outside the HMO, you may also need to buy a Medicare-supplement policy to shield you from the financial consequences of a serious illness. You might do better to choose an HMO that offers either a risk or cost arrangement, rather than pay the premium for supplemental insurance plus the premium for the HMO prepayment plan. Furthermore, fewer safeguards are built into these kinds of plans.

9

Health Insurance from Your Employer

If you're like most workers preparing for retirement, you probably have counted on your employer to pay for your health insurance after you leave the work force. In 1986, 58 percent of all employees who worked for medium- and large-size firms did have some employer-financed health insurance benefits when they reached age 65. Even those taking early retirement had some coverage. But by 1988, those numbers had dropped.

The explosion in health-care costs and new government rules have made many employers reluctant to fund health insurance for retirees. Corporations now have to show on their books the expected cost of retiree health benefits and account for a potentially huge liability that will take a large chunk of their pretax earnings. Consequently, employers are now requiring their retirees to pay a greater portion of their medical bills, and some workers will have no coverage at all when they retire.

If your employer won't pay for your health insurance, it's important to know what options you have for buying your own coverage. Health insurance is vital and if you have few options, you may have to postpone your retirement.

The first step in assessing your health coverage is to know what your employer will provide and how much you will have to pay. Then you can compare that coverage and premium with other policies on the market.

A common mistake retirees make is buying too much health insurance or the wrong kind. One good policy that supplements Medicare, whether from your former employer or from a private insurance company, is enough. Coverage from a former employer is often cheaper and more comprehensive than a policy purchased from an insurance company. But if coverage from your employer is skimpy or too expensive, a Medicare-supplement policy from a private carrier is the better choice.

Sometimes a combination of policies is appropriate. For example, if your employer offers coverage only for inpatient hospital stays and no benefits for outpatient or other medical services, you will need a supplemental policy.

IF YOU RETIRE EARLY

Whether your employer offers retiree health coverage usually depends on your age when you leave the work force. Some companies provide no benefits for workers who retire before age 65. Others give early retirees health coverage for only a short time. For example, your employer may offer health coverage for only three years. That's fine if you plan to retire at age 62 and will have three years' worth of coverage before becoming eligible for Medicare. But if you retire at age 60, your benefits will run out before Medicare picks up your medical bills, and you'll have to find your own insurance to cover the two remaining years. In addition, when coverage ends for you, it may end for your nonworking spouse as well.

Obviously, it's important to check to see if your employer will continue coverage for your spouse when you retire and after you become eligible for Medicare. If your spouse will have no coverage, and also must wait several years before becoming eligible for Medicare, he or she will have to find other health coverage.

If your employer offers no coverage and you retire several years before you're eligible for Medicare, you (and your spouse) have four options: (1) continue existing coverage from your employer for a short time; (2) convert to an individual health-insurance policy offered by the same carrier that provided your group coverage; (3) buy a new policy from another carrier; or (4) buy coverage from your state's high-risk pool, if there is one. The best choice is the plan that gives you the greatest coverage at the lowest price for the longest time.

Coverage Under COBRA

If you worked for a business with 20 or more employees, the Consolidated Omnibus Budget Reconciliation Act of 1985 (COBRA) entitles you and your dependents to continued coverage for at least 18 months under your former employer's plan. If you are disabled and eligible for Social Security disability benefits when your employment ends, you get an additional 11 months of coverage, or a total of 29 months. Your COBRA coverage can last up to 36 months if you are insured through your spouse's plan at work and your spouse dies, if you divorce or separate, or if your spouse becomes eligible for Medicare.

COBRA coverage isn't free. You have to pay 102 percent of the premium (the 2 percent is for administrative expenses). If you're disabled, you pay 150 percent for the extra 11 months of coverage. If you were not paying for any of your health insurance before leaving the company, or were only paying for part of the premium, you will undoubtedly have to pay a hefty bill for COBRA coverage.

Employers pay an average of $2,400 a year to insure workers and their dependents, and anywhere from $1,200 to $1,600 to insure employees who are single. Depending on the plan, your bill could be more or less. If you choose to go with COBRA, find out well in advance what your premiums will be so you can accommodate them in your retirement budget. Plan also for higher costs—premiums on some health policies have been rising as much as 50 percent a year.

You can lose COBRA coverage if you don't pay your premiums, if you become eligible for Medicare, if your employer discontinues health benefits for employees still working, or if you join another plan. However, if you or your spouse join another plan that imposes a waiting period for preexisting health conditions, you can keep your COBRA benefits until they normally would run out. By that time your preexisting condition may be covered under the new plan. You could be without coverage for that condition if COBRA benefits stop before the waiting period on the new plan is over.

An increasingly common way to lose benefits is for your former employer to drop coverage for employees still working or to change insurance carriers. Sometimes the new carrier "underwrites" all employees, active and retired. This means it scrutinizes your health and decides whether it wants to insure you. If it doesn't, you may have no coverage. The new plan may also provide fewer benefits.

Despite such uncertainties, COBRA coverage can be vital. If you retire early and are too young for Medicare unless you are seriously disabled, a preexisting health condition may make it difficult or impossible to buy insurance on your own. If you want or must retire early, try to coordinate your retirement with the length of time you'll receive COBRA benefits. If you can wait until you are 63½ to retire, you'll have protection until Medicare begins. When you do qualify for Medicare, your spouse can continue COBRA coverage for an additional 18 months, assuming he or she is not yet eligible for Medicare. Coverage for your spouse is a crucial factor in choosing the best time to retire.

If you work for a company that has self-insured its workers' health coverage, you are entitled to COBRA benefits even though such plans are normally exempt from other insurance regulations.

If you are not eligible for COBRA because your former firm employs fewer than 20 workers or is a church organization, you may still have some protection under state laws.

Some states provide for continuation of benefits, and you may be able to stay on your employer's group policy for as long as 18 months. (But in others you may get coverage for only three months.) These continuation benefits are usually not available to workers in self-insured plans or in states without comprehensive continuation laws. These states are Alabama, Alaska, Arizona, Delaware, Florida, Hawaii, Idaho, Indiana, Louisiana, Michigan, Mississippi, Nebraska, Pennsylvania, Wisconsin, and Wyoming.

Many employers don't like to offer COBRA coverage, claiming it is an administrative nightmare and costs them too much money. Consequently, some employers offer you the option of taking an accident-only policy instead of full-fledged health benefits under COBRA. These policies do not cover illness; they pay only if you're injured in an accident. Even though such a policy is much cheaper, you give up valuable protection, so we don't recommend these substitutes.

Conversion Policies

If COBRA benefits stop before you qualify for Medicare, your employer must give you the right to convert to an individual policy. If you're not eligible for COBRA, your state's insurance laws may require your employer to offer conversion policies. All states except Alabama, Alaska, Connecticut, Delaware, the District of Columbia, Hawaii, Idaho, Indiana, Louisiana, Massachusetts, Michigan, Mississippi, Nebraska, New Jersey, North Dakota, and Oklahoma require such policies.

Conversion policy coverage is almost always inferior to what you received from your group plan when you were working. Only 24 states require companies to offer conversion policies with major-medical or comprehensive benefits. A major-medical policy usually covers hospital and surgical charges, outpatient care, and physicians' fees, but a conversion policy is likely to provide only hospital and surgical benefits and pay only a fixed amount each day for hospital room and board and surgical procedures.

The price of a conversion policy is high because people in

poor health usually buy this coverage. For example, one company would charge a 62-year-old man living in Chicago $13,084 for its most generous conversion policy, a large sum for someone planning to live on a fixed income.

Despite low benefits and high premiums, a conversion policy may be your only option if you have chronic health problems. Insurers aren't allowed to underwrite conversion coverage, so you can always get one no matter how bad your health. If you are unable to buy an individual policy or obtain coverage from your state's high-risk pool, if it has one, you may have to pay the price for conversion coverage or risk going uninsured until you turn 65.

Buying a Policy on Your Own

If you retire early and your employer does not provide health insurance, you can always forgo your COBRA benefits and try to find a policy in the private market. If you have health problems, you may not be able to do this. But if your health is good, and you can find a carrier willing to issue a policy at a price that's less than your COBRA coverage, you may want to choose this option. When your COBRA benefits stop, you may also want to shop for your own policy rather than opt for a costly conversion policy from your employer (assuming you're not eligible for Medicare).

Your shopping trip won't be easy, however. There are few sellers and the ones that do offer coverage make you pass strict health requirements before they issue a policy. Virtually no commercial carriers and only a handful of Blue Cross and Blue Shield plans sell policies to anyone who has had heart disease, internal cancer, diabetes, a stroke, adrenal disorders, epilepsy, or ulcerative colitis. Treatment for alcohol and substance abuse, depression, or even visits to a marriage counselor can disqualify you.

If you have less serious medical problems, you may get coverage, but on unfavorable terms. Conditions that usually affect one part of the body are candidates for *exclusion riders.* This means a carrier offers a policy but excludes coverage for those conditions or that affected body part either for a short period or for as long as the policy is in force. For example, if you have had a recent knee operation, glaucoma, migraine headaches, varicose veins, or arthritis, your policy will probably carry an exclusion rider. If you have a medical condition that affects your general health—you're significantly overweight or have mild high blood pressure—you may get coverage but at a price 15 to 100 percent higher than the standard premium.

Pay particular attention to a policy's renewability clause. Few companies guarantee to renew your coverage. Most policies are "conditionally renewable," that is, the company can refuse to renew your policy, but only if it does so for all other similar policies in your state. You have some protection, then, because the company can't single you out for cancellation. But you can still lose your coverage eventually. Some companies use conditionally renewable policies as a lever to force insurance regulators to grant them rate increases, and a number of carriers have canceled policies in states where regulators were unwilling to raise rates. Ask whether the company you're considering has canceled any health policies. Past practice may give you a clue to what it will do in the future.

A few policies are "optionally renewable." A company can choose not to renew your insurance whether or not it renews coverage for others who have the same policy. Avoid these policies if you can.

High-Risk Pools

A fourth option is your state's high-risk pool. Twenty-three states have established such pools as the insurer of last resort for people with serious health problems. (See Appendix C for a list of pools and their addresses.) When your COBRA benefits run out, look to the pool if you are not in good health.

To obtain coverage, you must be a state resident for at least six months (a year in some states) and have received a rejection notice from at least one carrier. (A few states require two rejections.) If a carrier will insure you only at a premium that exceeds the price of coverage from the pool, or if the insurance you're offered carries exclusion riders, you are also eligible for a pool policy in most states.

Florida, Illinois, Iowa, Minnesota, North Dakota, Tennessee, Washington, and Wisconsin make Medicare-supplement policies available through their pools. That's a boon if you are disabled and under age 65 and rely on Medicare but can't find insurance to cover Medicare's gaps.

Pool coverage is similar to that offered by a major-medical policy, although benefits for mental and nervous disorders, organ transplants, and pregnancy may be less comprehensive. You may, however, pay more out-of-pocket than you would with a major-medical policy. Some plans require high deductibles, greater coinsurance, and have relatively low lifetime benefit maximums.

Premiums are very high, which is not surprising, since policyholders will almost certainly file claims. A 62-year-old man living in Chicago would pay $6,807 a year for a policy with a $500 deductible from the Illinois pool.

IF YOU RETIRE AT 65

If you are 65 and your employer offers you health insurance, you have to decide whether to take that coverage and/or buy a Medicare-supplement policy. Consider your spouse's coverage as well. He or she may have no insurance from your employer, in which case you have to buy him or her a Medicare-supplement policy, assuming your spouse is eligible for Medicare.

Employers use three basic approaches in fashioning health coverage for their retirees.

Carve-Out Coordination of Benefits

This is the most common approach. You receive the same benefits as active employees. The insurer calculates the portion of the claim the policy covers if Medicare were not in the picture. It then adds the amount the active employee would pay under this arrangement to the amount Medicare pays for you. The insurer subtracts this total from the amount of the claim and pays the difference. You pay whatever Medicare and the insurance carrier do not pay.

Example: You incur $1,100 in medical expenses. Medicare's allowed charge is $750, of which it pays 80 percent, or $600. Your policy has a $100 deductible, which the carrier subtracts from the amount of the claim, leaving $1,000 that you are responsible for paying. Under the terms of the policy for active workers, the carrier pays 80 percent of $1,000, or $800, leaving the worker to pay the remaining $300. To determine what the carrier pays for you, it adds what the active employee would pay or $300 to Medicare's payment of $600 for a total of $900. The carrier then pays the difference between the $900 and the $1,100 claim, or $200. Medicare pays $600, the insurance company $200, and you $300.

Standard Coordination of Benefits with Medicare

This is the most generous method. The insurer determines the portion of your expenses eligible for payment, subtracts the deductible, then pays 80 percent of the remainder. But if that amount plus Medicare's payment is greater than the total claim, the insurance company reduces what it pays to you. You cannot profit from an illness. *Example:* Let's return to the $1,100 claim on which Medicare pays $600. Five hundred dollars remains unpaid. In calculating what you should receive, the insurance company subtracts the $100 deductible from the $1,100 claim, leaving $1,000 on which it bases its payment. The company then pays 80 percent, or $800. (In this example, we assume that the $1,000 is the company's "usual and customary" reimbursement level for the particular procedure.) The $800 plus the $600 Medicare payment exceed the amount of the claim, so the insurance company pays only the $400 that remains after Medicare pays its share. In this example, you pay only the $100 deductible, if you haven't already paid it for some other claim. If you have paid it, you have no out-of-pocket expenses.

Exclusion Coordination of Benefits

This method recognizes only the part of a claim Medicare does not reimburse. The deductible, if it has not been paid, is subtracted from the portion of the claim Medicare doesn't cover; the insurer pays 80 percent of what's left. *Example:* Medicare pays $600 of the $1,100 claim, leaving $500 unpaid. The insurer subtracts the $100 deductible, leaving $400, of which it pays 80 percent, or $320. The insurer's payment of $320 plus Medicare's contribution of $600 equals $920. That leaves $180 for you to pay, along with any deductible that hasn't been satisfied.

OTHER APPROACHES

Your employer may simply set aside a sum of money for you to spend on health care. These accounts can range in size from a few hundred dollars to $20,000, depending on whether your employer intends for the account to supplement other health insurance or provide major coverage. If you are offered such an account, you should also buy a good supplemental policy unless your employer sets up an extraordinarily large account, which is rare. Some companies offer retirees regular Medicare-supplement policies similar to those you can buy on your own (see chapter 10). Still others offer policies that pay only for hospital-related charges, which is limited coverage indeed.

Comparing Your Employer's Plan with Other Policies

Your out-of-pocket medical expenses are the lowest if your former employer uses the standard coordination-of-benefits approach; they are highest under a carve-out arrangement.

If your employer uses the standard coordination-of-benefits approach and pays the entire cost of your coverage, an additional Medicare-supplement policy is a waste of money. The same is true if your employer uses either the carve-out or the exclusion approach and pays the entire premium. Under these plans, you have small out-of-pocket expenses but pay nothing for the coverage. If you buy a generous supplemental policy that pays nearly all excess physicians' charges, you will spend $1,000 or more a year on premiums. Of course, if your employer terminates its health plan or goes out of business, your good coverage could evaporate. In that case, you would have to buy a Medicare-supplement policy anyway.

If you still want a supplement, consider a less expensive bare-bones policy that covers only the 20 percent Medicare copayment. Look for Medicare-supplement Plan A when you do your shopping around for a policy (see chapter 10). If your employer uses the carve-out or exclusion approach and requires that you pay most of the premium, you may be better off buying a Medicare-supplement policy that pays most of your bills and forgoing your employer's coverage. The premium may be less than what your employer would charge.

Example: Let's return again to our hypothetical claim of $1,100. As noted, Medicare's allowed charge is $750, of which Medicare pays 80 percent, or $600, assuming the $100 deductible has already been paid. You are responsible for the 20 percent copayment, or $150. But your physician refuses to accept assignment, does not take Medicare's $600 as full payment, and instead bills you for the remaining $350, which is the total charge minus the allowed charge ($1,100 minus 750 equals $350). Besides the $150 copayment, you also pay $350 of excess charges, for a total of $500. If you have neither coverage from your employer nor a supplemental policy, your out-of-pocket expenses are $500, again assuming you've already paid the annual deductible. If you have not paid the deductible, Medicare will pay only $500 and you'll have to come up with $600.

If you have insurance from your employer, who has used one of the three approaches outlined in this chapter, you pay, in addition to the deductible, $0, $180, or $300, depending on the plan. If you have no employer-provided coverage but carry a Medicare-supplement policy, the amount you pay depends on the policy you bought. All Medicare-supplement policies must cover the 20 percent copayment. But they don't all cover the Part B deductible or excess physicians' charges. If your supplemental policy pays just the coinsurance, your out-of-pocket expenses are $350. If it covers excess charges, either 80 percent or all of the $350 is paid, depending on the type of supplement you buy. Your deductible would also be paid if your supplement covers it.

If the premium for your employer's coverage is about the same as you would pay for a Medicare-supplement policy that covers excess physicians' fees, work through a few hypothetical claims to see which policy pays the most.

In making your decision, consider coverage for extras such as prescription drugs or preventive care. Sometimes employer-provided policies cover these; sometimes Medicare-supplemental policies do. If your employer's plan pays for prescriptions, you may be asked to use a mail-order drug company and pay a small copayment ranging from $2 to $10. This coverage could be valuable if you regularly use prescription drugs. If the basic coverage of two competing policies is equal, coverage for these extras might tip the balance in favor of one policy or another. In a few instances, you might want both.

If your employer's plan is generally inferior but covers prescription drugs that you need to take on a regular basis, you may want to keep the plan and buy a 20 percent supplemental policy. Likewise, check policy exclusions. If you have a preexisting health condition for which you might need immediate coverage, you are probably better off staying with your employer's coverage.

Remember, if you have just turned 65 and you buy a Medicare-supplement policy, the insurance company cannot ask you any questions about your health. You have a six-month period during which insurance companies cannot "underwrite" you (see chapter 10).

10

Insurance to Supplement Medicare

From the beginning, Medicare was never meant to cover the entire health-care bill for the elderly. Initially, the gaps left by Medicare coverage were small—and so were the premiums for supplemental policies. But the gaps widened considerably as health-care costs escalated, and now Medicare-supplement insurance has become a major item in the budgets of older Americans. Today almost 80 percent of all Medicare beneficiaries own a supplemental policy.

The growth of supplemental insurance policies has also spawned an industry of questionable mailing and telemarketing practices. Lead-card companies, for example, buy names from firms that compile mailing lists and then send out deceptive mailings to the names on the list. If you fill in and return the card enclosed in the mailing, your name is sold to insurance agents who then contact you as a potential customer. A few lead-card companies masquerade under names that are easily confused with well-known consumer and retiree organizations, and others try to give the impression of a government connection.

Insurance agents can also use questionable tactics in their sales presentations. *Twisting,* for example, is the practice of inducing someone to switch policies unnecessarily by using false and misleading data; *loading up* is selling duplicate coverage or multiple policies that cover the same service.

If you have any doubts about an agent's sales tactics or are confused about whether or not you need another policy, contact your state insurance counseling program, if there is one (see Appendix D). Counselors can help you sort out the insurance coverage you already have, tell you what you need, and advise you whether the policy you are considering is right for you.

ASSESSING YOUR NEEDS

When you review your health-insurance needs in preparation for retirement, first see if you can continue coverage under your employer's health plan (or your spouse's, if he or she is still working). If that insurance covers Medicare's gaps, and if the employer picks up most of the bill, you probably don't need another policy. But if coverage from an employer is inadequate, or you must pay for it by yourself and the cost is greater than coverage purchased on your own, you must buy your supplement from private insurance carriers.

Of course, if your income is low enough to qualify you for Medicaid, you don't need a policy. Similarly, if your income is moderate to low, but not low enough for Medicaid, consider joining an HMO (health maintenance organization). HMOs usually take members who are already part of employer groups, but some accept people, especially senior citizens, who are not. Monthly fees for HMO membership are often lower than the monthly premiums for supplemental policies.

In beginning your search for a supplement, you must first understand what Medicare pays and what gaps remain in your coverage. Once you know what Medicare leaves uncovered, you need to become familiar with the coverage supplied by each policy.

THE 10 STANDARDIZED PLANS

In 1990, Congress passed legislation that put an end to much of the confusion about Medicare-supplement insurance. It delegated the National Association of Insurance Commissioners (NAIC), an organization composed of state insurance regulators, to create 10 standardized Medicare-supplement policies. Companies can now offer only the prescribed plans.

The plans are designated by the letters A through J and offer different combinations of benefits. Each plan is the same from insurer to insurer. For example, one company's Plan C is identical to another's Plan C. Therefore, the main differences among policies are price and the quality of the service provided by the insurance company.

Not all 10 policies may be approved for sale in your state, however, and not every insurance company offers every plan. Once you decide which plan suits your needs, seek out the companies that sell that particular plan. If the plan of your choice is not offered in your state (your state insurance department can tell you this) then choose the one that is available and comes closest to meeting your requirements.

THE PLANS AND THEIR BENEFITS

The following is a guide to the types of coverage provided by each Medicare-supplement plan (also see Table 15).

Plan A

Every insurer must offer Plan A, which provides certain core, or basic, benefits. These include:

1. Coverage for Part A coinsurance—the daily amount you must pay for a hospital stay if you're hospitalized from 61 to 90 days. In 1992, Part A coinsurance is $163 a day.

2. Coverage for Part A coinsurance—the daily amount you must pay for a hospital stay that lasts from 91 to 150 days. In 1992, that amount is $326.
3. Coverage for an extra 365 days of hospital care after you have exhausted all of your Medicare benefits. Insurance companies usually reimburse hospitals according to the prospective payment system that Medicare uses.
4. Coverage for the cost of the first three pints of blood you may need as an inpatient in a hospital. In other words, policies will cover the Part A blood deductible.
5. Coverage for Part B coinsurance—20 percent of Medicare's allowable charge.

Plan B

Plan B must include the core benefits plus the Part A hospital deductible. This was $652 in 1992.

Plan C

Plan C must include the core benefits plus the following:

1. Coverage for coinsurance for a stay in skilled-nursing facility. Medicare requires beneficiaries needing skilled-nursing care to pay coinsurance for stays that last from 21 to 100 days. In 1992, the amount of the coinsurance was $81.50. After that, neither Medicare nor Medicare-supplement insurance pays any part of the bill.
2. Part A hospital deductible.
3. Emergency medical care in foreign countries.
4. Part B deductible—$100 in 1992.

Plan D

Plan D includes the core benefits plus:

1. Coverage for coinsurance for a stay in a skilled-nursing facility.
2. Part A hospital deductible.
3. Emergency medical care in foreign countries.
4. Coverage for at-home care following an injury, illness, or surgery. This benefit covers assistance with activities of daily living such as eating, bathing, and dressing. *Note:* The at-home care coverage provided is limited to a short period. For example, the benefit is limited to $1,600 per year, and your physician must certify that visits by a licensed home-health aide or homemaker or personal-care worker are necessary because of a condition for which Medicare has already approved a home–health care treatment plan for you.

Plan E

Plan E includes the core benefits plus the following:

1. Coverage for coinsurance for a stay in a skilled-nursing facility.
2. Part A hospital deductible.
3. Emergency medical care in foreign countries.
4. Preventive medical care. This benefit covers the cost of an annual physical, fecal occult blood tests, mammograms, thyroid and diabetes screening, a pure-tone hearing test, and cholesterol screening every five years.

Plan F

Plan F contains the core benefits plus the following:

1. Coverage for coinsurance for a stay in a skilled-nursing facility.
2. Part A hospital deductible.
3. Part B deductible.
4. Emergency medical care in foreign countries.

5. One hundred percent of Medicare Part B excess charges. An excess charge is the difference between Medicare's approved amount or allowed charge (see chapter 8) and the amount the physician actually bills.

Plan G

Plan G includes the core benefits plus the following:

1. Coverage for coinsurance for a stay in a skilled-nursing facility.
2. Part A hospital deductible.
3. Emergency medical care in foreign countries.
4. Coverage for at-home care following an injury, illness, or surgery.
5. Eighty percent of Medicare Part B excess charges.

Plan H

Plan H includes the core benefits plus the following:

1. Coverage for coinsurance for a stay in a skilled-nursing facility.
2. Part A hospital deductible.
3. Emergency medical care in foreign countries.
4. Coverage for at-home care following an injury, illness, or surgery.
5. Fifty percent of the cost of prescription drugs up to an annual maximum benefit of $1,250 after the policyholder satisfies a $250 annual deductible. This is the basic prescription drug benefit.

Plan I

Plan I includes the core benefits plus the following:

1. Coverage for coinsurance for a stay in a skilled-nursing facility.

2. Part A hospital deductible.
3. Emergency medical care in foreign countries.
4. Coverage for at-home care following an injury, illness, or surgery.
5. One hundred percent of Part B excess charges.
6. The basic prescription drug benefit.

Plan J

Plan J includes the core benefits plus the following:

1. Coverage for coinsurance for a stay in a skilled-nursing facility.
2. Part A hospital deductible.
3. Part B deductible.
4. Emergency medical care in foreign countries.
5. Coverage for at-home care following an injury, illness, or surgery.
6. Preventive medical care.
7. One hundred percent of Part B excess charges.
8. Fifty percent of the cost of prescription drugs up to an annual maximum benefit of $3,000 after the policyholder meets an annual $250 deductible. This is the extended drug benefit.

The chart that follows gives a clear picture of the benefits covered by each policy.

THE COST

What you pay for a supplemental policy largely depends on how much coverage you want. The more coverage, the more it costs. Plan A, with only the most basic benefits, could cost as little as $300 or $400 a year, while Plan J, which offers the most comprehensive benefits, could cost as much as $2,000 a year. The other plans are priced somewhere in between these extremes.

TABLE 15
What the Policies Cover

Plan	Part A Hospital Coinsurance, Days 61–90 ($157 per Day)	Part A Hospital Coinsurance, Days 91–150 ($314 per Day)	All Charges for Extra 365 Days in Hospital	Part A Blood Deductible, 3 Pints	Part B Blood Deductible, 3 Pints	Part B Coinsurance (20% of Allowable Charges)	Skilled-Nursing Facility Coinsurance, Days 21–100	Part A Deductible ($628 per Year)	Emergency Care in Foreign Countries	Part B Deductible ($100 per Year)	Part B Excess Charges	At-Home Care Needed After an Injury, Illness, or Surgery	Prescription Drugs	Preventive Medical Care
A	✓	✓	✓	✓	✓	✓	—	—	—	—	—	—	—	—
B	✓	✓	✓	✓	✓	✓	—	✓	—	—	—	—	—	—
C	✓	✓	✓	✓	✓	✓	✓	✓	✓	✓	—	—	—	—
D	✓	✓	✓	✓	✓	✓	✓	✓	✓	—	—	✓	—	—
E	✓	✓	✓	✓	✓	✓	✓	✓	✓	—	—	—	—	✓
F	✓	✓	✓	✓	✓	✓	✓	✓	✓	✓	[1]	—	—	—
G	✓	✓	✓	✓	✓	✓	✓	✓	✓	—	[2]	✓	—	—
H	✓	✓	✓	✓	✓	✓	✓	✓	✓	—	—	—	[3]	—
I	✓	✓	✓	✓	✓	✓	✓	✓	✓	—	[1]	✓	[3]	—
J	✓	✓	✓	✓	✓	✓	✓	✓	✓	✓	[1]	✓	[4]	✓

[1] Pays 100 percent of difference between doctor's bill and amount Medicare pays.
[2] Pays 80 percent of difference between doctor's bill and amount Medicare pays.
[3] $1,250 maximum yearly benefit; $250 deductible; 50 percent coinsurance.
[4] $3,000 maximum yearly benefit; $250 deductible; 50 percent coinsurance.

What you pay may also depend on how thoroughly the insurance company underwrites—that is, scrutinizes the health of prospective policyholders. A carrier that underwrites stringently is able to charge less because it accepts only the healthiest people as customers.

THE SIX-MONTH RULE

A new rule prohibits insurance companies from checking on the health of applicants 65 and older during the first six months after they sign up for Medicare Part B. This rule is helpful if you have a chronic health condition. In that case, you should buy your Medicare-supplement policy as soon as you sign up for Part B. Don't let this six-month window slip by. If you wait too long, you run the risk of not being able to buy a policy because your health condition is unacceptable to some carriers. If you do get coverage after the six-month window, you may end up paying a far higher premium, since insurance companies try to compensate for the greater risk you present to them. During the six-month window, companies are not allowed to charge you a higher premium.

Companies that offer prescription drug plans are also likely to check applicants' health more carefully. This means people who already must use prescription medications on a regular basis may have a hard time buying drug coverage. The six-month window may help these people, too.

If you are 65, still working, and have not applied for Part B, you can remain under your employer's plan and still be eligible for the open window. When you stop working or are no longer covered by your employer, you can apply for Part B during the seven-month period that begins with the month you are no longer working. When you do, you are still eligible for the six-month open enrollment window and can buy a policy without meeting the insurer's underwriting requirements.

The same holds true if you are over 65 and retired, and are covered under your spouse's employer's insurance. When you and your spouse are no longer covered by that plan and apply for Part B, you are still eligible for the six-month window.

If you are over 65 and retired, but so far have chosen not to enroll in Part B, you can still do so, subject to the requirements described previously. When you do enroll, your six-month window begins.

SHOPPING FOR A POLICY

As you begin your shopping trip, we suggest you contact your state insurance department (see Appendix E) and find out what plans are available in your state. Also ask the department for a list of the companies licensed to sell Medicare-supplement insurance. Once you have this information, here are some points to keep in mind:

Part B excess charges. If you can afford it, we recommend that you buy a policy that pays for excess physicians' charges. Even though physicians will eventually be able to bill no more than 15 percent of Medicare's allowed charge, and your doctor may take assignment (that is, accept Medicare's allowed charge as payment in full), a serious illness may involve a team of specialists whose bills you'll have to pay out of your own pocket. Your insurance should cover such a catastrophic risk.

However, only four policies pay for these excess charges. Plan I and Plan J cover 100 percent of excess charges, plus prescription drugs. They are likely to be the most expensive plans, and if you already use prescription drugs, companies may not be eager to sell you this coverage (except during the six-month window). Or you may not want prescription drug benefits. In that case, you can choose only Plan F or Plan G if you want coverage for excess charges.

Part B deductible. Buying deductible coverage that pays the first $100 of any physician or hospital outpatient charge is simply dollar trading, since you may pay $100 in extra premiums for the coverage. However, one of the plans that covers excess physicians' charges also includes coverage for the Part B deductible. If your choice comes down to Plan F because you want coverage for excess physicians' charges, and you can afford that plan, you may get the coverage for the Part B deductible anyway.

At-home care following an injury, illness, or surgery. This benefit is somewhat limited. For that reason, it may not be high on your list of needed coverages. Furthermore, if you already own a long-term-care policy that has such a benefit, you don't need to pay another premium for a similar coverage.

Preventive medical care. This coverage is unnecessary if you can cover the costs of flu vaccines and screening tests yourself. But in reality you may have little choice. Only two plans offer preventive-care benefits—Plan E and Plan J. If Plan E is similar in price to Plan C, which has the same benefits (though it covers the Part B deductible instead of preventive care), we recommend that you take the preventive-care benefits instead of the coverage for the Part B deductible. Because Plan J is expensive, many people are unlikely to buy it.

Emergency care in foreign countries. All policies except Plan A include coverage for emergency care while you're in a foreign country. You may wonder why you need this coverage if you rarely or never travel abroad, but you have little choice in the matter. Insurance companies claim that this benefit adds only a negligible amount to the premium.

Prescription drugs. As you can see, only three plans—H, I, and J—cover prescription drugs. In theory, this is a good benefit to have, especially if you already take maintenance drugs. However, as we've pointed out before, you may not be able to obtain a policy that offers drug coverage if you currently take prescription drugs on a regular basis. Furthermore, you'll have to meet a high deductible ($250) before the policy begins to pay, and these policies are usually very expensive. Before committing yourself to a high annual premium for prescription drug coverage, total your annual prescription drug bill. If you pay far less than the $250 deductible, the coverage probably isn't worth the extra premium, although you may need such coverage in the future. You have to weigh the value of paying more now against the likelihood you may use the benefit later.

Preexisting conditions clauses. This clause imposes a waiting period before the policy covers you for medical conditions you have at the time the policy is written. Policies specify how long you must have had such a condition—typically three or six months—for the waiting period to apply, and then state how long you must wait before coverage begins for that condition. On most policies the waiting period is six months, but it may be shorter. A few companies offer coverage from day one for any health condition.

Automatic claims handling. A company that offers this service receives, directly from Medicare, the claims information that appears on a policyholder's Explanation of Medicare Benefits (EOMB). It then pays policyholders whatever benefits are due. Policyholders don't have to wait for their EOMBs and then submit them to the insurance carrier. This shortcut is important and could tip the balance in favor of one company's plan over another.

Renewability. All policies sold now must be guaranteed renewable. This means the company can't cancel your coverage so long as you continue to pay the premiums. Older policies, however, can be conditionally renewable; a company can cancel your coverage but has to do so for all those who had purchased similar policies.

If your policy is issued through a group, you also have some protection if the group terminates its master contract with the insurer or if you leave the group. You have the right to buy an individual policy with substantially the same benefits and premiums as the group policy.

SWITCHING POLICIES

If you are over 65 and already own a Medicare-supplement policy that provides you with adequate coverage, don't buy one of the new standardized policies. If your current policy pays for private-duty nurses and private rooms, you may want to keep it if this coverage is important to you. The new standardized policies do not cover either of those services.

You may also find that agents may try to sell you a new supplement, perhaps at a lower price than you're now paying. It's tempting to switch for a better price. But premiums for most Medicare-supplement policies rise every year, and today's bargain may be next year's costliest contract. Remember, too, that you may have to satisfy a new preexisting conditions requirement for a new policy, although you won't have to if the new policy is substantially similar to the one you currently have.

Then, too, your health may have changed, and you won't qualify for a new policy or perhaps not the one you want. If you do decide to switch, don't cancel your old policy until you're sure the new company will accept you.

SUPPLEMENTAL POLICIES AND MANAGED CARE PLANS

If you currently belong to an HMO (health maintenance organization) or a CMP (competitive medical plan), you don't need to buy a supplemental policy. At some HMOs, Medicare makes a monthly payment to the plan on your behalf, and you simply pay a monthly fee in return for all the medical services you need. However, you must agree to use the physicians and medical facilities that are part of the plan. (Some plans also pay for preventive care, drugs, hearing aids, and eyeglasses.) For a discussion of other types of HMO plans, see chapter 8.

However, if you later decide to quit the plan and return to a fee-for-service physician, you will probably need a Medicare-supplement policy. It may be harder to buy one if you have preexisting health problems that some companies don't want to cover.

SUPPLEMENTAL POLICIES AND THE DISABLED

If you have been disabled for 24 months and are receiving Social Security disability benefits, you are eligible for Medicare. Unfortunately, you will have a hard time finding a supplemental policy to fill in Medicare's gaps, because most companies sell such policies only to those who've turned 65. Contact several companies to see if they will sell a supplement to someone in your situation. If you live in one of the states that has a high-risk pool for people with health problems, contact the pool to see if it offers a Medicare-supplement policy. Some do (see Appendix C).

HOSPITAL-INDEMNITY AND DREAD-DISEASE POLICIES

Hospital-indemnity policies pay a fixed amount each day you're in the hospital. Dread-disease policies pay benefits only if you contract cancer or some other specified illness.

Such policies are among the worst buys in health insurance. They're sold to buyers through enticing but often misleading advertising: "Cash benefits of $2,250 a month, $525 a week, $75 a day. . . . You cannot be turned down. . . . No salesman will call," reads a flyer for one policy.

How does a hospital-indemnity policy work? You get a fixed dollar amount for each day you spend in the hospital. This policy has no complicated deductibles or coinsurance.

The trouble is, the fixed benefit is skimpy to start with and grows less valuable each year.

Plans usually offer daily benefits of $30, $50, or $75. But with the cost of a day in the hospital averaging around $800 in 1990, such policies barely dent your bill. Furthermore, to collect the high benefits touted by some of the ads, you'll need to be hospitalized for as long as a month—an unlikely prospect, since the average hospital stay is only about seven days. Finally, the benefit is fixed. In time, inflation in hospital and medical costs inevitably shrinks its value. Dread-disease policies offer similarly inadequate benefits.

Although the premiums for these coverages are low, running anywhere from $200 to around $500 a year, these policies are generally superfluous. Since Medicare pays virtually all of your hospital bill, there's no need for an additional policy that pays for the same service. If you choose a supplement that covers the Part A deductible, you certainly don't need a hospital-indemnity policy that also pays the deductible. You're better off taking the few hundred dollars you would spend on hospital-indemnity premiums and buying a good Medicare-supplement, and perhaps a long-term-care policy that offers inflation protection.

HOW TO COMPARE POLICIES

Worksheet 6, Medicare-Supplement Policy Checklist, in Appendix A helps you select a Medicare supplement. We suggest you compare policies sold by at least three companies. That way you'll be able to note any big price swings among the various offerings. Once you decide on the plan you want, list the annual premium the company is quoting. Now note the preexisting conditions requirements and whether the company offers automatic claims handling. If two policies are similarly priced but one has a more liberal preexisting conditions clause and the company also offers automatic claims handling, then that is the policy to buy.

Worksheet 6 also has a space to note the insurer's underwriting requirements. On this line, write whether the company has any stipulations and what they are. Does the company require a doctor's examination and a copy of all your medical records, or does it just ask a few questions about your health on the application? Look for a correlation between restrictive underwriting and the price of the policy. A company that looks carefully at your medical history may offer a lower-cost policy. If you can qualify, then that's the policy to buy.

11

Insurance for Long-Term Care

Forty-three percent of all Americans who turn 65 in 1991 eventually enter a nursing home. Twenty-five percent of that group will stay at least one year, at a cost of $30,000 to $40,000 or more. Currently there is no federal entitlement program similar to Medicare that pays long-term-care expenses for the elderly. Some people pay their entire nursing home bill with their savings. Others begin with their own savings, then turn to Medicaid when their money runs out. Still others rely on Medicaid from the beginning.

Nursing home patients and their families currently pay about half the $42 billion annual tab for nursing home care. Medicare pays for 2 percent of all nursing home stays, and private insurance policies pay for about 1 percent. Medicaid, the federal-state program that pays medical expenses for the poor, covers most of the rest. To qualify for Medicaid, patients must make themselves poor by spending down, that is, by using up all of their assets to pay for their nursing home expenses. Medicaid then steps in and pays the bill.

Given these facts, it's no surprise that many older people are increasingly turning to insurance as a way to pay for eventual long-term care. But the decision to buy a policy is one that must be made carefully and judiciously. There are several points to consider beforehand.

BEFORE YOU BUY

Why Do You Want the Coverage?

Insurance companies promote long-term-care insurance as a protection for assets that are built up over a lifetime. In other words, if you are confined to a nursing home, you won't have to tap into your savings so long as you have the policy to cover your expenses. Your money is safe both for you and for your heirs. For many people, this alone is a good reason to buy the coverage. If asset protection is your goal, though, there are other ways of preserving your savings, such as giving gifts or setting up irrevocable trusts (see chapter 17 and chapter 18).

Another reason for insurance is to protect your assets for your spouse or a dependent member of your family. Or you may simply feel more comfortable having a policy that helps you avoid impoverishment or reliance on government programs or family members in your later years.

Some people also decide to buy a policy as a means of getting into a more desirable nursing home. Many institutions don't like to take Medicaid patients. If you don't have to rely on Medicaid when you first enter, you may have a choice of nursing homes. Finally, some policyholders believe long-term-care insurance pays for care at home, keeping them out of a nursing facility. However, only policies that have home-care benefits pay for that service.

Can You Afford It?

If you have realistically thought about why you want long-term-care coverage and still feel having a policy is better than not, think about the cost. Ask yourself if you can pay the premium out of your retirement income. For most retirees, the answer is no. The average annual per capita income for someone 65 or over is about $17,000. A 65-year-old with average income could pay about $2,000 each year for a good long-term-care policy with inflation protection. That's 12 percent of his or her annual income. Add another $1,000 or so for Medicare-supplement insurance, and decent health and long-term-care insurance comes to more than $3,000 a year, or $6,000 for a couple. And the premiums are likely to increase over the years.

Of course, if the value of your assets (excluding your house) is $10,000 or less, you probably don't need insurance coverage—you would qualify fairly quickly in most states for Medicaid. If your assets are between $10,000 and $30,000, you probably don't need a policy either. Your need for long-term-care coverage is marginal at best, especially if these assets produce some of the income you are living on. And you probably can't afford current or future premiums.

If your assets are between $30,000 and $50,000 or more, and your current income is sufficient to pay the premiums, you might seriously consider buying a long-term-care policy. If your assets far exceed $50,000, you should contact an attorney specializing in estate planning to find other suitable alternatives.

Are You Married or Single?

Unfortunately, older married women often have far less income to live on once their husbands die, especially if they have not worked outside the home for most of their adult lives. And, even though a widow may have less income to pay expensive premiums, her need for long-term care may increase as she gets older. Married men are often cared for at home by their wives, while single women (and men) are more likely to end up in nursing homes because no one is at home to care for them when they are ill or infirm.

Are You in Good Health?

If you have only minor health problems, you should be able to buy a long-term-care policy. But if you have had strokes, heart or respiratory disease, or have limited mobility, a company may not want to insure you. Sometimes people with specific medical problems can get coverage, but they pay a higher premium to compensate the insurance company for the greater risk they pose.

WHAT LONG-TERM-CARE POLICIES COVER

After you have evaluated these key questions, take the time to review the policies themselves carefully. Insurance companies sell three kinds of long-term-care policies covering: (1) only nursing home stays; (2) only care at home; (3) both nursing home care and care at home. Some life insurance policies have riders that pay for long-term care (see chapter 5).

Nursing Home Coverage

Nursing home coverage typically includes all levels of nursing care—skilled, intermediate, and custodial. Skilled care is intensive medical care provided 24 hours a day by trained, licensed personnel; intermediate care is similar but less intensive; and custodial or personal care helps patients with everyday activities, such as eating, bathing, dressing, and moving about.

Today long-term-care policies cover all three levels of nursing care; many make no distinction among them, simply saying they will pay for any nursing care needed by a patient. But the policyholder still may not collect benefits, since a company can deny a claim if care is not provided in what it defines as an eligible facility.

Home-Care Coverage

Home-care coverage is more complicated. When you think of home care, you may envision someone coming to your house to prepare meals, clean, help with dressing, and run a few errands. But most insurance companies don't mean that at all.

A few pay home-care benefits only for skilled-nursing care

performed by registered nurses, licensed practical nurses, and occupational, speech, or physical therapists. Others cover the services of home-health aides employed by licensed agencies. Such aides have less training and primarily help patients with personal or custodial care. A policy that covers home-health aides is obviously better than one that pays only for skilled personnel.

Better still are policies that pay for homemaker services, such as cooking, cleaning, and running errands. Only a few companies, however, offer this benefit, and some of those limit how much they will pay. Several others may be willing to pay home-health aides to do a little housekeeping, so long as they also provide personal care. But they won't pay your sister or granddaughter to help out. Policies do not pay benefits to family members who perform home-care services.

A few policies offer what are called recuperative, home again, or postconfinement benefits, usually as a substitute for real home-care coverage. These are of limited value, since they typically pay only for a short period following a nursing home or hospital stay.

Other Policy Provisions

Once the company has begun paying benefits, a *waiver of premium* allows the policyholder to stop paying premiums during a nursing home stay. A few companies waive the premium as soon as a policyholder receives the first payment. But waits of between 60 and 90 days are more typical. Most don't waive premiums if the policyholder receives nursing care at home.

Nonforfeiture benefits return to policyholders some of their equity if they drop their coverage. Without that benefit, your loss could be sizable if you drop the policy after 10 or 20 years. To minimize such losses, policyholders may buy a policy with a *reduced paid-up* arrangement, in which part of the benefits are payable after the policy is dropped.

Other carriers offer a *return of premium* nonforfeiture benefit, under which they return all or a portion of the premiums after a certain number of years if the policyholder decides to drop the policy.

Nonforfeiture benefits are not common in individual policies. They are more likely to be found as an option in group plans offered through employers.

Death benefits refund to the policyholder's estate any premiums paid (minus any benefits the company paid on the policyholder's behalf). This benefit is usually payable only if the policyholder dies before a certain age, typically 65 or 70.

GETTING INTO THE RIGHT FACILITY

Long-term-care policies usually dictate the type of facility where policyholders can receive care. Whether or not you adhere to their requirements can mean the difference between receiving payment on a claim or having the claim denied.

Nursing Home Facilities

The most liberal coverage would allow policyholders to obtain health-care services wherever they wished. Ideally, once policyholders qualified for benefits, the insurance company would simply give them the money to spend on any kind of long-term care. But such "disability-based" policies are rare.

All other policies are "service-based," that is, most policyholders must obtain services from providers that meet the qualifications set by the insurance company. True, some of these policies are more liberal than others—the best pay for care in any licensed facility. But the majority are more restrictive, particularly when it comes to custodial care, which is the kind of service people are more likely to need as they grow older. For example, some policies do not cover custodial care unless it is provided in a skilled- or intermediate-nursing facility.

Other policies cover custodial care but exclude by name some types of facilities that are licensed to provide such services. For example, most policies do not pay for custodial care in homes for the aged, although such homes are licensed in several states to provide just those services.

Still other carriers use the fine print in their contracts to restrict coverage. One policy pays for care in a custodial-care facility, so long as the facility has at least 25 residents. But in Arizona, for instance, custodial-care facilities may legally care for fewer than 10 people, and in Oregon, fewer than 5. Another policy may require that nursing services must be under the supervision of a physician or a graduate registered nurse, but homes that provide custodial care in Pennsylvania don't need supervisory nurses on duty.

Care in Your Own Home

Most home care takes place in a person's residence. More generous policies also allow their policyholders to receive such benefits in adult day-care centers. These policies, however, may define the term adult day-care center more restrictively than do certain states, effectively preventing policyholders in some state-approved facilities from collecting their benefits.

RESTRICTIONS ON ELIGIBILITY

All long-term-care policies have *gatekeepers*—those restrictions that determine who is eligible to receive benefits. In fact, these gatekeepers are the most important feature of a policy but the one prospective buyers hear least about. And no wonder. Few agents understand them, because few companies teach the agents how they work. Outlines of coverage (a document summarizing the policy provisions) seldom discuss these rules, and sales brochures are usually silent on the matter as well.

Under the least restrictive policies, a policyholder qualifies for benefits simply if his or her doctor orders the care. More restrictive policies require that any care provided be medically necessary, either for sickness or injury. Yet many nursing home patients, especially those needing only custodial care, are not acutely sick or injured, so they may not qualify for benefits under such a policy. Furthermore, the standard is often subjective. A company may interpret its requirements liberally today, but several years from now, after experiencing costly claims, the carrier could argue that a policyholder's stay is not medically necessary.

A third type of gatekeeper requires policyholders to be unable to perform a certain number of "activities of daily living" (commonly referred to as ADLs) before the company pays benefits. The activities usually include bathing, dressing, eating, using the toilet, walking, maintaining continence, taking medicine, and ability to move themselves from bed to chair. Sometimes a company with an activity standard allows policyholders who fail certain mental (cognitive) tests to qualify for benefits anyway. These are called "cognitive" gatekeepers, and are highly desirable to have in a policy.

Most policies define activities of daily living vaguely, leaving the final decision in each individual case to a company claims analyst. Policies also differ about which activities, and how many, policyholders must be unable to perform before they are eligible for benefits. The most restrictive policies require that policyholders be unable to perform activities of daily living because of sickness or injury.

Even though state regulators require all policies to cover Alzheimer's disease, policyholders with the disease may be denied benefits if they are still physically able to perform the activities of daily living. If a company uses an activities standard to judge whether the policyholder is entitled to benefits, and if it doesn't specifically allow people whose only problem is severe memory loss to qualify, patients with Alzheimer's disease may not be covered.

A fourth type of policy gatekeeper requires a hospital stay of at least three days before the company pays nursing home benefits. That requirement is illegal in 38 states, and such policies should be avoided.

A few policies have different gatekeepers for home-care benefits. Watch for these restrictions when shopping around for a policy.

BENEFIT BASICS

Insurance companies offer policyholders a choice of daily benefits for nursing home care that typically range from $40 to $120. If home-care coverage is included as part of the policy, the dollar benefit is often half that for nursing home care.

Home-care-only policies pay up to a fixed daily amount or up to a fixed number of dollars per hour of service—$50 a day or $14 an hour, for example. A few policies don't limit the daily amounts but instead set a lifetime dollar maximum for policyholders to use as needed; $50,000 is typical.

Policies generally pay nursing home benefits for a minimum of one year. Insurers also offer 2-, 5-, and 6-year plans. Others pay for 10 years or for the rest of a policyholder's life. While most nursing home stays are short—the average is only 19 months—longer coverage can protect policyholders and their families from the financial ravages of a catastrophic illness that might continue for several years.

When home care is combined with nursing home coverage, the home-care benefit period is sometimes shorter than for a nursing home stay. With home-care-only plans, benefit periods are often one to two years.

Benefits can start as soon as the policyholder enters a nursing home, or they can begin after a *waiting, elimination,* or *deductible* period of 20, 30, 60, 90, or 100 days. Some policies have shorter waiting periods for home-care benefits.

For policyholders who can afford to pay for several days or months of care from their own savings, a longer waiting period can mean a lower premium. However, consumers are given little choice. Instead, agents often make the selection for them, basing their decision on what that particular company wants to sell.

INFLATION PROTECTION

A 65-year-old who buys a long-term-care policy today may not need it for 20 years. A nursing home that costs an average of $86 today will cost $228 in 20 years, assuming a relatively modest inflation rate of 5 percent a year. These statistics underscore the importance of buying good inflation protection on a long-term-care policy.

Unfortunately, companies that sell policies with inflation protection report that less than half their policyholders buy it. We think policyholders who forgo good inflation protection are ill-advised.

Not all inflation protection is the same. Insurers use two methods to increase coverage to account for inflation. One method lets policyholders buy additional coverage every few years at the then current price, based on their age at that time, usually without having to prove they are still insurable. The price of that additional coverage, however, can increase so rapidly that the additional protection becomes virtually unaffordable. And those who don't buy the additional benefits when they are first offered may lose their right to buy any in the future. For most people, this method is unacceptable.

The second method automatically increases the daily benefit by some percentage, usually 5 percent. But these increases are generally not compounded, a serious shortcoming in our view. A common $80 benefit that increases at 5 percent a year is worth $160 in 20 years; an $80 benefit that's compounded is worth $212 in 20 years. Only a few companies offer inflation protection that continues so long as the policy stays in force. Most discontinue inflation increases after 10 or 20 years, regardless of the method used. Those who purchase a long-term-care policy at 55 or 60 may discover that their ability to increase coverage has ended long before they need nursing care—in effect, freezing their benefits at an inadequate level. A few companies terminate increases when a policyholder reaches 80 or 85, the age when someone is most likely to enter a nursing home.

Good inflation protection is expensive. The annual cost of such protection for a 65-year-old ranged from $97 to $1,163 in a 1991 *Consumer Reports* study of long-term-care policies. Such protection adds between 25 and 40 percent to the cost of the premium. The more expensive inflation benefits are far better—their protection compounds forever, while the cost of the benefit doesn't increase.

Some companies using the automatic-increase approach charge a level premium for the inflation rider even though the benefit goes up each year. Others increase the premium at the same rate as the benefits, that is, 5 percent a year. Beware of the latter. Those riders may be less expensive initially, but they eventually cost more than most people can comfortably afford. You may have to drop the coverage just when you are most likely to need it.

WHO IS INSURABLE

Not everyone who applies for a long-term-care policy can get one. Your chances depend on your health and how carefully a company scrutinizes your medical history. Generally, companies don't want to sign up people who suffer from diabetes, multiple sclerosis, asthma, macular degeneration (an eye disease), severe high blood pressure, or Alzheimer's disease. Nor are they anxious to insure those who have had strokes or recent cancer surgery. But some companies are more selective than others; one may not accept someone who has had hip-replacement surgery within the last 18 months, while another company has no such restriction.

Several insurers accept people with certain health problems but charge them more or offer slimmer benefits. One carrier, for example, insures people who already have Alzheimer's disease, but it charges two and a half times more and allows only a $50 daily benefit. Another company has three classes of rates for people whose health is considered substandard. A severe illness might mean a doubling of the standard rate. A milder one results in only a 15 percent increase.

Some companies also have preferred rates for applicants who are in better health or meet other conditions. Keep in mind the rates labeled *preferred, standard,* and *substandard* are not comparable across companies. A preferred rate at one company may be the same as the standard rate at another.

Some insurers reject as many as 40 percent of those who apply. Others don't bother checking out applicants very thoroughly and enroll practically all comers. But don't be deceived about the practices of these seemingly lax companies. Certainly these insurers may turn you down if you answer yes on their application to any questions concerning your medical history; in that case the agent may not even submit the application to the home office. If you answer no to each question, coverage may begin in a few days or weeks. However, when you submit a claim, these companies may then carefully review your medical history to make sure you didn't lie on the application. During the contestable period—two years in most states—a company can legally rescind a policy and return all premiums that you've paid if it discovers you have misrepresented relevant facts on the application and it had relied on those facts in issuing coverage. It can do this even if an agent has "clean-sheeted" the application, that is, not told the truth about your health. Even after the contestability period is over, companies can still deny coverage if they can prove fraudulent statements were made on the application.

To protect yourself from this practice—called *post-claims underwriting*—answer all questions on the application truthfully and completely. Even if an agent tells you not to list some chronic or current health problem, do it anyway. When you receive the policy, carefully check out the signed application to make sure it's correct. The application becomes part of the policy, and the company can later use it to rescind your coverage if any questions arise about the veracity of your answers. If you spot any errors, notify the company at once.

Most states allow you 30 days to examine your policy; if you wish, you can return it and get your money back. Don't work with agents who insist they can obtain coverage in 24 or 48 hours or with one who *field underwrites,* that is, issues coverage immediately. Such practices may mean that the company waits until you file a claim to determine your fitness for coverage. You're better off with a company that carefully examines your medical history and requires a doctor's statement before issuing a policy.

Insurers also differ in how they handle preexisting conditions—those health problems that already exist when the policyholder purchases a policy. Some companies make customers wait six months before they cover preexisting conditions, while others impose no waiting period at all. Insurers that carefully check an applicant's health before issuing a policy are more likely to have no waiting period.

PAYMENT OF CLAIMS

Insurance carriers rarely pay all the claims that are submitted to them. And most companies are reluctant to reveal what percentage of claims are denied.

We have data from some companies indicating that a large number of claims are often turned down because policyholders don't understand the limitations built into their contracts. One company reported to us that in 1989 it denied 80 percent of the claims made under its home-care-only policy. Another turned down about a third of the claims submitted, and a third company refused 22 percent of its claims.

HOW COSTS ESCALATE

Long-term-care insurance is not cheap. A 65-year-old can expect to pay around $1,000 a year at most companies for a policy covering both nursing home and home care; a 75-year-old pays upward of $2,000. The older you are when you take out the policy, the more you will pay. Table 16 shows how premiums increased at three companies selling long-term-care insurance in 1991.

Prices vary considerably among carriers. An $80 benefit payable for four years with a 30-day waiting period could cost a 65-year-old as much as $3,020 or as little as $766.

Not surprisingly, the larger the benefit, the longer it lasts. Also, the sooner it begins, the higher the price. *Example:* A 65-year-old buying a $100 benefit for four years with no waiting period and no inflation protection pays $895 a year at one company. At the same insurer, a $60 benefit lasting

TABLE 16
The Older You Are, the More You Pay

Company	Age 55	Age 65	Age 75
Amex Life[1]	$311	$828	$2,249
Equitable Life and Casualty[2]	259	875	3,108
Bankers Life and Casualty[3]	636	996	2,616

[1]$100 daily benefit, payable for 4 years, 20-day waiting period, no inflation rider.
[2]$110 daily benefit, payable for 4 years, 30-day waiting period, no inflation rider.
[3]$100 daily benefit, payable for 5 years, 20-day waiting period, no inflation rider.

two years with a 90-day wait costs $439. Inflation protection can add as much as $1,200 per year to the premium; home-care coverage adds $150 to $600.

Home-care-only policies are somewhat cheaper. A 65-year-old could pay as much as $675 or as little as $254 for a policy, according to our 1991 survey.

All long-term-care policies are guaranteed renewable. That means a carrier must renew your coverage every year, but it doesn't guarantee the rates you pay.

Most policies have level premiums, that is, they don't rise as the policyholder ages. However, premiums can go up if an insurer experiences more claims expenses than anticipated. We found only one company that offered to guarantee rates for the life of the policy. A few offer rate guarantees for a short period—three years, for example, but those guarantees are not very valuable.

All this means the policy with the lowest price today may well turn out to be the worst buy later on. "The next five years will produce rate increases as the rule rather than the exception for most companies currently marketing long-term-care insurance," predicts one actuary. But right now, companies are actually lowering premiums and raising benefit levels as a way to stimulate sales. At the same time, some carriers are also paying extraordinary commissions to sales agents, sometimes as much as 70 to 80 percent of the first-year premium.

That recipe for today's sales success may be tomorrow's prescription for disaster. Companies can justify lower premiums by underestimating the dollar value of claims they eventually have to pay, or by overestimating the number of policyholders who drop their coverage before they ever file a claim. Some insurers are doing both. Either way, if more claims materialize than the company has counted on, it will have to raise policyholders' premiums or risk going out of business.

A few companies use attained-age pricing to make their policies look less expensive. Unlike policies with level premiums, these premiums start out low but rise as a policyholder ages. If policyholders keep their coverage for 12 years or so, the total premiums are greater than those for a policy that doesn't increase with the policyholder's age. *Example:* A 65-year-old who buys one attained-age policy initially pays $458 a year for an $80 benefit payable for four years with a 30-day elimination period. At 80, he or she has to pay $3,470; at 85 the annual premium is $5,676. The same person who buys the company's sister product, a policy without attained-age rates, pays $1,111 a year for as long as the policy stays in force.

CHOOSING THE RIGHT CARRIER

An insurer's financial reliability is especially important with long-term-care policies, since the company is called upon to pay benefits far in the future. Over the past few years, a number of carriers selling this type of insurance have experienced financial difficulties. When that happens, insurance regulators often step in and find another company to take over the insolvent company's policies.

A state's guaranty association can also make good on the company's promises (see chapter 4). (Although the states have created these associations, they are not state agencies, are not part of state insurance departments, and the states themselves do not guarantee anyone's insurance coverage.)

If the guaranty association does take over a policy, it may cancel it if the policy is not guaranteed renewable. (Long-term-care policies sold today are guaranteed renewable, but many earlier versions were not.) Even if their coverage is not canceled, policyholders may face serious delays in getting their claims paid, because records of the insolvent company are often confusing and incomplete. Also, most associations guarantee only $100,000 of benefits for long-term-care insurance. This means a nursing home stay that lasts for several years may not be fully covered. Furthermore, associations do not cover policies issued by fraternal organizations or by special trusts that employers have set up to provide health coverage. With the exception of 16 states, they do not cover Blue Cross and Blue Shield plans.

Even more limiting, most associations cover only their own state residents if a company in that state becomes insolvent. Policyholders in other states must look to their own state's guaranty fund for redress. In most cases, the funds pay only if the insurance company was licensed to sell in that state—a potential problem for people who move to another state after buying a policy. In only 11 states will funds cover all policyholders of an insolvent carrier, regardless of where they live.

What can you do to make sure a carrier is financially reliable? The conventional advice to buy from a company rated A or A+ by A. M. Best is no longer foolproof. You can also check the ratings of a particular company provided by other ratings services such as Standard & Poor's, but again a high rating is not an ironclad guarantee of fiscal strength. Aside from avoiding companies that are already in trouble, there's little you can do to assure yourself absolutely that the company you select today will be still with you tomorrow.

EMPLOYER-PROVIDED INSURANCE

Some insurance companies think the future market for long-term-care policies lies with younger people who can be persuaded to buy the insurance when they're young and the premiums are lower. This strategy gives insurers a longer time to build up reserves from which to pay claims submitted 20 or 30 years later. To meet this goal, some companies, through employers, are selling policies to people at their workplace. But unlike other kinds of employer-provided insurance, employers don't pay any part of the premium.

There are two drawbacks to buying long-term-care insurance when you're young. First, unless companies offer inflation protection, the policy may be worthless by the time you need care many years later. We do not recommend that you buy any long-term-care insurance through your employer, no matter how cheap, unless the benefits keep pace with inflation. Second, we recommend that some kind of nonforfeiture or return-of-premium benefit be attached, or you could pay premiums for years only to lose your entire equity if you let the policy lapse.

If you are in your fifties and your employer offers long-term-care coverage, you might consider buying it so long as these two conditions are met. Some companies selling through employers provide these benefits. Others don't. We cannot recommend this coverage for younger people, since too many years intervene before they actually need the benefits and most younger people are raising families and have far more pressing financial obligations.

There are some advantages to employer-provided policies. Some companies selling to employers do not underwrite as stringently as they do for individuals buying policies on their own. If you have chronic health problems, that's a plus. Most sellers also allow parents of active employees to buy coverage through the group, although the parents must pass the company's underwriting requirements. If you have a child who works for a company offering this insurance, seriously consider purchasing the plan, especially if it comes with a nonforfeiture benefit. If you're a retiree and your former employer offers long-term-care coverage, by all means consider it.

HOW TO COMPARE POLICIES

When you are looking for a long-term-care policy, compare features and price. If you are shopping among several companies and agents, obtain and use the outlines of coverage they provide to fill in the checklist on Worksheet 7, Long-Term-Care Policy Checklist, in Appendix A. Companies don't offer identical benefits, and almost every policy is different in some way from another.

Here's a list of recommendations to follow as you draw up your list of advantages and disadvantages:

1. Decide how large a daily benefit you need and want and how long you wish to wait before benefits begin. For example, you may want a 20-day waiting period, but the company only offers 30 days. If that's the case, use the policy with the 30-day waiting period in your comparison chart.
2. Make sure you thoroughly understand the gatekeepers—those restrictions in the policy that determine if you are eligible for benefits. This is the most important aspect of any policy.
3. In which facilities is custodial care covered? Many policies limit the places where you can receive care. Since this is the care you are most likely to need, you want a policy that pays for custodial care in many types of facilities.
4. Check on home-care benefits. Many policies don't pay for homemaker services.
5. Buy a policy with inflation coverage. Although such coverage is expensive, we think it's worth the extra cost. Without it, a prolonged nursing home stay may require you to spend part or all of your assets, despite all your attempts to protect them.
6. Buy one good policy. If you already have a policy and

want higher benefits or less restrictive coverage, ask your present company about upgrading. This may be cheaper than buying a new policy from a different company and paying additional commissions. If you can't upgrade, we suggest you keep the policy and buy additional coverage. If you own a policy that's very restrictive, you have to weigh the likelihood of collecting benefits against the cost of higher premiums for a new, less restrictive policy, as well as the loss of equity you may have built up.

After you have selected and bought your policy, use the "free-look" period to check the policy provisions and to make sure your application has been completed correctly. Also try to pay your premiums through an automatic draft arrangement with your bank. That minimizes your chances of letting the policy lapse if you forget or are physically unable to pay your premiums. Make sure a friend, family member, or your lawyer knows where the policy is located, when the premiums are due, and how to submit claims to the insurance company.

If you have any questions or need advice, contact the insurance counseling program in your state (see Appendix D).

12

MEDICAID *and* Long-Term Care

Medicaid is a government program that pays medical bills for people who are poor. Even though you probably don't consider yourself poor and may even have substantial assets and income when you retire, you may nevertheless qualify for Medicaid if you or your spouse eventually needs nursing or custodial care. At that point in your life, Medicaid is not a poverty program; it is a lifeline for survival.

Medicaid covers a variety of medical services, including services needed by people with long-term or chronic impairments. All states cover care provided in a nursing facility, or at home. In some states, Medicaid also pays for care in adult day-care centers as well as for nonmedical custodial care that helps with such activities as bathing, dressing, preparing meals, or eating. This kind of care can be given in your home, but the home-care agency that provides your home attendant must be licensed or certified by Medicaid in order for Medicaid to pay the bills. The number of Medicaid-certified providers of long-term-care services around the country is limited, so even if you do qualify for the program, it may be difficult to find a provider you can use.

The federal and state governments share the cost for Medicaid. (In a few states, local governments also participate in the cost.) The federal government pays at least 50 percent of each state's Medicaid budget, and states (and local governments) fund the rest, usually out of general tax revenues. States administer the program within broad federal guidelines. In all states, people receiving Aid to Families with Dependent Children (AFDC) or Supplemental Security Income (SSI) from the Social Security Administration are eligible for Medicaid, usually on an automatic basis. Most states cover the "medically needy"—people who have some income but are still considered poor. If you are not poor but eventually need Medicaid's help to pay for long-term nursing care, you'll most likely come under the medically needy program in your state. In states that don't have a medically needy program, you can still qualify for benefits. Eligibility requirements vary, and it's more difficult to qualify for benefits in some states than in others. In each state, though, you must meet an income and asset or resource test, which means you must have neither income nor assets that exceed a prescribed amount.

SPENDING DOWN

Many people who enter a nursing home begin by paying the bills themselves. But if their stay is prolonged, they quickly exhaust their resources and are able to meet their states' income and asset test. If you start out paying the bills yourself, you may get into a better facility, since many nursing homes refuse to accept Medicaid patients. (Medicaid claims many homes use illegal methods to refuse needy patients.) But if Medicaid later picks up the bills, the nursing home usually lets you stay.

The process by which Medicaid comes to pay your nursing home bills is called a *spend-down.* That means when you have spent enough of your assets to reach your state's Medicaid limits, and your income is not too high, Medicaid begins to pay your bills. You also have to turn over all your monthly income (except for a personal needs allowance) to the nursing home. The more assets you have, of course, the longer it takes to spend down.

Example: Imagine you are a widow living alone in New York City. Your annual income is $15,000, or $1,250 a month. You also have $25,000 in certificates of deposit. Nursing home costs in New York City run about $5,000 a month, so your income is insufficient to cover the cost. You must turn to Medicaid for help. But at the time you enter the nursing home, your assets and income exceed New York's Medicaid limits—$6,000 in annual income and $3,500 in assets for a single person. You enter the nursing home and for a while pay the bills out of your savings. You must spend $20,000 of the $25,000 before Medicaid steps in. (New York allows you to keep $5,000: a $3,500 allowance plus $1,500 for burial expenses.) If you turn over *all* your monthly income to the nursing home (excluding the personal needs allowance), you have to withdraw $3,750 from your savings each month to cover the $5,000 monthly bill. At that rate, you would spend the $20,000 "excess" assets in about six months. After that, you are eligible for Medicaid. Once you qualify for coverage, Medicaid requires you to spend virtually all your monthly income for your nursing care. You can keep $50 of your $1,250 monthly income for personal needs and deduct medical expenses, including health insurance premiums if there are any. The rest must go to the nursing home. You keep the $50 personal needs allowance and contribute $1,200 toward your care; the state of New York pays the rest—$3,800 a month.

IMPOVERISHING YOUR SPOUSE

For many families, a spend-down once meant poverty for the spouse who remained at home, since all the family's assets went toward nursing home care for the other spouse. However, Congress has made it easier for spouses to maintain a more comfortable standard of living. (This also means that a spend-down occurs faster, since more of the family's assets are sheltered.)

Each state determines how much of a couple's assets the spouse living at home can keep. (A couple's home, household goods, and personal effects are not included.) Both the asset and income limits are adjusted for inflation and change each year. If your family members would suffer financial hardship because of the limits, they can petition the state to allow them to keep more money.

Let's see how these provisions work in New York, a state that has adopted the maximum limits for both income and assets. In 1992, after adjusting for inflation, the asset limit was $62,580 and income limit was $1,565. Suppose a couple's monthly income is $1,000 and their assets total $25,000 when the husband enters a nursing home. After deducting the $50 personal allowance for the husband, $950 of their $1,000 monthly income is left. His wife, who remains at home, can keep all of that, since it is less than $1,565. The husband keeps $5,000 of the couple's $25,000 of assets ($3,500 for personal needs plus a $1,500 burial allowance), and the wife keeps the remaining $20,000, since it is less than the state's $62,580 maximum asset limit. Medicaid then pays all the nursing home bills, which run around $5,000 a month.

But suppose the couple has a monthly income of $2,500 and $100,000 of assets. After deducting the $50 personal needs allowance, $2,450 remains. The wife gets to keep only $1,565; $885 goes to the nursing home. Medicaid's share of the monthly nursing home bill is $4,115. But before it pays, Medicaid requires the couple to spend down. As in the previous example, the husband keeps $5,000, which leaves $95,000. His wife can retain $62,580, and they have to spend the remaining $32,420 on nursing home care before Medicaid steps in. In other words, they have to pay for about 6½ months of care.

PROTECTING YOUR ASSETS

In states like New York, California, and Florida, which have adopted high income and asset limits, middle-income people qualify more quickly for Medicaid than they would in states that have lower limits. In a state that allows the spouse at home to keep $12,000, for instance, a couple whose assets are $100,000 would have to spend $88,000 on nursing care before qualifying for Medicaid. If nursing costs average $5,000 a month, that sum would pay for about 17½ months of care compared to about 7½ months in a state that allowed the spouse at home to keep $62,580.

In determining your eligibility for Medicaid, a state carefully reviews all the assets available to you and your spouse. Certain assets such as limited amounts set aside for burial, your car, and personal property are not counted in determining your eligibility for Medicaid. Putting an asset in your spouse's name usually doesn't protect it from Medicaid, and most states consider money held in joint bank accounts as an available asset to pay for nursing home care.

The law does, however, allow you to give away your assets as gifts, or put them in an irrevocable trust (see chapters 17 and 18) so long as you do it at least 30 months before you apply for Medicaid. If you effect the transfer in fewer than 30 months or transfer assets for less than their fair market value, you are usually ineligible for Medicaid coverage for nursing facility services, or for services obtained under a special home and community program, for a period equaling the total uncompensated value of your assets divided by the average monthly cost of nursing home care in your area. This penalty may not exceed 30 months. The period of ineligibility begins in the month you transferred the asset. (This provision applies only to transfers made on or after October 1, 1989.) You also encounter these restrictions if you apply for Medicaid benefits provided under a special home and community program and Medicaid determines that you are at risk for needing nursing home care in the future.

The time limit for transferring assets, however, does not apply if you receive care in your home or in a community facility, such as an adult day-care center, that provides medical treatment and whose services are covered under your state's Medicaid program. In that case, you can transfer assets one day, and Medicaid begins paying for your care the next.

However, if you subsequently need care in a nursing facility, your transfer could trigger the penalty.

You can also make some kinds of transfers regardless of the 30-month limitation and not jeopardize your eligibility for Medicaid benefits. For example, you can transfer your home to your spouse; to a minor, disabled, or blind child; or to a sibling who had an equity interest in your home and who has lived there for at least one year before you need nursing home care. You can also transfer your home to a child who has lived with you for at least the two years before you were institutionalized and who provided care that delayed your nursing home stay. If you, your spouse, or a dependent relative remain in your home, Medicaid cannot count it as an asset in determining your eligibility for benefits. If you transfer your home to someone who Medicaid says is not eligible to live there, or your home is no longer your residence, Medicaid can sue your estate and force the sale of the house to obtain reimbursement for your care. Transferring your home to a spouse may be a worthwhile move to avoid a Medicaid lien after your death or if you are too sick to return home. (In some states, Medicaid can't put a lien on your home if a surviving child lives there who is under age 31 and is blind or disabled.)

As we explain in chapter 18, you can try to set up a Medicaid qualifying trust so long as you do it 30 months before applying for Medicaid. The trust must be written in such a way that neither you nor the trustee can tap the principal for your benefit. You may receive only the income from the assets held in the trust. This requires some careful planning. If you set up a trust and the trustee has the power to invade the principal for your benefit, Medicaid considers that you own the trust even though you have no control over the principal, never receive any benefits, and have named other beneficiaries. And if the income from the trust is greater than your state's Medicaid income limit, a trust isn't much help. Medicaid still requires you to use any income that exceeds the state limit before it pays its share of your nursing home bills.

If you set up a trust, Medicaid asks for a copy of the trust agreement when you apply for benefits. Officials scrutinize it to see whether it complies with the rules and whether the assets you put into the trust should in fact be counted in determining your eligibility. When you set up a Medicaid qualifying trust, you are also gambling that you'll eventually need nursing home care. If your principal is tied up in the trust, and you live a long time without seeing the inside of a nursing home, you could well find yourself in a financial bind. You'll be unable to tap the trust for more money. If you have substantial assets, buying a good long-term-care insurance policy may be a better strategy.

Another device for protecting your assets is to give them away as gifts at least 30 months before you require a nursing home level of care.* Medicaid usually does not count these assets in determining your eligibility. Obviously, if you give money or property away, you won't have the assets or the income from those assets to live on, and may find yourself in the position of having to go to your children or the other recipients of your assets and asking for money. Nevertheless, such gifts may be an effective way to retain eligibility for Medicaid. Taking such a serious step requires careful planning and coordination with all your sources of income.

APPLYING FOR MEDICAID

When the time comes to apply for Medicaid benefits, the nursing home will help you or your spouse do so. If it turns out that you qualify for benefits, Medicaid pays the nursing home directly. For the portion of the bills you must pay, Medicaid may collect directly from you or from a surrogate, usually a relative who handles your personal business. In some cases, Medicaid helps arrange to have your Social Security check sent directly to the nursing home. The nursing

*Whether or not you want to pursue the strategy of divesting your assets to qualify for Medicaid is an individual decision for you, your family, and your lawyer or financial adviser to make. However, Consumers Union believes that the nation would be better served by a public program—like Medicare—that protects all Americans from the devastating costs of long-term care.

home may keep your personal needs allowance in a special account for you.

Because rules governing Medicaid are complicated and change frequently, nursing home personnel may not always be aware of all the requirements. Even state officials may not keep track of changes in the rules. So if you or your family has been told by Medicaid or a nursing home administrator that you're ineligible for benefits because you've set up a trust or transferred assets, seek another opinion.

13

◆

Special Health-Care Decisions

Fifteen or twenty years ago, if someone was terminally ill or critically injured, he or she would simply die within a "normal" period of time. But with advances in medical technology, it's possible to keep critically ill and comatose people alive for years. We all must confront that reality of modern life when we plan for the years after our retirement.

You can keep some control over these life and death decisions by making a living will or drawing up a health-care proxy.

LIVING WILLS

A *living will* is a declaration that if you should become terminally ill you do not want any extraordinary measures taken to prolong your life. (It has nothing to do with the will that disposes of your estate upon your death. Nor is it related to living trusts.)

A living will gives guidance to your family and to the medical professionals who will eventually care for you. You can

Living Will

TO MY FAMILY, MY PHYSICIANS, AND ANY COMMITTEE, CONSERVATOR, OR OTHER LEGAL REPRESENTATIVE APPOINTED FOR ME

I, __________________________, make this statement as an expression of my wishes if the time comes when I can no longer take part in decisions for my own future:

If there is no reasonable expectation of my recovery from physical or mental disability, I request that I be allowed to die and not be kept alive by life-sustaining means or heroic measures, and I direct that any such life-sustaining treatments or procedures shall be withheld or withdrawn, as the case may be. I do not fear death as much as I fear the indignity of deterioration, dependence, and hopeless pain. Accordingly, I ask that drugs be mercifully administered to me to alleviate terminal suffering even if they may hasten the moment of death. I also do not wish to receive futile medical treatment, which I define as treatment that will provide no benefit to me and will only prolong my inevitable death or irreversible coma. If the best medical advice you can obtain indicates that my condition is incurable and imminently terminal, or if I am in an irreversible coma, with no reasonable possibility of my ever regaining consciousness regardless of what medical treatment I may receive, I would like you to be guided by this expression of my wishes in authorizing discontinuance of treatment (including not only medical treatment, but also providing me with nourishment or liquids) and permitting me to die, as painlessly as possible.

direct them not to use sophisticated and expensive technology to prolong your life if there is no reasonable expectation that you will recover or if the treatment is not likely to do any good. You can specify when your instructions will apply—

These directions to my family and physicians and any legal representative who may be appointed for me are written while I am in good health and spirits so that they may be advised of my sincere wishes and considered judgment in this regard. Although this statement may not be legally binding, I ask that it be honored as an expression of my legal right to refuse medical or surgical treatment, and I direct that such persons shall be free from any liability for having carried out my directions.

I hope that you who care for me will feel morally bound to follow the mandates contained in this statement. I recognize that it places a heavy burden of responsibility upon you, and it is with the intention of sharing that responsibility and of mitigating any feelings of guilt that this statement is made.

Signed: ______________________

Dated: ______________________

Witnessed by: ______________

Address: ________________

____

Witnessed by: ______________

Address: ________________

____

for example, if you are conscious but have irreversible brain damage. You can state which medical procedures you don't want—being resuscitated or put on a mechanical respirator or being a subject for experimental procedures, for example.

Your living will can also specify what you *do* want: drugs that help alleviate pain or procedures that keep you alive as long as possible. Currently, withholding food and water is still a gray area—if you want your doctors to take such a step, check with a lawyer in your state before you make such a notation in your living will.

For most people, a written expression of their wishes is essential, and we recommend that you sign one. However, a living will is not an ironclad guarantee that your wishes will be carried out. Because you cannot anticipate every medical situation that could arise, doctors, hospitals, and family members may still have to make their own decisions. Nevertheless, such a will is an expression of your intent, and courts often look at intent in deciding right-to-die cases. The health-care proxy discussed later in this chapter helps overcome the shortcomings of living wills.

How to Execute a Living Will

Forty-nine states (all but Nebraska) plus the District of Columbia have statutes that permit their citizens to execute a living will. That right is often supplemented by case-by-case court decisions that are still evolving. There is no standard form that can be used in all states. The Society for the Right to Die (250 West 57 Street, New York, NY 10107) has copies of forms that are used in various states. You can also use the form that follows if your state does not have its own form. Be sure to date the will and have it witnessed by two people who are not family members who stand to inherit your estate.

Give copies to your spouse and other family members and to your primary-care doctor. Also keep a copy among your personal papers but *not* in your safe-deposit box, because no one except you may have access to it. After you have written a living will, you can revoke or amend it as your thinking changes. Hospitals and hospices that are certified by Medicare and Medicaid must tell patients about their right to execute a living will, and note in your medical records whether such a document has been made.

HEALTH-CARE PROXIES

A health-care proxy is similar to the durable power of attorney discussed in chapter 7. You may even hear it called a "durable power of attorney for health care." Whatever its name, the document gives another person the authority to make health-care decisions for you should you be unable to do so. The powers you delegate can be as comprehensive or as limited as you want. For instance, you can direct your surrogate to instruct physicians not to resuscitate you, to withhold certain treatments, or to administer pain-relieving medications. You can specify how long you are willing to remain in a coma—for example, 6 months, 30 days, 15 days—before being removed from life-support systems. You can ask your surrogate to take you out of the hospital if you wish to die at home. And if you choose to remain on life supports until you die, you can also make that desire known through your health-care proxy.

So far, 40 states recognize health-care proxies (see Appendix F). If you live in one of them, the person you name to make health-care decisions for you is usually legally bound to carry out your wishes. Nevertheless, some states have rules that might run contrary to your wishes. For example, in New York, a person acting as a surrogate can order a doctor not to administer food or drink *only* if he or she has specific knowledge of your wishes on the subject that were made clear in conversations or through a living will. In Tennessee and Kentucky, a surrogate cannot ask that food and drink be withheld for patients who have been in comas, unless death is imminent.

A few states that recognize health-care proxies do not specifically allow your surrogate to authorize withdrawal or withholding of life support. In states that have no statute, the powers given to a surrogate have been interpreted through court decisions. In these states, consult an attorney for guidance on the legal fine points of what you can include in your directive.

If your state has a specific form, you can obtain it from the Society for the Right to Die. If your state has no form, you can

California Directive to Physicians

Directive made this ________ day of ______________ (month, year).

I, ______________________, being of sound mind, willfully and voluntarily make known my desire that my life shall not be artificially prolonged under the circumstances set forth below, and do hereby declare:

1. If at any time I should have an incurable injury, disease, or illness certified to be a terminal condition by two physicians, and where the application of life-sustaining procedures would serve only to prolong artificially the moment of my death, and where my physician determines that my death is imminent whether or not life-sustaining procedures are utilized, I direct that such procedures be withheld or withdrawn, and that I be permitted to die naturally.

2. In the absence of my ability to give directions regarding the use of such life-sustaining procedures, it is my intention that this directive shall be honored by my family and physician(s) as the final expression of my legal right to refuse medical or surgical treatment and accept the consequences of such refusal.

3. If I have been diagnosed as pregnant and the diagnosis is known to my physician, this directive shall have no force or effect during the course of my pregnancy.

write your own. However, we recommend the California Directive to Physicians that follows as a guide. In any case, it is imperative that you discuss your wishes carefully with the person you choose as your surrogate. Make sure he or she understands what treatments you want and don't want. The document you sign should be witnessed by two people, but not the person you name to carry out your wishes. Give copies of the document to your surrogate as well as to family members and your primary physician.

We recommend that you execute both a living will *and* a

4. I have been diagnosed and notified at least 14 days ago as having a terminal condition by ________________________ M.D., whose address is ________________________, and whose telephone number is ________________________. I understand that if I have not filled in the physician's name and address, it shall be presumed that I did not have a terminal condition when I made out this directive.

5. This directive shall have no force or effect five years from the date filled in above.

6. I understand the full import of this directive and I am emotionally and mentally competent to make this directive.

____

City, County, and State of
Residence ________________________________

The declarant has been personally known to me and I believe him or her to be of sound mind.

____
Witness

____
Witness

health-care proxy. The living will is an expression of your philosophy on dying. The proxy directs someone to carry it out when you are unable to do so.

ANATOMICAL GIFTS

You can donate your body or parts of your body for organ transplants, research, or other medical purposes after your death.

In many states, an organ donor card is attached to your driver's license. If you wish to make an anatomical gift, simply follow the instructions on your license. Usually this means signing the card and asking two witnesses to sign it. If you change your mind, you can revoke the card by destroying it. If your state does not use the driver's license procedure, you can obtain a Uniform Donor Card from one of the organizations listed in Appendix G. Once you have signed either card, carry it at all times. Also make sure that your doctor and the family members who will first learn of your death know that you have signed an organ donor card. If you die unexpectedly, they then should be able to arrange for the organs you have donated to be removed at a nearby hospital or preservation laboratory.

You can also wear a metal tag engraved with the words "Organ Donor." You can get these from Medic Alert, 777 United Nations Plaza, New York, NY 10017. In addition, you can make your desires known by registering at any of the several central organ donor registries, which coordinate anatomical gifts and keep records of potential donors (see Appendix G). You can express your desire to make an anatomical gift when you write your will, but as a practical matter, this isn't a good idea. By the time your will is read, it is usually too late.

PART THREE

◆

Housing

14

Tapping the Equity in Your Home

Your home is probably your largest asset. Thanks to the increase in real estate values in the past decade, your house may now be worth much more than you paid for it, and what's more, you may well own it free and clear. Recognizing that older Americans have a virtual gold mine in their home equity, lenders have fashioned a number of *home equity conversion* plans that allow homeowners to tap some of that money during their lifetimes.

Don't confuse home equity conversion arrangements with the widely advertised home equity loans, which require homeowners to repay the amount borrowed, usually in regular monthly installments. If you fail to repay, the lender can foreclose on the loan, forcing you to sell your house. We don't recommend such loans for people already retired or about to retire. Repaying the loan may prove especially burdensome if you are living on a fixed income.

On the other hand, home equity conversion plans offer advantages if you are cash poor and need extra money to continue living in your home. With these plans, you usually don't have to repay your loan until you move or sell your house. If you die, your estate repays the loan. Home equity conversion plans, however, do carry some risk. With some arrangements, you might use up all your equity, leaving no financial cushion in your later years, or your lender might default or the loan payments you receive may not keep up with inflation. So it pays to proceed with caution when considering a home equity conversion loan.

There are two basic types of home equity conversion plans—*special-purpose* loans for anything from deferring property taxes to making home repairs, and *reverse mortgages,* which return your equity in the form of monthly payments, a line of credit, or a lump sum that you can use for living expenses.

A third kind of home equity conversion plan lets you sell your house and lease it back from the buyer (sometimes your children or other relatives) while you continue to live in it. These *sale-leaseback* plans are complicated, and you need a real estate attorney to arrange one. We discuss only the first two arrangements.

SPECIAL-PURPOSE LOANS TO PAY PROPERTY TAXES

Special-purpose loans used to defer property taxes are the most common home equity conversion plan. Eighteen states plus the District of Columbia allow homeowners to borrow money from either the state or a local government to pay their property taxes (see Appendix I). The money does not have to be repaid until you die, move, or sell the house. With these arrangements, you in effect use the equity in your home to pay your property taxes.

Here's how property tax deferral works: Once you sign up for a program, you decide each year whether you want to defer that year's property taxes. If you do, some states require that you file an application before your taxes are due. The state then sends a check in the amount of your taxes to the local tax collector, or it may send a check made out to both you and the tax collector, and you pay the taxes yourself.

The amount of deferral turns into a loan on which the state government charges interest, usually 6 to 8 percent. (You don't have to pay points, loan fees, or other costs associated with mortgage loans.) The loan is secured by a lien against your property. When the property is sold either before or after your death, the state can collect the amount of taxes you have deferred, plus accumulated interest, and the amount of the deferral is subtracted from the equity. If you defer the full amount of your taxes each year for several years, it's possible to have little equity left in your home when you move or at your death. In the first case, you'll have little money left to buy another home, and in the second case, your heirs won't receive much money from the sale of your house. On the other hand, if your home continues to appreciate in value, the amount of equity keeps building (although your property taxes are likely to keep increasing, too). States offering these programs usually don't ask you to repay your loans before you sell your home, but you can often do so without prepayment penalties. The loan balance is usually paid from your estate.

Are You Eligible?

In most states, you must be at least 65 to take advantage of a property tax deferral program. A few states, such as Iowa and Florida, and the District of Columbia, have no age requirement. Many states also have income limitations. Usually your household income must not exceed $20,000. A few states allow anyone to qualify regardless of annual income.

To be eligible for property tax deferral, states usually require that your home be debt-free or nearly so. If you owe a substantial amount on your mortgage, or if you've taken a second mortgage or a home equity loan, you are not eligible to defer your property taxes under most programs. Check Appendix I to see if your state has a property tax deferral program. If it does, contact the state department of revenue for details.

SPECIAL-PURPOSE LOANS FOR PROPERTY REPAIRS

Using Community Development Block grant funds and other funding sources, state and local governments offer loans to homeowners to replace roofs, porches, plumbing, and heating equipment; install storm windows; or modify a home to accommodate a resident with a physical disability. Such loans, however, can't be used for merely cosmetic improvements. For example, you can't add a family room, but you can widen doorways to accommodate a wheelchair. Often agencies make loan funds available so older homes can be brought into line with recent local housing codes.

How They Work

Like property tax deferral loans, these loans carry a very low interest rate. In some localities, they are interest-free. There are no fees or other costs involved in taking out the loan. You usually don't have to repay the loan until you move, sell your house, or die (then your heirs have to worry about repaying it). So long as you live in your home, you are not required to repay. Some programs even forgive all or part of the loan the longer you remain in your house. However, with some programs, you have to begin repayment as soon as the repairs are completed.

When the time comes for you or your heirs to repay, the money no doubt will come from the sale of the house. It's possible that the improvements you made will increase the value of the house to the point where the loan actually pays for itself. (Of course, that depends on the amount you borrowed.) *Example:* If your house is now worth $100,000 and you take out a $10,000 loan and make improvements, your home may immediately increase in value to, say, $108,000. Assuming it appreciates 5 percent each year, after 8 years the house is worth $160,000. If you then sell the house, the appreciation more than covers the amount you borrowed.

Are You Eligible?

Eligibility requirements can be stiff. Usually your income cannot exceed a certain amount; in some states it can't exceed the poverty level. But you may be surprised at how high an income you can have and still be eligible for a loan. In Maryland, for example, your income cannot be greater than 80 percent of the state's median income. In 1991, for a family of two, 80 percent of the median income was $30,150 (in certain counties, it was higher). Maryland residents who apply for loans to make their homes more energy efficient may be eligible regardless of income.

Some jurisdictions require that a residence be in a certain location. In Kentucky, such loan programs are often targeted to rural areas.

Deferred-payment arrangements sometimes go by different names, such as home repair loans or accessibility loans. Their availability also varies from time to time and from locale to locale. A local agency may have money available to lend only at certain times of the year. To locate a program, call your state's department of aging (see Appendix B) or community economic development agency.

Should You Take a Deferred-Payment Loan?

If you have trouble paying your property taxes or need to repair your home to make it more energy efficient, to bring it up to code or to modify it for a disability, these loans may be just what you need. Their low cost (or no cost) makes them exceptionally attractive. However, once you assume such a loan, it may be difficult, if not impossible, to borrow more money against your home equity. If you think you need more cash than you can get from one of these loans, a reverse mortgage may be a better option, even though the costs may be greater. You should also consider how your heirs will repay the loan or how you will repay the money if it turns out your property doesn't appreciate as much as you expect. If you take a loan that requires immediate repayment, make sure your budget can accommodate the payments.

REVERSE MORTGAGES

With a reverse mortgage you can withdraw the equity in your house in the form of a loan and use the money for living expenses. Typically, the loan proceeds are paid out monthly, but you can make other arrangements. The loan balance increases each month as you receive payments. In addition, interest is added to the growing balance.

The mortgage balance must be repaid when you die, move, or sell the house. If you are away from the house for a long time—in a nursing home, for example—most lenders require that the loan balance be repaid in full. You retain the title to your property, but if the loan is not repaid, the lender can foreclose on the property just the same as if you defaulted on a traditional mortgage. But the lender cannot require payment from assets other than your home and cannot make claims against your estate or against your heirs to collect the balance.

The amount you can borrow depends on the amount of equity you've built up, the interest rate on the loan, and the loan term. Typically, the more equity you have, the lower the interest rate; the shorter the loan term, the more you can borrow.

Reverse mortgages may be insured—either by the lender through a risk pool created by fees that borrowers pay, or by the Federal Housing Administration (FHA)—or they may remain uninsured. Insurance protects you if the lender defaults and is unable to make the required payments, and also protects the lender if you outlive the term of the loan. If that happens, the insurer pays the lender the amount of the principal plus interest due, allowing you to remain in your home as long as you wish, even if you have outlived the equity in your home.

There are other significant differences between insured and uninsured loans. FHA-insured mortgages offer a variety of loan options, such as monthly payments for a fixed term, monthly payments for as long as you remain in your home, and a line of credit that lets you decide when to take your payments. Uninsured mortgages offer monthly payments for a fixed term only. At the end of the term, the loan must be repaid. Insured loans do not require repayments until you die, sell the house, or move. With an uninsured loan, you must repay the loan in full when the loan term ends. Typically you are able to borrow more with self- or lender-insured loans but will have to pay a substantial up-front fee that is added to the loan balance.

Today insured mortgages are the predominant type of reverse mortgage, and most of them are insured by the FHA.

FHA-Insured Mortgages

The FHA program began in 1989 and is expanding. The agency can insure up to 25,000 reverse mortgages originated through September 1995. Let's see how these mortgages work.

Any lender can write an FHA reverse mortgage, but not all do. To find a lender in your area, contact the nearest Housing and Urban Development field office (see Appendix H). You can also call "HUD User" at 800-245-2691 to obtain a list of lenders participating in the program. The FHA requires all potential borrowers to receive counseling in a HUD-approved counseling program before they can obtain a mortgage. A counselor (someone other than the lender) must discuss alternatives for getting cash, the financial consequences of taking a mortgage, the tax implications, and the effects of reverse mortgages on eligibility for government benefit programs, such as Medicaid.

How these loans work. To determine the amount you can borrow, the lender must first appraise your home, using an independent appraiser. Next the lender calculates a *maximum claim amount.* This is the lesser of the house's appraised value or the amount HUD lends for traditional mortgages in different parts of the country. It's possible for the appraised value to far exceed the maximum claim amount. If that's the case, you might find other types of reverse mortgages that are more suitable. The amount you can actually borrow is a portion of the maximum claim amount and is based on your life expectancy. A 62-year-old can borrow less than an 80-year-old with the same maximum claim amount. In the case of a couple, the FHA requires a lender to use the age of the younger spouse in figuring the loan amount. Borrowers must be age 62 or older.

Lenders use two interest rates in preparing a mortgage loan. The 1-year Treasury-bill rate plus a margin of 1.6 percent is used to calculate the interest accruing on the growing balance; the 10-year Treasury-bill rate plus a margin of 1.6 percent is used to figure the monthly payments you receive. For example, if 1-year rates are 5 percent and 10-year rates are 7 percent, your payments would be figured using a rate of 8.6 percent, and interest would be accruing on your unpaid balance at a rate of 6.6 percent. Since reverse mortgages are usually adjustable-rate loans, the interest rate applied to the increasing loan balance fluctuates with swings in the Treasury-bill rates. The rate can't increase more than 2 percent each year and no more than 5 percent over the life of the loan. The adjustable rate does not affect the amount of your payments, but a higher rate causes the balance to increase faster. Conversely, a lower rate results in slower growth.

You pay closing costs plus an origination fee of 1 to 2 percent of the house's value. Most of the closing costs—2 percent of the maximum claim amount—pay the initial insurance premium. You also must pay for the credit report and appraisal fee, typically $275 to $300. The FHA allows you to pay closing costs out of the loan proceeds.

Besides closing costs, you pay additional fees each month. These include a monthly mortgage insurance premium of one-half of 1 percent of the maximum claim amount and a monthly service fee of around $25.

Payment Options

You can receive money from your loan in three ways: (1) a payment each month for the rest of your life (called a *tenure* arrangement); (2) a line of credit you draw on whenever you need cash; or (3) monthly payments for a fixed term, usually 10 years. You can combine a line of credit with a tenure or a fixed-term arrangement. The FHA lets you switch from one form of payment to another anytime you wish.

The line of credit is not fixed. It grows as the house value appreciates and as you grow older. We recommend that you add a line of credit with any payment arrangement. Since the credit line increases over time, that money could come in handy in your later years when you might need cash to pay medical bills or make repairs to sell your house. With any of the payment options, you are allowed to take a sum off the top of your total loan proceeds. This is called an *initial draw*, and it's not uncommon for borrowers to use this sum to pay off other loans against their property. (The FHA requires that the property be free from other mortgages.)

Tables 17, 18, and 19 show how a loan balance increases for a 72-year-old homeowner whose property is valued at $100,000 and whose maximum claim amount is $90,950 and who takes a tenure arrangement, a line-of-credit option, or a loan with a 10-year fixed term. In all cases, the example assumes an interest rate of 10 percent and a 4 percent rate of appreciation in the house. With the monthly payment or tenure option, the borrower takes an initial draw of $2,000 and finances the closing costs. In the line-of-credit example, the borrower finances the closing costs.

Are Reverse Mortgages for You?

Reverse mortgages are complicated financial transactions with serious consequences. Discuss your plans with a family member or accountant before proceeding. Although reverse mortgages offer financial salvation for many of the house-rich and cash-poor elderly, they have their drawbacks.

These mortgages don't make sense if you plan to move in a year or two. Consider them only if you plan to stay in your home permanently. They also are not suitable if you already have a large mortgage on your home, since you will most likely have to pay off that mortgage before you will be eligi-

TABLE 17
FHA-Insured Reverse Mortgage—Tenure

Age of youngest borrower	72	Maximum claim amount	$90,950
Expected interest rate	10%	Expected appreciation	4%
Initial draw	$2,000	Initial line of credit	$2,000
Total closing costs	$3,319	Monthly payment	$216.32
Beginning mortgage balance	$5,319	Monthly servicing fee	$25
Initial property value	$100,000		

		Annual Totals				End-of-Year Projections		
Year	Age	Service Fee	Payment	Monthly Insurance Premium	Interest	Loan Balance	Line of Credit	Property Value
1	72	$300	$2,596	$ 36	$ 720	$ 8,971	$ 2,220	$104,000
2	73	300	2,596	55	1,104	13,026	2,465	108,160
3	74	300	2,596	76	1,529	17,527	2,736	112,486
4	75	300	2,596	100	2,002	22,525	3,038	116,985
5	76	300	2,596	126	2,526	28,073	3,373	121,665
6	77	300	2,596	155	3,108	34,233	3,744	126,531
7	78	300	2,596	188	3,755	41,071	4,157	131,593

8	79	300	2,596	224	4,473	48,663	4,615	136,856
9	80	300	2,596	263	5,269	57,092	5,124	142,331
10	81	300	2,596	308	6,154	66,450	5,689	148,024
11	82	300	2,596	357	7,136	76,838	6,316	153,945
12	83	300	2,596	411	8,227	88,372	7,012	160,103
13	84	300	2,596	472	9,437	101,177	7,785	166,507
14	85	300	2,596	539	10,781	115,393	8,643	173,167
15	86	300	2,596	614	12,273	131,176	9,595	180,094
16	87	300	2,596	696	13,930	148,698	10,652	187,298
17	88	300	2,596	788	15,769	168,151	11,826	194,790
18	89	300	2,596	891	17,810	189,748	13,130	202,581
19	90	300	2,596	1,004	20,077	213,724	14,577	210,684
20	91	300	2,596	1,130	22,594	240,343	16,183	219,112
21	92	300	2,596	1,269	25,387	269,896	17,967	227,876
22	93	300	2,597	1,424	28,489	302,705	19,947	236,991
23	94	300	2,596	1,597	31,933	339,131	22,145	246,471
24	95	300	2,596	1,788	35,756	379,570	24,586	256,330
25	96	300	2,596	2,000	40,000	424,466	27,295	266,583
26	97	300	2,596	2,236	44,712	474,309	30,303	277,246
27	98	300	2,596	2,497	49,943	529,646	33,643	288,336
28	99	300	2,596	2,788	55,751	591,080	37,350	299,870

TABLE 18
FHA-Insured Reverse Mortgage—Line of Credit

Age of youngest borrower	72	Maximum claim amount	$90,950
Expected interest rate	10%	Expected appreciation	4%
Initial draw	$0	Initial line of credit	$27,603
Total closing costs	$3,319	Monthly payment	$0
Beginning mortgage balance	$3,319	Monthly servicing fee	$25
Initial property value	$100,000		

		Annual Totals				End-of-Year Projections		
Year	Age	Service Fee	Payment	Monthly Insurance Premium	Interest	Loan Balance	Line of Credit	Property Value
1	72	$300	$0	$ 18	$ 365	$ 8,971	$ 30,644	$104,000
2	73	300	0	22	437	13,026	34,022	108,160
3	74	300	0	26	516	17,527	37,771	112,486
4	75	300	0	30	605	22,525	41,934	116,985
5	76	300	0	35	703	28,073	46,555	121,665
6	77	300	0	41	812	34,233	51,685	126,531
7	78	300	0	47	933	41,071	57,381	131,593

8	79	300	0	53	1,067	48,663	63,705	136,856
9	80	300	0	61	1,216	57,092	70,726	142,331
10	81	300	0	69	1,382	66,450	78,520	148,024
11	82	300	0	78	1,566	76,838	87,173	153,945
12	83	300	0	88	1,770	88,372	96,780	160,103
13	84	300	0	100	1,996	101,177	107,445	166,507
14	85	300	0	112	2,248	115,393	119,286	173,167
15	86	300	0	126	2,527	131,176	132,432	180,094
16	87	300	0	142	2,837	148,698	147,027	187,298
17	88	300	0	159	3,181	168,151	163,230	194,790
18	89	300	0	178	3,563	189,748	181,218	202,581
19	90	300	0	199	3,987	213,724	201,189	210,684
20	91	300	0	223	4,458	240,343	223,361	219,112
21	92	300	0	249	4,981	269,896	247,976	227,876
22	93	300	0	278	5,561	302,705	275,304	236,991
23	94	300	0	310	6,206	339,131	305,643	246,471
24	95	300	0	346	6,921	379,570	339,326	256,330
25	96	300	0	386	7,715	424,466	376,721	266,583
26	97	300	0	430	8,597	474,309	418,237	277,246
27	98	300	0	479	9,576	529,646	464,328	288,336
28	99	300	0	533	10,663	591,080	515,499	299,870

TABLE 19
FHA-Insured Reverse Mortgage—10-Year Term

Age of youngest borrower	72	Maximum claim amount	$90,950
Expected interest rate	10%	Expected appreciation	4%
Initial draw	$2,000	Initial line of credit	$2,000
Total closing costs	$3,319	Monthly payment	$216.32
Beginning mortgage balance	$5,319	Monthly servicing fee	$25
Initial property value	$100,000		

		Annual Totals				End-of-Year Projections		
Year	Age	Service Fee	Payment	Monthly Insurance Premium	Interest	Loan Balance	Line of Credit	Property Value
1	72	$300	$4,110	$ 30	$ 595	$ 8,354	$ 2,220	$104,000
2	73	300	4,110	56	1,123	13,943	2,465	108,160
3	74	300	4,110	86	1,710	20,149	2,736	112,486
4	75	300	4,110	118	2,361	27,038	3,038	116,985
5	76	300	4,110	154	3,085	34,687	3,373	121,665
6	77	300	4,110	194	3,887	43,178	3,744	126,531
7	78	300	4,110	239	4,779	52,606	4,157	131,593

8	79	300	4,110	288	5,768	63,072	4,615	136,856
9	80	300	4,110	343	6,866	74,691	5,124	142,331
10	81	300	4,110	404	8,086	87,592	5,689	148,024
11	82	300	0	461	9,210	97,562	6,316	153,945
12	83	300	0	513	10,256	108,631	7,012	160,103
13	84	300	0	571	11,418	120,921	7,785	166,507
14	85	300	0	635	12,708	134,564	8,643	173,167
15	86	300	0	707	14,140	149,711	9,595	180,094
16	87	300	0	786	15,730	166,527	10,652	187,298
17	88	300	0	875	17,495	185,197	11,826	194,790
18	89	300	0	973	19,454	205,924	13,130	202,581
19	90	300	0	1,081	21,630	228,935	14,577	210,684
20	91	300	0	1,202	24,045	254,482	16,183	219,112
21	92	300	0	1,336	26,726	282,844	17,967	227,876
22	93	300	0	1,485	29,703	314,332	19,947	236,991
23	94	300	0	1,650	33,008	349,291	22,145	246,471
24	95	300	0	1,834	36,677	388,101	24,586	256,330
25	96	300	0	2,038	40,750	431,189	27,295	266,583
26	97	300	0	2,064	45,273	479,025	30,303	277,246
27	98	300	0	2,515	55,293	532,133	33,643	288,336
28	99	300	0	2,793	55,867	591,093	37,350	299,870

ble for a reverse mortgage. If you want to preserve the equity in your home for your children, then reverse mortgages are not a good option. The lender—not your children—gets most, if not all, of the equity when the house is sold.

Make sure you know the circumstances under which the loan becomes due and payable. Under the FHA program, the loan is due when you die or have not used the house as a primary residence for 12 or more consecutive months. If you go to a nursing home and have no prospects for returning to your home, your relatives or whoever is acting on your behalf has three options for paying off the loan: sell the house, refinance your reverse mortgage balance with a traditional mortgage, or pay the balance out of other assets. Other types of loans have other rules. Uninsured loans, for example, are payable at the end of a fixed term or when you die, sell the house, or move, if that happens first. The lender can foreclose on the loan and force you to move.

A number of safeguards are built into the FHA program, so if you're seriously thinking of a reverse mortgage, consider an FHA loan. However, with this arrangement, your mortgage is based on the total value of your home. If you want a mortgage based on less than your home's full value, you have to consider other types of reverse mortgage loans, which allow you to free up some cash and still save part of the equity for your heirs. In the near future, the FHA program will offer this kind of plan, called an *equity reserve* feature. Check with your FHA lender to see if it is available before seeking other types of reverse mortgages.

15

Housing Tax Breaks

If you own your home, deciding whether to stay put or move is one of the biggest financial decisions you face as you plan for retirement. If you do move, the tax consequences of selling your house and obtaining another can determine your financial well-being in your later years. The federal government allows you to use the *rollover* provisions of the tax code and the *$125,000 exclusion* to shield some of your profits from taxes. Knowing when and how to use these tax breaks helps you maximize income from your house and protect your equity from a painful tax bite.

ROLLOVERS

Ordinarily when you sell a house, your profit is taxable at the capital gains rate. But under a special tax code provision, you can invest or "roll over" some of that profit in a new house so long as it is more expensive than the one you sold. You do not have to pay taxes on the amount rolled over until a later time, if ever. In fact, it's possible to avoid paying taxes on your profits until you die if you continue buying bigger and more expensive homes. Your death wipes out the gain you've been rolling over. Eventually, though, the IRS may catch up with your heirs, who may have to pay estate or inheritance taxes on your home. However, if you're over age 55 when you sell, you may not have to pay taxes on as much as $125,000 of your profit. (This exclusion is discussed more fully later in this chapter.)

The government doesn't treat losses on the sale of a home kindly. You can't deduct a loss unless part of your home was used for business, and that part of the loss is then treated like any other business loss.

Are You Eligible?

You are eligible for the rollover only if the house you sell is your principal residence. If you live in a rented house or apartment but sell your vacation home when you retire, you do not qualify. To take advantage of the tax break, you must be able to prove that the house you're selling is where you live and that you spend more time there than at any other residence. *Example:* You own a house in Chicago and a vacation condominium in Florida. You spend seven months of the year in Chicago and five in Florida. If you sell the condo, you won't get the deferral because your Chicago house is your principal residence. But if you move to Florida and return to Chicago for a couple of months in the summer, you qualify when you sell the condo.

From a financial standpoint, if you have two homes and are considering selling one, sell your principal residence. Or else you may want to change addresses for a while. If you're unsure which property to sell, consider selling the one that will yield the biggest profit, thereby increasing the value of your rollover.

When Are You Eligible?

Timing is critical in taking advantage of the rollover. You must buy the new home two years before or within two years after selling your old house. *Example:* You have lived in the Chicago home for 30 years and bought the condo in Florida on September 1, 1990, using it only for vacations. On June 1, 1992, you sell the Chicago residence at a profit and move to Florida. Since you bought the condo two years before selling the Chicago home, you qualify for the rollover. But that is not the case if you purchased the condo in 1989.

The IRS strictly adheres to this time period, unless you can prove you were out of the country or serving in the armed forces.

FIGURING THE BASIS

To figure the profit or gain on your home, first establish its *basis,* which in IRS parlance means its total cost. The basis is what you paid for your house, including the down payment, the amount of the original mortgage, and closing costs. If you built your house, it includes the cost of land and construction. To this amount, add the value of any additions or permanent improvements—new rooms, new plumbing, wiring, or a finished basement, for example. You can also include the cost of fixtures that can't be removed without damaging the house structure, but not the cost of paint jobs and repairs. Once you've made all the additions to the original cost of your home, subtract certain items if they are applicable. If you have claimed tax losses for fire, flood, or storm damage, reduce your basis by the amount of those deductions. And if you use part of your home for business and have taken deductions for depreciation, subtract the value of those deductions from your basis.

(If you inherited your home, its basis is its value in the estate of the person from whom you inherited, at the time you inherited it. This is usually the value reported for tax purposes. If there were no estate proceedings, you may need an independent appraisal to assess its value.)

Once you establish your basis, determine the selling price. You can reduce the gross proceeds from the sale by the amount of any sales expenses, such as real estate commissions, advertising costs, and legal fees. The gross proceeds minus sales expenses is the *net selling price.*

Next, subtract the basis from the net selling price to arrive at the gain. *Example:* If your basis is $55,000, and the net selling price is $141,000, your gain is $86,000. That is the amount on which your tax rate is applied. If your marginal rate is 28 percent, the tax on the gain comes to $24,080 ($141,000 – $55,000 = $86,000 × .28 = $24,080). If you buy another residence that costs more, you can postpone paying some of that tax. If you reinvest in a smaller, less expensive house, you will have to pay some tax. If you rent an apartment and don't reinvest at all, you'll have to pay all the tax on your gain within two years.

If you trade up to a more expensive home, you need to calculate the amount that must be rolled over or invested in the new house. That amount is called the *adjusted selling price* and equals the net selling price minus any "fixing-up" expenses (costs you incurred getting the house ready for sale). The work, however, must be finished within 90 days before you sign a sales contract and paid for within 30 days after the contract is signed. (You can't deduct fixing-up expenses as a regular itemized deduction; nor are they used to determine the basis.)

Example: You sell your house for $150,000 and pay a sales commission of $9,000. As in the previous example, your net selling price is $141,000. You spent $5,000 fixing up the house. Subtract $5,000 from $141,000 to get an adjusted selling price of $136,000. Your new house costs $120,000. Subtracting $120,000 from $136,000 results in a gain of $16,000 on which you must pay $4,480 in taxes ($16,000 × .28 = $4,480). By rolling over part of your profit, you save $19,600 ($24,080 – $4,480).

RESIDENCE/BUSINESS TAX RULES

If you have a home office, use part of your home as a professional office, or live in one apartment of the two-family home or apartment house that you are selling, you can defer the taxes only on the part of your gain that is allocated to your residence. When you sell the property, the IRS treats the sale as if you had sold two separate properties—your home and your business. *Example:* You bought your home for $200,000 and used three-quarters of it for living space and one-quarter for a home office. You then sell the property for $300,000. The rollover applies only to $225,000, which represents three-quarters of the selling price, the same proportion of the house you actually lived in. You have at least a $25,000 gain on the business portion. (The gain is higher if you claimed depreciation, which is subtracted from your basis.) If you plan to use your new residence for business, the same rules apply. Only the portion of the purchase price allocated to the residential portion of your home is considered the cost of your new home for purposes of figuring the gain.

THE $125,000 EXCLUSION

The rollover lets you escape paying taxes for a while; the $125,000 exclusion allows you to avoid paying them altogether if you have reached your fifty-fifth birthday by the time you sell your principal residence. This is a valuable tax break that can help fund a secure retirement.

Unlike the rollover, the exclusion is optional; you don't have to take it when you sell your home, but once you do, it's gone. You can use it only once. The exclusion rule forces you to make some hard decisions about where you'll live. For example, if your gain from the sale is less than $125,000 and you want to buy another house, you could forgo the exclusion and save it for another time. That way you have another chance at using the entire amount (assuming, of course, that your house appreciates substantially). In that case, you pay the taxes that are due and use the rollover provision if you buy a more expensive house. Suppose you realize a $50,000 gain from your house and you plan to buy a retirement home in a part of the country where housing prices are rising. You might be better off rolling over your gain and saving the exclusion until you sell your new home, which may yield a profit greater than $125,000.

If the gain is less than $125,000 and you're sure the residence you are currently buying is your last one, go ahead and take the exclusion, even if it means you don't use the entire $125,000.

Who Is Eligible?

You must be 55 or older on the date you sell the house, which must be your principal residence, before you can take advantage of the exclusion rule. (The rules that apply to a principal residence for the rollover also apply to the exclusion.) You must have owned and lived in the house for at least three years during the five-year period ending with the date of the sale. And neither you nor your spouse can have previously used the exclusion for any sale concluded after July 26, 1978. The first requirement is easy to meet; the other two may be harder to fulfill.

The three-year requirement. You don't have to live in the house for three continuous years, nor do the three years you own the residence have to be the same three years you live there. As long as you have owned the house for at least 1,095 days and lived in it for any period totaling 1,095 days, you are eligible for the exclusion.

Example: In 1983 you moved into a house that your daughter owns in Illinois. You lived there until June 16, 1987, when you bought the house from her. You stayed in the house until December 1, 1989, when you sold it and moved to Florida. Although you lived in the house for three years, you can't claim the exclusion because you didn't own it for three years.

You don't have to be in the house every minute to qualify. Temporary absences for vacations don't count against you. You can even rent your house while you are away. But lengthy absences could disqualify you from taking the exclusion. A construction worker, for example, who is away from home on short assignments won't lose the exclusion. But such eligibility might be sacrificed if he or she is on a long-term project that takes six months or more.

If you have a similar situation, consult a tax adviser before selling your home and trying to claim the exclusion.

Requirements for spouses. If you and your spouse own a house together, but your spouse has been married before and used the exclusion selling a previous house, you are not eligible to take the exclusion when you sell your jointly owned home. But if your spouse dies and you sell the house, you can claim the exclusion. Similarly, if you plan to remarry and both you and your intended spouse own houses and want to sell them and reinvest together in a new residence, sell both properties before you get married. That way each of you can use your own $125,000 exclusion. If you sell one of the houses after the marriage, one of you loses the exclusion.

More than one owner. If you sell your house after your spouse has died, you can claim that tax break if you are over 55, have not remarried, and your spouse had qualified for the exclusion. *Example:* Your husband bought his home in 1986 and used it as a principal residence. You were married in 1989 but your husband died a year later and had never claimed the $125,000 exclusion. If you continue to live in the house and then sell it in 1993 when you turn 55, you are eligible for the exclusion because your husband had been eligible and you are over 55.

If the joint owners are not husband and wife, each owner who qualifies for the exclusion can shield from taxes his or her proportionate share of the gain. *Example:* You and your brother own a house together. You paid three-fourths of the cost; your brother paid one-fourth. You are both over 55 and have lived in the house for five years when you decide to sell it. The selling price is $240,000, the basis $40,000, and the gain $200,000. Your share of the gain is $150,000 and your brother's is $50,000.

Both of you can use the exclusion. You will pay some tax, however, unless you roll over part of your gain into a new house. Your brother will waste part of his exclusion because his portion of the gain is less than $125,000. But if he doesn't plan to buy another home, he should use the exclusion. If you are under 55 and your brother over 55, he can use his exclusion, and doing so doesn't disqualify you from using yours in the future.

How to Claim the Exclusion

If you want to claim the exclusion, you must file Form 2119 with your income tax return for the year you sold your house. If you take the exclusion but later change your mind, you can file an amended return on Form 1040X and attach a copy of Form 2119 to it. You can file an amended return any time up to three years from the due date of the return for the year of sale, three years from the date that the return was actually filed, or two years after you paid tax on the gain, whichever date comes later. The same time limits apply if you do not elect the exclusion and later change your mind. In any case, seek help from a tax adviser.

HOMESTEAD EXEMPTIONS AND OTHER REDUCTIONS IN STATE TAXES

Many states provide real estate tax reductions or tax deferrals for homes occupied by senior citizens. These tax breaks are designed to allow older residents, living on fixed incomes, to remain in their homes, despite the rising burden of local property taxes. These reductions take many forms and often include corresponding state income tax credits for renters. Most states also provide some kind of arrangement to preserve your benefits while you're in a nursing home.

For example, New York municipalities, at their option, may exempt older, low-income residents from up to 50 percent of their real estate tax bills. Married couples are eligible for this benefit if either of them is 65 or older; for other joint owners, both must be 65 or older. To qualify, your income must be under $12,025; this figure is periodically adjusted for inflation. The real estate tax bills you receive from the city or town where you live will tell you how to apply for the exemption.

California residents who are 62 or over and have less than $20,000 of income are entitled to a property tax credit on the first $34,000 of assessed value. The credit is on a sliding scale, from 96 percent for incomes under $3,000 down to 4 percent if your income is $12,000 or more.

In other states, such as Illinois and Hawaii, the break takes the form of a *homestead exemption,* which eliminates the tax on part of the assessed value of your home. New Jersey gives most homeowners a homestead rebate, with a larger amount going to qualified senior citizens.

One popular retirement destination, Florida, has several layers of homestead exemptions. If you or a dependent are permanent residents of Florida, the first $5,000 of your home's assessed value is exempt from municipal and school taxes. This exemption goes up to $10,000 for residents who are over 65 and up to $9,500 for disabled persons once they've lived in Florida for five years (but you can't claim both exemptions). If you occupy the residence yourself, the first $25,000 of assessed value is exempt, regardless of your age.

States with deferral provisions, such as Georgia and Colorado, let qualified senior citizens postpone paying their property taxes. The accumulated taxes, plus interest, are a lien against the property that becomes payable when they sell the house or die. The deferral saves cash for those living on fixed incomes but shifts the tax burden to their children or other heirs.

And some states, such as New Mexico, combine their real estate and income tax systems by allowing real estate tax rebates (up to $250) as state income tax deductions. If your rebate is more than your tax, you get a refund.

You can get information on property tax breaks from your state department of revenue or the state agencies on aging, listed in Appendix B. If you move to a retirement home in a new area or enter a nursing home or other care facility, be sure to check on your real estate tax status—the rules may be very different from what you are familiar with.

16

Continuing-Care Retirement Communities

Today, continuing-care retirement communities (CCRCs) are the fastest-growing segment of the housing market for older Americans. In return for substantial entrance fees, these communities promise you a place to live for the rest of your life; some, if not all, of your meals; and most important, nursing care should the need for it arise.

CCRCs come in many shapes and sizes: luxury high-rises with balconies, modest mid-rises, one- and two-bedroom cottages with carports and patios, and ranchlike structures with apartment wings radiating from a central common area. Most communities provide transportation, housekeeping services, craft or activity rooms, gardens, libraries, beauty shops, and a steady supply of bridge games, movies, tours, parties, exercise classes, concerts, and religious services. All have communal dining rooms.

Round-the-clock personnel provide skilled nursing in nursing wings, or on special floors in the main building, or in a separate building that's part of the entire complex.

HOW A CCRC WORKS

The communities, built largely with tax-exempt bonds and some conventional mortgage financing, work on the insurance principle of risk pooling. Not all residents will need nursing care, but for those who do, their care is funded with the fees paid by all the residents. In this sense, CCRCs work like any insurance policy—premiums paid by all policyholders are pooled to pay benefits to those who suffer some misfortune. Some CCRCs also work on another insurance principle—the life annuity. When you buy an annuity, you pay an insurance company a sum of money, and the company sends you a monthly check for the rest of your life (see chapter 4). When you sign a CCRC contract, you receive your payments in the form of services and care. With an annuity, you can't outlive your income; with a CCRC, you can't outlive your lifetime care. What kind of services and how much care you receive depend on the generosity of the sponsor, the facility you select, and the amount of money you pay.

TYPES OF COMMUNITIES

There are three basic types of continuing-care retirement communities: the Type A or "all-inclusive," Type B or "modified," and Type C or "fee-for-service."

Type A or "All-Inclusive"

These facilities guarantee residents *fully paid* nursing care. If you spend 10 years in the nursing wing, the community is obligated to provide care at no cost other than your monthly fee. You are, in effect, buying a long-term-care insurance policy.

Some Type A communities provide care for certain acute illnesses and offer other medical services, such as eye and podiatric clinics. Many offer personal and assisted care, such as help with bathing, dressing, and taking medications. A Type A CCRC may also provide apartment cleaning, laundering linens, tray service, utilities (though usually not telephones), transportation, private dining rooms, cable television, banks, saunas, and swimming pools. About one-third include three meals a day in the monthly fee; the rest, one or two. Some communities require you to buy a certain number of meals each month, sometimes for an extra charge. Meals not included in the basic fee are also extra.

Type B or "Modified"

These communities do not guarantee unlimited nursing care. Instead, they provide nursing care for only a specified number of days each year or during your lifetime. When the days (usually fewer than 15) are used up, you pay the regular per diem charge for nursing care, although many communities give discounts from the going daily rate. Many of these communities offer personal care, such as help with bathing and dressing, but less than half include those services in the basic fees. Services and amenities offered by Type B communities are similar to those found in Type A facilities, and most include at least one meal a day in the monthly charge.

Type C or "Fee-for-Service"

These communities guarantee access to their nursing wings but usually charge the full per diem rate. Occasionally, you find a Type C community that reduces the daily charge for its residents. These communities typically do not include meals or personal care services in their basic monthly fees. They do offer some of the same amenities as Type A and B facilities, although they are less likely to provide private dining rooms for parties, swimming pools, and woodworking shops.

The major difference among CCRCs is the amount of prepaid nursing care the entrance fee buys. Type B and C facilities shift the cost of future care to you. And you may still be at the mercy of Medicaid and face the prospect of spending down your assets so Medicaid will pay your nursing bills (see chapter 12).

COST

Entrance fees are high, and most people entering a facility use the equity in their homes to pay for them. In Type A CCRCs, entrance fees average from about $75,000 for one-bedroom apartments to about $96,000 for two bedrooms. For a larger unit, often a cottage or penthouse, entrance fees average around $120,000. Fees also vary by locality: Facilities in rural areas usually charge less than those in large urban areas. Monthly charges, too, vary by the size of the living unit. For one-bedroom apartments, the average monthly fee is $1,144; for two-bedroom units, $1,362.

For Type B communities, entrance fees average about $50,800 for one bedroom to $76,200 for two. The average monthly fees are $948 and $1,162 respectively.

Type C communities usually have lower fees and offer fewer services; entrance charges average about $42,000 for one-bedroom apartments and about $62,000 for two-bedroom units. Monthly fees go from about $766 for one bedroom to $864 for two bedrooms.

Couples almost always pay more than single people. Older residents usually pay the same entrance and monthly fees as younger ones, even though they have shorter life expectancies and will have less time to use the facilities. On the other hand, older people are more likely to need the expensive nursing care, which communities say justifies charging the same price. Nevertheless, older residents who enter a CCRC and then leave or die before needing nursing care get less for their money. In that sense, going into a CCRC is a financial gamble. A few communities do recognize that younger residents will need services longer and so charge them more. It is rare, however, that people in their late fifties and sixties move into a CCRC. The median age of someone moving in is 78; the average age of all residents is 82.

Once you're in a CCRC, the facility can't retroactively

raise the entrance fee, although it may charge a higher entrance fee to newcomers. But monthly fees can and do increase as the cost of providing services increases. Fee increases of between 4 and 6 percent have been typical per year. Sometimes the frequency and the basis for the increases are spelled out in the contracts. Often they are not. In terms of equity, your entrance fee buys security rather than real estate, and in most facilities you don't have an equity interest in your living unit. When you die or leave, the community reclaims the apartment. Whether you or your estate get back any portion of the entrance fee depends on whether your facility has made its fees refundable.

Refundable Fees

Historically, CCRC entrance fees were not refundable. If you paid a substantial sum to enter one, and died two days after moving in, your heirs would be out of luck. But to gain a marketing edge, many communities now make their fees refundable, or at least offer a choice between an entrance fee that is refundable and one that is not.

Refundable fees appeal mainly to those who want to leave an estate. Nonrefundable plans appeal to those who have no heirs and prefer to pay a fee that may be as much as 40 to 50 percent lower. To refund fees and still cover the cost of promised services, communities necessarily must make refundable fees higher. Sometimes the fees are as much as 65 percent higher. (Thus facilities with refundable fees may attract wealthier residents.) But communities rarely refund 100 percent of the fee. You might receive 100 percent if you leave in the first year, but only 90 percent or even 80 percent if you leave after that. Or it could be the other way around. You get 80 percent back the first year, 90 percent the next year, and 100 percent the third year. Typically, though, the amount of the refund will decline by 1 or 2 percent a month, so that after a number of years, you are entitled to no refund at all.

Some communities refund entrance fees only if you die; others only if you leave. Still others return your money in either case. Most communities attach an additional string. They refund your money only after your unit is reoccupied, using the entrance fee paid by the new resident to reimburse you.

CCRC LOOK-ALIKES

The definition of a CCRC is blurring as more and more retirement communities offer a "continuum of care" but *not* continuing care. This subtle distinction has enormous financial consequences.

CCRC look-alikes, which outnumber all Types A, B, and C combined, offer the same services and amenities. Indeed, there may even be a nursing wing or an assisted-living unit down the hall from the residents' apartments. But the financial arrangements are very different from the traditional continuing-care community.

Look-alikes rent their apartments on a monthly basis. You often have neither the burden of an entrance fee nor the protection of a contract or lease. If you need nursing care, you pay the going daily rate—that is, if you can get into the nursing wing. Many communities rent their nursing beds to people who live outside the CCRC. Residents are not assured of a bed in the nursing center, only a priority spot on the waiting list. If the beds are full when you need care, you have to go somewhere else. Other services, including meals, also cost extra.

The number of look-alikes is growing rapidly. Even some traditional communities that have gotten into financial trouble have converted to simpler continuum-of-care arrangements without entrance fees.

Without the protection of a lease, skyrocketing fees could force you to leave if you can't afford the increases. At one facility, monthly fees rose from $950 to $1,500 in four years. In the long run, you may pay more at a CCRC look-alike than at a community charging an entrance fee, especially if you need extended nursing care.

PROFIT OR NONPROFIT?

The continuing-care industry has traditionally been nonprofit, since most communities sprouted from religious and fraternal organizations. The industry is still overwhelmingly not-for-profit, but in recent years, for-profit corporations, notably hotel chains, have begun to supply housing for the elderly. You can find both profit and nonprofit arrangements among all types of CCRCs, including the look-alikes.

Nonprofit sponsors of CCRCs, who believe they have a spiritual mission to care for the elderly, don't like for-profit businesses invading their territory and question whether for-profit organizations always have the residents' best interests at heart. However, there's no evidence that for-profit companies have deceived or harmed residents of continuing-care communities, and the nonprofits have had their share of problems. Nevertheless, many residents feel more comfortable with the nonprofit label, which many CCRCs exploit. Some communities, however, are not as nonprofit as they first appear. They may have a nonprofit board of directors, but the community is managed by a for-profit management company hired by the board. It's not always clear whether the board and the management firm are at arm's length. If they aren't, it's possible you will face increased costs or reduced services that wouldn't otherwise occur.

COMMUNITIES IN TROUBLE

Nobody knows how many CCRCs are in financial trouble. If they are having financial difficulties, low occupancy rate is usually the reason. Low occupancy means fewer fees and less money for services. It's a problem that plagues both old and new communities.

If an old community doesn't have adequate reserves to spruce up its aging facilities, it can quickly find itself at a disadvantage when it tries to attract new residents to replace those who leave or die. As with any real estate development, if the location of a new community is wrong, or if the buildings are unattractive, it can fail to attract interested prospective residents. If a community is undercapitalized, too small, fails to project future costs accurately, or fails to project correctly the sources of future dollars to pay those costs, its residents may find that the security they were buying has suddenly evaporated.

How do you know whether a CCRC you're considering is in financial difficulty? It's not easy to find out. You may have to dig deeply to get the necessary information.

The industry's trade association, the American Association of Homes for the Aging, says that buyers are entitled to specific information about each community. Soon there may be laws in many states that require a community to give such information to prospective buyers as well as to current residents. Before investing your money, find out what your state requires a CCRC to give you.

Partly in response to prospective state regulations and partly to elevate the quality of the communities, the industry has formed a commission to accredit CCRCs that meet certain minimum standards in the areas of finance, governance, resident life, and health care. Communities applying for accreditation conduct a self-examination of their operations and open their books and facilities to a three-day inspection by an industry team. So far, some 111 communities in 21 states have won the stamp of approval.

Between 5 and 10 percent of those applying for accreditation are found unfit, mostly because of too many liabilities and too few reserves to cover their health-care commitments. Some communities are "conditionally accredited"; that is, they have a few deficiencies, such as a poorly written contract or no long-range plan. However, the names of these communities are not made public by the commission.

Do not depend on a CCRC salesperson to give you accurate information about accreditation. Nevertheless, accreditation may be a helpful guide to a community's financial picture. Be sure to ask for some official document to prove that the CCRC you're considering is indeed accredited by the Continuing Care Accreditation Commission. (Don't confuse this kind of accreditation with approvals given to a community by a state health department.)

To obtain a list of accredited communities, send a self-addressed, stamped envelope to the Continuing Care Accreditation Commission, 901 E Street, N.W., Suite 500, Washington, DC 20004.

IS A CCRC FOR YOU?

A CCRC is usually your last residence, and moving into one often means exhausting most, if not all, of your remaining assets. Selecting a community requires careful planning and shopping to protect the security you're buying. If you wait until the need for continuing care suddenly appears, you may hastily choose the wrong community or may not even be able to get into the one of your choice. The better CCRCs have long waiting lists, and the larger the unit, the longer the wait. For example, at many CCRCs there is often a one- to five-year wait for a two-bedroom apartment. All communities have entrance requirements relating to your health and ability to pay. Communities require physical examinations, performed either by your own doctor or one selected by the community. Some require a psychiatric exam as well. CCRCs also scrutinize your finances. As a general rule, you must have a monthly income that's twice the monthly fee. This requirement is intended to assure the CCRC that you can afford the inevitable fee increases.

If you wait until you need long-term care, your health has probably deteriorated to the point where a community will not accept you. Few communities accept people who are already debilitated by a stroke or Alzheimer's disease and are certain candidates for nursing care. That doesn't mean if you need a wheelchair or a walker to get around, you shouldn't apply. So long as you can care for yourself, most communities will consider you. The community may, however, make you pay extra for nursing care arising from certain health conditions you have when you enter.

If you do qualify for a CCRC, then ask yourself some basic questions.

1. Will you be happy living in a community? Administrators say that people who have worked in large, institutional

settings adjust to communal living better than those who have worked and lived alone. Make sure the community has the amenities and services you're looking for. You may want to spend a few nights as a guest to see how residents interact and if the daily routines appeal to you.

2. How much prepaid health care do you want to buy? If you like the security of knowing that any long-term care is paid for, and you can afford it, go first-class at a Type A community, bearing in mind that you pay much larger entrance and monthly fees.

If you are a risk taker and think you'll never need nursing care, a community that prefunds little or no care through an entrance fee may be a good choice. A facility without an entrance fee may be attractive initially but could cost you dearly later. If you do need care, you may end up paying more than you would have at a community with an entrance fee.

3. If you choose a CCRC with an entrance fee, do you want it to be refundable or nonrefundable? If your assets are limited, or you don't care about leaving an estate, consider communities with nonrefundable fees, since they are likely to be much lower. If money is no object, or you want to leave money to your children, explore communities with refundable fees. (This decision is similar to one you might have to make about an annuity payment.)

Both refundable and nonrefundable fees have income tax implications. Some fees, usually those at Type A facilities, are considered below-market loans to the CCRC and are subject to a tax on the imputed interest. (The IRS assumes that a resident receives something of value instead of interest on the "loan," and therefore "imputes" interest income to the lender.) CCRCs should warn you of this and advise you to consult a tax adviser. On the other hand, a substantial portion of nonrefundable entrance fees is tax deductible as a prepayment for future health care. A portion of the monthly fee is similarly deductible. Consider this in determining your tax bill in retirement (see chapter 6).

4. Once you make the basic decision, look carefully at the finances of each community you're considering, then evaluate whether each is a good financial investment.

Evaluating a CCRC

On your first visit, obtain a copy of the contract and study it thoroughly. It spells out the rights residents have and the conditions under which they receive nursing care (see contract checklist that follows). If a community doesn't include the contract in its information packet, insist on seeing it. You may need a lawyer's assistance to review the contract properly.

Obtain *complete* audited financial statements. These may be in the community's *disclosure statement*, a thick document available for inspection at the facility. If a community does not have audited statements, or if it refuses to give you financial information, look for another community. It's important to obtain financial information even from communities that don't charge entrance fees. A shaky community may have to raise its monthly fees to the point where you can't afford them, and if the community offers no lease, you might have to find another place to live at a time when you are least able to do so.

Once you get the statements, look at the auditor's notes or have your accountant review them. They often reveal important information about a community's financial health. For example, the notes may disclose how the community treats entrance fees on its income statement. Fees should be amortized over the resident's lifetime, and only a portion recognized as income in any year. If the entire fee is counted as income the year it's received, the community may project an overly rosy financial picture.

Look at the community's debt. A CCRC with heavy debt, few assets, and little income to cover it may be headed for trouble. Also look at the *current ratio*, a measure of the facility's current assets and current liabilities. A CCRC with plenty of assets in the form of buildings and equipment might nevertheless not have enough cash on hand to pay everyday expenses.

For nonprofit CCRCs, look at the fund balance. Most nonprofit facilities try to achieve a fund balance close to zero. A negative balance is not necessarily bad, but if the community is running substantially negative balances year after year, ask why.

Ask for a history of fee increases. Most communities raise fees yearly, in line with the cost of living. A community that has not raised its fees in several years could have an inadequate cash flow rather than a benevolent management. It may have inadequate cash to pay its bills.

Find out the occupancy rate. For most facilities, the break-even rate is around 90 percent. If a community's rate is lower than that after several years of operation, the community may be in trouble.

Ask whether the community has conducted actuarial studies and found out whether it has adequate reserves for paying future health-care costs and refurbishing the facility. A community that has conducted such a study has at least thought about how it will fund future costs. You might have trouble getting this information. Persevere, or look elsewhere.

Learn who the sponsors and managers are and their experience with CCRCs. Understand the financial structure of the community and know something about the financial entity whose name appears on your contract.

CONTRACT CHECKLIST

When shopping for a continuing-care community, it's critical to review the contract. If you don't have a contract in hand you may be misled by the claims of the facility's sales personnel. Once you obtain a contract, have a lawyer look it over, paying attention to the following provisions:

Refunds. Are entrance fees refundable? If so, under what conditions? The contract should be clear on the issue.

Transfer decisions. Contracts should spell out what triggers the transfer of a resident from his or her apartment to the nursing center or assisted-living unit. Many contracts say the community alone makes the decision to transfer. Others require consultation with the resident, his or her physician, and the resident's family. What right of appeal do you have if you don't agree with the community's decision?

Availability of nursing beds. What responsibility does the community have to provide nursing care? Contracts should state what your rights are if no beds are available in the nursing center when you need one. Does it guarantee that any off-site care will be comparable in quality?

Fees if you are transferred to a nursing center. Residents in Type A communities who transfer permanently to the nursing center usually pay a monthly fee equal to that for the smallest one-bedroom apartment. In Type B and C communities, residents who go to the nursing center typically pay the normal daily rate for nursing care after any days of prepaid care are used up. (These rates generally range from $50 to $100 a day, depending on the locality.)

Fees if spouse is transferred to nursing center. In many Type A communities, if one spouse is in the nursing center temporarily (some facilities use 60 days as the cutoff), the spouse remaining in the apartment continues to pay the regular monthly fee. The spouse in the nursing center pays only for two extra meals. If he or she needs permanent nursing care, the monthly charge then becomes the fee for the smallest one-bedroom apartment. The spouse still living independently continues to pay the regular monthly fee for the apartment. In Type B and C communities, spouses transferred to the nursing center pay the normal daily charges after any days of prepaid care are exhausted.

Fee increases. The contract should specify how the community raises or lowers the monthly fee. Many contracts give communities the right to raise (or lower) fees if the cost of operations increases (or decreases). It should also say how much notice will be given to residents and specify the frequency of increases. It should also explain any caps on the amount of those increases.

To maintain their tax-exempt status, nonprofit continuing-care communities can't evict you if you run out of money. In fact, most contracts say that communities won't evict residents so long as the community's finances are not jeopardized. Some CCRCs have special funds to subsidize residents who fall on hard times.

Rights upon remarriage. What are your rights if you remarry? Can your new spouse live in the community? This is an important issue often overlooked in contracts.

Some communities stipulate that a new spouse who is not a resident must meet the community's entrance requirements and pay an entrance fee equal to the fee for a studio apartment at the time you moved in. The couple must also pay the monthly fees for a couple. (If the new spouse fails to meet the entrance requirements, you are free to move out.) Other communities have a more reasonable approach. If new spouses don't meet the entrance requirements, they can remain in the community as nonresidents and even receive care in the nursing center *if* they pay for it themselves.

Grounds for contract termination. Generally, communities can ask you to leave if you are (1) disruptive or (2) if you lied about your health or finances on the application. For your part, you can cancel during a probationary period of residency, usually 7 to 90 days, and the community refunds almost all the entrance fee, even if the entrance fee is normally not refundable. If, however, you die during the probationary period, some communities refund nothing.

Requirements for health insurance. Many communities require you to carry a Medicare-supplement policy in addition to Parts A and B of Medicare. Some even specify the amount of coverage. That requirement, often written into the contract, ensures that the CCRC doesn't have to pay for your acute illnesses.

Some communities, mostly Types B and C, also require you to carry long-term-care insurance. Since these facilities don't fund in advance much, if any, nursing care, the policies help pay for residents' care. Be wary of any Type A facility that makes you buy a long-term-care policy. Since you are already prefunding nursing care through the entrance fees, it makes no sense to pay for it twice.

Some facilities that require long-term-care policies want you to buy the one they have preselected. Others may require you to buy but don't specify the policy. In cases where you have a choice, shop carefully just as you would if you were not going to live in a CCRC (see chapter 11).

PART FOUR

Estate Planning

17

Transferring Your Estate

Estate planning is an integral part of retirement preparation. It involves gathering information about your assets, providing for your family's financial needs, making sure the right people benefit from your estate, and appointing the appropriate executors, trustees, and guardians to carry out your wishes.

Estate planning can include writing a will, giving away assets while you're alive, setting up a trust for someone to manage your money, and minimizing taxes. (Most estates do not have to pay federal estate taxes, but they may be subject to state death taxes and both state and federal income taxes. Good planning can minimize the bite.)

You almost always need the help of a lawyer if either your family situation or your financial circumstances are complicated. For example, a lawyer is essential if you've been married more than once, have children from all your marriages, own an interest in a closely held corporation or partnership, own investment real estate, or have significant assets in more than one state. Furthermore, if you expect the value of your qualified pension or profit-sharing plan to exceed $100,000, see an accountant or tax adviser before choosing payout provisions (see chapter 3).

SETTING UP AN ESTATE PLAN

Estate planning should focus on the following:

The Right Beneficiaries

Provide for the most important beneficiaries first—usually your spouse and children—before leaving any property to others.

The Right Plan

Don't hesitate to use trusts or other tax-saving arrangements just because they are complex. You may, for example, want to establish a trust for a child you believe will squander the family fortune. At the same time, don't make your affairs unnecessarily complicated. If a trust isn't really necessary, it's foolish to spend money setting one up.

Competent Management

Pick one or more executors (and trustees, if necessary) who can manage your estate effectively and who are acquainted with your family's needs. Competent trustees are especially important if your heirs include minor children or grandchildren who are inexperienced in handling money.

Liquidity

After you figure the taxes and administrative expenses that will be charged to your estate, make sure that there are enough liquid assets to pay them. If a large part of your estate consists of a family business or investment real estate, there may be insufficient cash to cover these expenses. If you're short, one option is to buy more life insurance. With sufficient coverage, your heirs may be able to keep the family business. Other ways to find cash include drawing up a shareholders' or partners' agreement during your lifetime or a corporate stock redemption plan to tap the cash in the corporation after your death. You need professional help for both options.

Special Situations

If your estate includes a closely held business or investment real estate, proper management is essential. A second marriage also requires careful planning, especially if children from a first marriage are to receive part of your estate.

WHAT ESTATE PLANNING COSTS

The cost of planning your estate and drawing up a will varies, depending on the complexity of your situation, where you live, and your lawyer's customary fee. Some lawyers regard wills as loss leaders and charge a small fee in the hope of someday handling your estate. If a lawyer insists on being named executor of your estate, a seemingly cheap will could turn out to be very expensive. Furthermore, you may not want your lawyer as the executor of your estate. He or she may have personal interests that conflict with your interests or those of your beneficiaries.

Some lawyers charge a flat fee—$250 for a simple will, $500 for a will with trusts. Others charge an hourly rate. A simple will may cost less than $100 in a small town, $500 or more in a large city. If you want to create trusts for your spouse and children, the cost may exceed $1,000.

If you don't have a lawyer, ask friends for references. If that doesn't work, contact your local bar association; most have referral services. When you find a lawyer, ask what his or her charges are. If the lawyer can't give a precise figure, find out the basis for the fee and how long it will take to draw up your plan.

MAKING A WILL

Some of your property automatically passes to others whether or not you write a will. For example, joint accounts with right of survivorship pass to the surviving joint owner, and "in trust for" bank accounts go to the named beneficiary (see chapter 7). The proceeds from life insurance policies, pension and profit-sharing plans, and IRAs also go to the person you name as beneficiary.

None of these devices alone may be sufficient to dispose of your estate. Even if you have put all your investments into joint accounts, you still must decide who gets your furniture and other personal property. If the person who is joint owner of your accounts (usually your spouse) dies before you do, you definitely need a will to establish who inherits your accounts.

Everyone should have a will that legally establishes who is to receive what part of his or her estate and who will manage it after death. If you don't have a will when you die, you are said to die *intestate,* and your property passes according to the intestacy laws of your state. These laws are rigid, and you run the risk of having your estate disposed of in a way you do not approve.

If you are survived by both a spouse and children, all usually share your estate under most state intestacy laws. In some states the division is equal; in others, children receive larger shares than surviving spouses. If you have no spouse, your children generally inherit the entire estate. If your children are under 18, the court appoints a guardian to manage their inheritance until they turn 18. At that time, they have control over all your property. The court also appoints a guardian to supervise the daily activities of minor children.

If you have no spouse or children, your estate usually passes to any surviving relatives. However, distant relatives may not receive a thing. If the only person who survives is your second cousin, your estate could *escheat* to the state, meaning the state gets whatever property you leave.

Intestacy laws typically grant the right to become administrators or personal representatives to those who inherit. Administrators control the estate. If your assets pass to a group of heirs, such as your children or your brothers and sisters, they can all administer your estate. Obviously, this can lead to trouble. If the heirs can't agree, or if the estate involves conflicts that can't be resolved amicably, the court appoints someone else to manage your estate.

There are other reasons not to rely on intestacy laws. These laws create an "average" estate plan that may or may not fit your needs. Even if you are pleased with the state-mandated plan where you live now, you might move after you retire to a state whose intestacy laws are unsatisfactory.

For example, your assets may pass to some relative who doesn't need the money. Your children may receive more than your spouse, or they may inherit your money outright when they might be better served by a trust. Your parents may inherit your assets, which could be depleted paying for their nursing home expenses. Or your aged parents could end up as guardians for minor children.

Nor do intestacy laws recognize common-law marriages, nonmarital relationships, or other nontraditional arrangements. Unless each partner in such an arrangement has a will, the survivor usually cannot inherit the estate of the first to die.

When you write a will, you decide who gets your assets and who manages them. The first step is to figure out what assets you have and how liquid they are.

Use Worksheet 9, Taking Stock of Your Assets and Liabilities, in Appendix A to determine the current value of your assets, project what your assets and liabilities are likely to be when you die, and estimate the remainder after all bills and taxes are paid. You can give this worksheet to your attorney or tax adviser to use as a starting point in devising your estate plan.

If the calculation shows that your spouse will need most or all of your assets to live on, then you probably want to leave those assets to him or her. If there's more than enough for your spouse, then consider leaving money to your children, friends, or favorite charities.

If the worksheet reveals that your assets are substantial and that you can amply provide for your spouse and children, your next step is to consider how your estate can save on taxes.

PROBATE AND NONPROBATE ASSETS

After completing Worksheet 9, make a list of your probate and nonprobate assets on Worksheet 10, List of Probate and Nonprobate Assets, in Appendix A. (Probate is the process by which a court validates your will and makes sure that your wishes are carried out.) *Probate* assets are those that pass to your heirs under the terms of your will. *Nonprobate* assets pass directly to a named beneficiary. For example, if most of your property is in joint accounts and you don't want the joint tenant to retain ownership of the property, change the ownership of those assets. (Even though nonprobate assets don't pass under the terms of your will, they may become part of your estate for purposes of calculating estate taxes.)

Nonprobate assets include:

Joint accounts with right of survivorship. Your residence, bank accounts, stocks, and mutual funds automatically pass to the surviving joint tenant. They are not controlled by your will, although when the survivor dies, the asset may be covered by his or her will.

Half the value of assets owned jointly with your spouse is included in your estate for calculating federal estate taxes. Whether these assets are counted in figuring state death taxes depends on your state's law. If you own property with someone other than your spouse, for example your child, the entire value is taxable in your estate, unless your child can prove how much he or she paid for the asset.

Life insurance. Life insurance proceeds can be nonprobate property or they can pass under your will. As explained in chapter 18, they can also be included as part of a trust. If you name a beneficiary when you take out the policy, the proceeds go to that person when you die. For life insurance to pass under your will, you must designate your estate as the beneficiary.

When it comes to figuring federal taxes, life insurance is considered part of your estate *if* you retain the right to change beneficiaries or borrow against the cash value. To keep life insurance out of your estate, you must make an irrevocable transfer of ownership and control of the policy more than three years before you die. (The owner has the right to decide who gets benefits. The owner and the insured—the person on whose life the policy is written—need not be the same.) Making gifts of life insurance to children may be one way to minimize taxes.

Qualified plans. The proceeds from pension and profit-sharing plans, IRAs, 401(k) plans, and SEP arrangements are nonprobate assets that pass to your beneficiary. You can, however, leave these assets to a trust created by your will, or you can name your estate as the beneficiary.

The assets from your qualified plan are subject to estate as well as federal income taxes (with an offset for any estate taxes paid). No taxes are due, however, if the payout qualifies for the "marital deduction" (see page 254). If, on the other hand, you leave your accumulation to someone other than your spouse, your heirs may have to pay both estate and federal income taxes.

In trust for accounts. These accounts, also called Totten Trusts, are not true trusts. The income from the account or "trust" is taxable to you during your lifetime. When you die, the account becomes part of your taxable estate, and the beneficiary becomes the new owner of the account. The beneficiary has no tax liability or ownership rights so long as you are alive, since you have the power to take back the account at any time.

SELECTING A TRUSTEE OR EXECUTOR

Every estate has an executor or personal representative who is responsible for managing the assets, paying the estate's bills including taxes, and making distributions. Sometimes the executor hires a lawyer or accountant to help with these tasks. The estate pays the fees.

When you establish a trust, you name a trustee to manage the trust's assets. The trustee invests the assets and pays out income and principal according to the terms of the trust.

If you have minor children, you also need to name a guardian for them. You can select one person to care for the child and another to manage the child's money; one person may not be suitable for both tasks.

ESTATE TAXES

Your estate may be subject to six different taxes.

Federal Estate Taxes

This tax is figured on your entire estate. The top rate is 55 percent on estates greater than $3 million. Estates under $600,000 are exempt from federal estate taxes.

State Death Taxes

States usually impose one of three kinds of death taxes: estate taxes that work like the federal version, inheritance taxes that are levied against what each heir receives, and credits against federal taxes.

In states with inheritance taxes, the tax on a spouse's share of an estate is likely to be lower than the tax on the portions inherited by other heirs. Some states tax the shares received by all relatives at lower rates than shares received by unrelated beneficiaries.

Most states, however, use a system of credits against federal estate taxes. *Example:* Suppose your estate owes federal taxes of $100,000. The federal government allows a credit against these taxes, which turns out to be $20,000. The state credit is subtracted from the amount of federal tax, and the estate owes $80,000 to the federal government. The state then claims the amount of the credit, or $20,000. If it turns out your estate owes no federal estate taxes, the state doesn't require any either.

Gift Taxes

The federal government and seven states (Delaware, Louisiana, New York, North Carolina, South Carolina, Tennessee, and Wisconsin) tax certain substantial gifts you make during your lifetime.

Generation-Skipping Taxes

The federal government and a few states tax assets that manage to escape estate taxes for at least one generation. A typical example of such a transfer is a trust in which the income is payable to your child for his or her life. When the child dies, the trust is then payable to his or her children.

Transfers of assets made to a grandchild or descendant two or more generations after you are also subject to this tax.

Income Taxes

The federal government and the states treat estates and trusts as separate taxpayers. After you die, your estate may well be subject to both income taxes.

Pension Plan Excise Taxes

The federal government imposes a 15 percent excise tax on taxpayers and estates that receive large distributions from qualified pension plans. Unless you are expecting a very large distribution each year (exceeding $125,000), you don't have to worry about this tax.

CREDITS AND DEDUCTIONS

Some of these taxes bite into many estates. But the government has provided credits and deductions that minimize the pain.

Unified Tax Credit

This credit exempts from federal estate taxes the first $600,000 of any estate. Most families don't have estates this large. But if you own a house and received a generous pension, a $600,000 estate is quite possible.

The same credit applies to gift taxes. During your lifetime, you can make gifts up to $600,000 and escape taxes on the money you give away. However, if you use most of your credit on gifts, less applies to your estate at death.

The Unlimited Marital Deduction

This deduction allows you to give any amount to a spouse when you are alive or when you die and pay no taxes on the amount given. You can give your spouse $100 or $1 million either outright or as part of a qualified trust, and the gift is exempt from federal estate taxes. (Some states also allow a similar exemption.) If you leave all your property to your spouse, the deduction means that no estate taxes are due.

If your spouse is not a U.S. citizen, you are eligible for the $600,000 unified credit, but usually you cannot exempt further assets from taxation (unless you use a Q-DOT—see chapter 18). In other words, the unlimited marital deduction generally doesn't apply.

Annual Gift-Tax Exclusion

This provision lets you give up to $10,000 a year to children, relatives, and friends. Married couples can give up to $20,000 by splitting their gifts. If your gift exceeds the amount of the exclusion, the unified credit comes into play—the value of your gift is charged against the credit. Of course, that reduces the credit available to offset estate taxes, as we have noted.

In states that impose gift taxes, taxpayers can also make use of a gift tax exclusion.

PLANNING FOR TAX SAVINGS

The marital deduction lets you defer estate taxes if you leave everything to your spouse. When the spouse dies, his or her estate is taxed. There are ways, however, to minimize those estate taxes.

Begin using the $600,000 unified credit during your lifetime. The federal government doesn't care whether you use the $600,000 tax exemption during your lifetime or at death. Removing assets from your estate while you are alive and allowing them to escape estate taxes makes sense for many people. Any appreciation and income aren't subject to taxes. If both the appreciation and income are considerable, the tax savings can be great as well. Undeveloped land, life insurance, and shares of a family business are examples of assets that can be disposed of during your lifetime at a significant tax savings.

Create a bypass trust to maximize the $600,000 unified credit. Consider a bypass trust to avoid having money left to a spouse being taxed as part of his or her estate. Couples with large estates, generally $1 million or more, find this device useful. *Example:* Your estate is valued at $1.2 million. You can put $600,000 in a bypass trust and leave the balance of the money to your spouse. You can leave the money outright or create a Q-TIP (see chapter 18). The marital deduction allows the estate to escape all estate taxes. When the spouse dies, his or her estate contains only the $600,000 that was not part of the bypass trust. Since the spouse's estate is eligible for the unified tax credit of $600,000, no estate taxes are due.

Without a bypass trust, your estate is still not subject to

taxes, but your spouse's estate will be. Assuming no change in the estate's value, the $1.2 million will be taxable when your spouse dies. However, after deducting the $600,000 unified tax credit, your spouse's estate will owe tax on only $600,000. Federal estate taxes will total nearly $190,000.

To make a bypass trust work, you must have enough assets in your own name to fund the trust. To do that, you may have to split joint accounts or name your trust as the beneficiary of some of your life insurance. You may also have to rearrange your assets if you want the bypass trust to come into play no matter whether you or your spouse dies first. The spouse with the larger estate can take advantage of the unlimited lifetime marital deduction to shift assets to the other spouse so he or she has at least $600,000 in his or her own name.

Make the most of the gift-tax exclusion. As mentioned, you can give away $10,000 each year. (Married couples can give away $20,000.) A couple with two married children who each have two children of their own can make eight potential gifts each year, amounting to a total of $160,000. (Each can make four gifts: two to the children and two to the grandchildren.) Obviously not everyone is in a position to give away $160,000 annually, but if you can afford to give away some of your money and won't need it for living expenses, gifts to family are one way to keep your money from the IRS.

But don't be pressured into giving away so much that you are left to depend on others. Many overly generous parents have given most of their assets to their children only to find they later need that money.

SPECIAL GIFTS

Life Insurance

You can give away life insurance, keep it out of your estate, and incur no estate tax and little or no gift tax. The real value of life insurance manifests itself after your death. Before

Congress allowed the unlimited marital deduction, one spouse usually transferred ownership of a policy to the other to cut estate taxes. Since the marital deduction makes that unnecessary, the usual recipients of life insurance gifts are now children or irrevocable insurance trusts.

Think long and hard, however, before relinquishing the ownership of a policy. If you retain ownership, you can borrow against the policy and change the beneficiary. You lose these rights when you transfer ownership. If you transfer and later change your mind, you might be able to persuade a family member to return the policy. But if you give the policy to an insurance trust, the trustee may not have the power to return it or to change the terms of the trust. (As we note in chapter 18, any trust you have the power to change or revoke does not eliminate estate taxes.)

Example: You have assets in your name of $1.5 million, including $300,000 of whole life insurance and joint property totaling $250,000. Your spouse has no other assets. When you die, you leave the entire estate outright except for $600,000 placed in a bypass trust. There are no estate taxes at your death, since the unlimited marital deduction comes into play.

When your spouse dies, however, his or her estate is valued at $900,000 ($1.5 million minus the $600,000 in the nontaxable bypass trust) and is subject to taxes of about $115,000.

If your spouse won't need the income from the life insurance policy, you could transfer ownership of the insurance to your children, thus removing $300,000 from both your estate and your spouse's. Your $1.2 million estate now passes to your spouse. The marital deduction and the $600,000 unified credit protect the money from estate taxes when your spouse dies.

However, if your spouse needs the income from the insurance to live on, you might be better off creating an irrevocable insurance trust, which provides your spouse with necessary income. The trustee has the power to invade the principal in the trust for your spouse's benefit, but the trust is not required to pay estate taxes. When your spouse dies, the trust passes to your children.

Interest in a Family Business

Interests in a family business are well suited for gifts. By making small gifts of stock to your children, for example, you can eliminate future appreciation in stock values from your estate. The same applies to interests in real estate.

The complicated part of making such gifts is valuing the assets. The IRS requires that all assets be valued at *fair market value,* that is, the price a willing buyer would pay a willing seller. When estimating the value of your home or other real estate, use the price you would receive if you sold it, minus the mortgage amount. (You cannot use the original cost.) Special rules govern business real estate and farms, which may be taxed (for estate tax purposes) based on their business or agricultural value rather than their full market value. In valuing a business, the IRS usually looks first at the book value and then at earnings to determine what estate taxes are due.

A few strategies can help reduce taxes. A binding buy-sell agreement can effectively fix the value of your interest for estate tax purposes. It can also protect your family by assuring that they won't be locked into the business as absentee owners and that they will receive the current value of the stock when it's sold.

Your tax adviser may also be able to suggest various methods for reorganizing a family business to freeze the value of the older generation's interest while allocating future growth to younger generations. Recent changes in the tax law, however, have made this goal much harder to reach.

Gifts to Children or Grandchildren

These gifts may save income taxes if the recipients are in lower tax brackets than you are. However, here too, recent changes in tax laws have made any savings harder to come by. Children and parents are very often in the same tax bracket now, and the so-called kiddie tax causes most investment income earned by children under 14 to be taxed at their parents' rates. However, by using trusts and the Uniform Gifts to Minors Act to transfer money to children or grandchildren, you may still be able to lower the tax bill.

If you pay someone's school tuition or medical expenses, those payments don't count against the $10,000 gift-tax exclusion or the $600,000 unified credit. You must, however, pay the school or medical provider directly. This can be a valuable provision as you move into retirement. You may, for example, continue paying for a child or grandchild's education or a relative's medical expenses, in effect giving away more than $10,000 a year.

OTHER PLANNING CONSIDERATIONS

There are many other facets of estate planning to consider as you near retirement. Your lawyer or tax adviser can explain them in detail. Here are a few of these considerations.

Second Families

If you or your spouse have children from previous marriages, you may want to leave part of your estate to them. You can make these provisions in a prenuptial agreement, or through your will. You can, for example, earmark a life insurance policy or other assets for one set of children and leave the balance of your estate to the other.

Rights of a Spouse

In almost every state, a surviving spouse who does not receive at least some benefits from a deceased spouse's estate has the right to elect against the spouse's will to claim a share of the estate. Most states allow people in this predicament to claim up to one-third of the estate. If you are planning to remarry, you might ask your prospective spouse to waive any elective rights through a prenuptial agreement. That way you can preserve your assets for children from a prior marriage. In some states, a spouse's elective share can be left in a trust.

Children and other relatives usually have no elective rights. If you cut children out of your will, they can try to prove your will was invalid, alleging that you were mentally incompetent when you signed it or were pressured by those who do stand to inherit. If children succeed in the legal battle, a court can set aside your will, causing your estate to pass according to the intestacy laws.

Community Property

Arizona, California, Idaho, Louisiana, Nevada, New Mexico, Texas, Washington, and Wisconsin are community property states. That means husbands and wives each own half of their community property, or property that was acquired during marriage. A spouse can own separate property if it was acquired before marriage or by a special agreement.

If a spouse in a community property state dies, only half of the community property is included in his or her estate for tax purposes.

Moving to Another State

Moving to another state can complicate estate planning. You may have to comply with your new state's requirements. A spouse's elective rights may be different, and if you move to a community property state, you have to rearrange your estate plan to suit the different laws. It may also be easier or perhaps harder to file a will for probate if it is prepared and signed in the new state.

Provisions for Charity

Any assets you leave to a qualified charity are free from estate taxes. Before leaving significant gifts—paintings and other art, for example—be sure the charity is willing to accept them. Many museums and charities are very selective about their acquisitions and sometimes refuse a bequest unless it is accompanied by a cash gift for maintenance. If the charity you pick refuses your gift, the court has the power to choose another charity—perhaps one you might not have approved of.

You can also leave a gift to charity through a trust. Here the tax rules are very complex, so consult a lawyer first. Some charities have special arrangements for these types of gifts. These include annuity programs and pooled income funds. The charity may be able to give you guidance.

Federal Estate Tax Audits

The odds of an estate tax audit aren't great. The IRS usually examines only those few returns that raise significant issues of law or fact, such as the valuation of a family business or real estate, deductions for loans to family members, and the taxability of trusts in which you have retained interest or power.

During an audit, an examiner meets with the estate's lawyer or accountant. When valuation is an issue, the IRS calls on appraisers to prepare a report. The estate hires an appraiser too. The tax examiner then evaluates both reports and makes a decision. If the estate and examiner still disagree, the decision can be appealed.

Keeping Your Estate Plan Up-to-Date

Keep your will current. Reviewing it every three to five years is sufficient for most people. But if your financial or family situations are complicated or change, more frequent review is probably necessary. Certain events should automatically trigger a new look at your will. These include: divorce and remarriage; new grandchildren you haven't provided for; an increase or decrease in assets; changes in tax and pension laws; a move to another state; and the death of a trustee or executor.

18

Setting Up a Trust

Sooner or later, we all must consider where we want our money to go after our death. For many people, a simple will is the easiest and most suitable way to dispose of assets. However, for others, a will is not enough. The creation of a trust often offers more protection to both heirs and assets.

There are two major reasons for setting up a trust: managing assets and saving taxes. Although trusts come in many forms, almost all are designed to accomplish either or both purposes.

Long before there were income and estate taxes, trusts were used to preserve family lands for future generations. They are still used to control family fortunes. But you don't need millions to use some kinds of trusts. Trusts can help you provide for children, grandchildren, and other relatives. They can be a central feature of your estate plan. You should recognize, however, that for all their good points, trusts usually involve some expenses and inconvenience. Sometimes you may prefer a cheaper and easier way to safeguard modest amounts of money.

TRUST BASICS

A trust is a legal arrangement under which one person transfers ownership of assets to another person or to a corporation. A trustee then manages the assets for the benefit of yet another individual, who is known as the beneficiary. A trust created during your lifetime is called an *inter vivos* or living trust. A trust that is created under your will is called a *testamentary* trust. A few trusts, called *combination trusts,* have characteristics of both living and testamentary trusts. You set them up while you are alive, but they don't become effective until after your death. (Some types of insurance trusts are combination trusts.)

Trusts can be *revocable,* which means you can change or terminate them, or they can be *irrevocable,* which means you can't.

REVOCABLE TRUSTS

These trusts are used primarily to manage assets. For instance, if you are afraid that someday you will be unable to manage your money, you can set up a revocable trust. With this arrangement, you can name yourself one of the trustees (there must be more than one) and take an active role in managing the trust's assets. If health problems eventually force you to give up your role as trustee, the co-trustee takes over. Sometimes you can write a revocable trust so that you can continue as a trustee, but the power to handle the trust's investments goes to a bank or to another person.

Revocable trusts are useful if you own assets such as residences or a business in several states. If you travel extensively or find it inconvenient to look after property located where you no longer live, a family member or an independent trustee in the area can help manage it for you.

Revocable trusts don't save taxes during your lifetime. If you retain the right to receive income or decide how income or principal should be used, or even retain the right to vote stock in a family business, you have to pay taxes on the income generated by the trust's investments. The IRS still considers you the owner of the assets in the trust. That's the case even if someone else actually receives the income.

A Trust to Avoid Probate

Revocable trusts are a kind of living trust, and living trusts can be distributed after your death without any court proceedings. In other words, they can avoid probate, which can be a major advantage. If the trust is to continue for the benefit of others after your death, the trustee simply continues to administer the trust assets for them. If the trust is to end with your death, the trustee follows the instructions in the trust for making a final distribution.

Transferring an estate through such a trust is generally cheaper and faster than having an estate go through probate. If, for example, the trust is set up for your spouse and children, the trustee can begin paying them income almost immediately. But if your estate is part of a trust created by your will, the distribution may be delayed for months or even years until your estate is settled.

If you own property in another state, putting it into a revocable trust may avoid probate proceedings in both states. *Example:* You own a condominium in Florida and a single-family house in Michigan. Even though you are a legal resident of Florida, your estate will pass through probate in both Florida and Michigan to transfer ownership of your homes. But if you transfer your homes to a revocable trust, your family can skip probate proceedings in both states.

Avoiding probate may save commissions paid to an executor, but the estate could still face substantial bills for legal and accounting fees. And the assets in the trust are subject to federal estate and state death taxes. Assets transferred to a revocable trust are not considered gifts for purposes of the federal gift-tax exclusion. They do, however, qualify for the $600,000 unified tax credit and the unlimited marital deduction (see chapter 17).

Drawbacks of Revocable Trusts

Your assets must be in a suitable form. For example, if you and your spouse own all your property jointly or if your main source of retirement income is pension money that can't be transferred to a trust, a revocable trust may be inappropriate.

If you decide to establish a revocable trust, you may have to transfer a number of bank accounts or securities and set up a system for record keeping. Whenever you purchase a new investment that goes into the trust, you have to register it in the name of the trust. As we have pointed out, in most states you cannot be the sole trustee. But you may not want a co-trustee interfering in your financial affairs.

Creating a revocable trust also can be expensive. You almost certainly have to pay a lawyer to draft the trust. That can cost from a few hundred dollars to several thousand. There may be costs to transfer assets to the trust (real estate recording fees, for example). And you may have to pay the trustee for his or her services. A family member may choose not to charge for serving as a trustee, but a lawyer or a bank usually does. Bear in mind that trustee commissions are likely to be much lower than commissions paid to an executor who administers your estate. It is also a matter of deciding whether you want the money to come out of your pocket now or your heirs' later.

If the trust must file income taxes, consider the extra cost of having someone prepare the returns. To avoid tax problems, coordinate your will with any trust you set up.

Alternatives to Revocable Trusts

A revocable trust is not the only way to provide for someone to manage your financial affairs. As noted in chapter 7, you can give someone a durable power of attorney. However, if you have many types of investments or business and real estate interests, a revocable trust may be more suitable.

You may also allow the court to appoint a guardian, conservator, or committee to manage your affairs (see chapter 7). But, since court proceedings are necessary to appoint a guardian, conservator, or committee, there can be a long delay before any bills are paid, causing a potential hardship for family members. Court proceedings are also costly. The bill, which can include fees for lawyers and medical witnesses, usually exceeds the cost of drafting a trust. If relatives fight to control your financial destiny, costs can mount. So can the delay.

A trust is a cheaper and faster way to deal with the problem of incapacity. When you are no longer able to handle your affairs, your co-trustee can begin immediately to act on your behalf. For example, you could set up the trust in such a way that the co-trustee goes into action if two doctors certify you no longer have the mental capacity to manage the trust. Your co-trustee can then begin to collect your income and pay bills, including those from hospitals and nursing homes.

Setting up a trust before problems arise can also protect you and your family from an unpleasant and expensive battle, which may also draw unwanted publicity about your physical and mental abilities as well as your financial affairs. A trust also allows you to choose the person you want to handle your financial matters. If you appoint a co-trustee, you can see how he or she handles the duties assigned by the trust. If you don't like what the trustee does, you can appoint another or revoke the entire trust.

If you have cause to believe your relatives are trying to have a court declare you incompetent, set up a trust as soon as possible. Have your lawyer draw up a revocable trust, naming you and your lawyer or another independent professional as co-trustees. You retain the right to income for the rest of your life, but the co-trustee can tap the principal for your benefit. After you die, the balance in the trust passes to your family members or to charity. By taking this route, you protect your assets and take care of disposing of your estate without the necessity of probate. You also make it very difficult for any family member to interfere with your wishes.

Will contests are hard to win. It's even tougher to challenge the validity of a living trust successfully.

IRREVOCABLE LIVING TRUSTS

During your lifetime you can create another kind of trust, shift its income to a beneficiary, and remove assets from your estate. If you cannot change the terms of the trust and retain virtually no power over the assets, the trust is *irrevocable.*

Unlike revocable trusts, which are used primarily for management purposes, irrevocable trusts have several other uses. You can use them to manage assets—usually for someone other than yourself. In addition, you can use them to remove property from your estate and reduce your estate tax bill, and to save on income taxes while you are alive. If you want to set up a trust for this purpose, though, you have to shift control of the assets to someone else, and you (and your spouse) give up the right to income from the trust. Many people don't want to do this, and therefore they use irrevocable trusts for reasons other than saving income taxes.

You can set up an irrevocable trust to benefit specific people. For example, you may want to provide for a grandchild's education or a relative's medical needs. A trust allows you to give to beneficiaries, during your lifetime, money they would otherwise receive only after your death. You also can use such a trust to protect your beneficiaries. Suppose you have a child who can't manage money. Creating an irrevocable trust lets you set aside a fund that no one, including the beneficiary or creditors, can touch. Finally, irrevocable trusts can protect your estate from creditors, including your state's Medicaid program. In fact, protecting assets from Medicaid is a primary reason why people set up an irrevocable trust.

Weighing the Pros and Cons

Creating an irrevocable trust is a serious step. Once you set one up, it's hard to undo it. Sometimes the only way to reverse a trust is through a court proceeding, which can be costly and time-consuming. Although you sometimes can break a trust by obtaining the consent of all beneficiaries, this escape hatch won't do much good if you've named minor children, grandchildren born and unborn, or remote descendants as beneficiaries.

Before deciding to set up such a trust, think through your objectives carefully. If you want to save income taxes, are you sure you can live with the loss of control over your assets? Can you do without the income they would generate? If the answers are no, then be sure you have other good reasons for establishing an irrevocable trust. If you create a trust intending primarily to benefit your children, but you still control the income or disposition of principal, you may find yourself in the worst of both worlds: You have relinquished control over your assets but you still must pay income taxes.

Be sure you understand which powers you can retain and which ones you can't. For example, if you are a trustee of a trust you've created, you may still have to pay income taxes. Even if the income is not payable to you, the trust may not be effective in cutting your tax bill. Holding the purse strings on the assets in the trust may subject them to estate taxes as well. If you give away your assets to a trust, the tax law may require you to use your annual gift-tax exclusion and possibly some of the $600,000 unified credit. Decide if this is how you want to use these tax breaks. A lawyer who specializes in trusts can help with these decisions.

Also consider whether you can continue to pay the ongoing expenses of the trust. You not only have to pay a lawyer to draft the trust agreement, but you also need someone to prepare the trust's tax returns. The trust may have other record-keeping expenses as well. Trustees are also entitled to commissions for their services. State law usually determines the amount. In some states, however, a court that supervises the trust's administration sets the fee. A few states, such as New York, let banks that act as trustees charge more for their services than individuals who perform the same chores. Sometimes family members or friends are willing to act as trustees. But remember, you may be giving up competent and expert management to save a few dollars on fees. The loss of such guidance could be more costly in the long run.

Other Considerations

If you and your spouse own property jointly, both of you must create the trust. Depending on how the trust is written, this could mean that the assets in the trust wind up in the estate of the spouse who dies last and are subject to estate taxes—an unintended consequence of a joint trust.

If you own a cooperative or condominium apartment, the cooperative or condominium association may have rules barring ownership by a trust. If you want to transfer mortgaged property, you may have to get permission from the bank or other mortgagee. If you do put mortgaged property into a trust and later want to refinance, you may have a hard time finding a willing lender.

TYPES OF IRREVOCABLE TRUSTS

Medicaid Qualifying Trusts

As we discussed in chapter 12, Medicaid may eventually come to pay for most long-term nursing care, after all your assets are depleted. Some people try to avoid a Medicaid spend-down by putting all their assets in a trust. Doing so is tricky, and you must conform to all the rules or else your trust will not save your assets from a Medicaid spend-down.

Neither you nor the trustee can have any control over the assets in the trust or over the income they generate. If either of you does, then Medicaid counts both the income and assets in determining your eligibility for benefits. If you retain no control, then you have preserved your savings for your heirs. However, setting up a trust in which you cannot tap the income or principal may mean a lower standard of living in retirement.

Let's see how Medicaid looks at different kinds of qualifying trusts.

Suppose you name your child as trustee. You retain the right to all income from the trust's assets but give away all right to the principal. If the income is greater than your state's income limit to qualify for benefits, Medicaid requires you to spend that income for nursing home care. The principal, however, is safe.

Now suppose you retain the right to all income but also keep the ability to draw up to $5,000 each year from the principal. You not only have to spend your income on your care but also spend $5,000 of the principal each year you're confined in a nursing home. Even if you never draw the $5,000, Medicaid still counts it as income that can be used to pay for your care.

As a third example, you could retain the income but give the trustee power to invade the principal for your benefit. In that case, Medicaid counts all the assets in the trust in determining your eligibility. You have to spend all the assets on your care before Medicaid considers paying your bills.

Furthermore, if you decide to transfer your assets to a trust, you must usually do so at least 30 months before applying for Medicaid. If you transfer your assets for less than their fair market value, or if the transfer occurs fewer than 30 months before you apply for Medicaid, you may be temporarily ineligible for Medicaid for a period of up to 30 months, depending on the rules of the state where you live. The time limit also does not apply if you receive care in your home or in a Medicaid-approved facility, such as an adult day-care center that provides medical treatment. Under those circumstances, you can transfer your assets one day and Medicaid begins paying for your care the next.

Obviously, it's difficult, if not impossible, to predict the exact time when you might need nursing home care. Transferring assets to a trust years before you're confined to a nursing home can deprive you of money you need to maintain a comfortable standard of living in retirement.

As you can see, setting up a Medicaid qualifying trust is complicated and has several disadvantages. An alternative is a long-term-care insurance policy that helps defray nursing home expenses. But as noted in chapter 11, these policies, too, have their drawbacks. In short, there is no perfect way to protect your assets from a Medicaid spend-down.

Trusts for Children and Grandchildren

You can set up a college fund for children or grandchildren using an irrevocable trust. The gift-tax exclusion allows you and your spouse to give up to $20,000 each year to the trust and escape gift taxes. By shifting assets to the trust, you also avoid taxes on the income they generate. (Remember, however, to achieve the tax savings you must relinquish control over both income and assets.) Your children or grandchildren, or the trust itself, are responsible for any income taxes that are due. If they are in a lower tax bracket, such a trust has the potential for reducing income taxes. However, be aware that if you set up a trust for grandchildren who are under 14, any income they receive is taxed at their parents' rates. If the grandchild is over 14, and if income from the trust is used for such necessities as food and clothing, the IRS usually considers that it belongs to the child and also taxes it. The IRS has also ruled that income used to pay for a grandchild's college expenses is income to his or her parent—your child—and the parents must pay the taxes.

Grantor-Retained Interest Trust

This trust, which goes by the acronym GRIT, is a sophisticated irrevocable arrangement created solely to save taxes. In setting up a GRIT, you retain the right to receive an annuity or percentage payment from the trust for a specific period of years, usually not more than 10. If you live for the entire time period, your interest in the trust's assets ends, and the assets pass to the named beneficiaries. If you die before the trust term ends, the assets revert to your estate. You may be no worse off when it comes to estate taxes.

Wealthy people use GRITs to save estate taxes, but those with modest amounts of money can also use them. Any tax savings arise because the individual granting the trust is making a gift of the discounted future value of the property put into the trust. When the trust ends, you have not only removed from your estate the amount of money put into the trust but also the increase in its value during the 10 years it exists. The benefits from putting your home into a GRIT are especially great. But get competent legal advice. This is a tricky subject, and the rules change frequently.

Generally these trusts are recommended only for couples with estates larger than $600,000. If the amount put into the trust is too small, administrative expenses and the cost of drawing up the trust outweigh any potential tax savings.

UNIFORM GIFTS TO MINORS

Instead of a formal trust, consider making a gift under the *Uniform Gifts to Minors Act.* This may be a good choice if you have little money to spare and still want to do something for a grandchild. If you have less than $20,000 to give away, a gift made under the act is the way to go.

You can set up a Uniform Gifts to Minors account at a bank or a brokerage firm with any amount of money or securities. Some states allow residents to transfer insurance policies, real estate, or even limited partnership interests to these accounts, and there's no limit to how much you can contribute.

You can give money to a "custodian," who must use it for the child's health, welfare, and education, or you can be the custodian yourself, although it's usually not a good idea. (When you die, the money you put into the account is subject to estate taxes.)

When the child turns 18 (or 21 in some states), the money remaining in the account automatically belongs to the child. Therein lies the major disadvantage of these accounts. A child turns 18 and comes into a large sum of money that he or she may not be ready to handle. If you're worried about this possibility, it's better to put money into a trust where the child has far less discretion over the assets.

The child has to pay taxes on the income from the assets in the account (provided the income exceeds $1,000 each year). Until the child reaches 14, the tax rate is the same as that of the child's parents. Larger income tax savings may be possible with a trust.

TESTAMENTARY TRUSTS

A testamentary trust created under your will is always irrevocable. But while you are alive, you can change the terms of your will whenever you like. After your death, however, no one can change the provisions. Testamentary trusts can save both income and estate taxes and preserve assets for your family. The following testamentary trusts are used for saving taxes:

Credit Shelter or Bypass Trusts

These trusts take advantage of the federal unified estate and gift-tax credit by allowing up to $600,000 of assets left in trust by one spouse for the other to escape estate taxes in the survivor's estate.

Qualified Terminable Interest Property Trust (Q-TIP)

All the income from this type of trust must be paid to a spouse, and the executor of your estate sees that the trust is eligible for the marital deduction, thus exempting it from gift or estate taxes. The assets in a Q-TIP are taxed in the spouse's estate.

Example: Suppose your spouse does not have the experience to manage your finances. So you decide to leave your entire estate to him or her by creating two trusts under your will—a Q-TIP and a bypass trust. You name your spouse and your bank as co-trustees. Your spouse receives all the income from both trusts, and the bank can tap the principal if necessary. The assets in both trusts escape federal estate taxes, thanks to the marital deduction. When your spouse dies, the assets in the bypass trust also escape taxation, but assets in the Q-TIP do not. The remaining assets in both trusts then pass to your children.

You might want to give your spouse the power to dispose of part or all of the assets in the trusts under the terms of his or her will. But this power, technically known as a *power of appointment,* can result in significant estate and income taxes if you're not careful. Discuss this with an attorney before granting such powers.

Qualifying Domestic Trusts (Q-DOT)

If your spouse is not a U.S. citizen, this kind of trust preserves the marital deduction. (The marital deduction isn't otherwise available to spouses who are not citizens.) Without a Q-DOT, the portion of your estate that exceeds the unified credit is subject to federal estate taxes.

A Q-DOT is similar to a Q-TIP. The surviving spouse must receive all the income during his or her lifetime and the executor of your estate must choose to qualify the trust for the marital deduction. Using the trust results in a tax deferral until the surviving spouse receives certain principal payments or dies. Seek legal advice before setting up a Q-DOT.

COMBINATION TRUSTS

Insurance Trusts

You have three choices if you want to set up an insurance trust.

1. You can establish a revocable trust that does not actually own the insurance policy. You name the trust the beneficiary of the policy, and when you die, the trust collects the proceeds. Essentially, the trust is inactive during your lifetime but acts as a receptacle to consolidate your assets after your death. (The trust can collect other assets, too, and help eliminate some of the delay and expense of probate.)
2. You can set up a revocable insurance trust that actually owns the policy. Remember, though, you must transfer ownership of the policy to the trust and give up any rights associated with ownership, such as changing the beneficiary. The trust can buy the policy, but you have to pay the premiums.
3. You can set up an irrevocable living insurance trust

whose primary purpose is to save estate taxes. The trust owns the policy. You can design this kind of trust so that the policy is removed from your own taxable estate and also from the estate of your spouse or other beneficiaries. (But again, to achieve any tax savings you must give up ownership of the policies and control over the trust. You probably can't act as sole trustee, for example.)

Removing assets from an estate has gift-tax implications. To make sure your estate doesn't get stuck for gift taxes, it's usually safest to have the trust buy a new insurance policy. If you use an existing whole life policy with a high cash value, it may also be subject to gift taxes. If you have an old policy that you want to put into the trust, borrow the cash value before putting the policy in the trust, thus eliminating the potential for gift taxes. Remember, however, that any outstanding policy loans reduce the amount of the death benefit available to your heirs. You may also want to pay the insurance premiums out of income from other assets you put into the trust. If you pay the premiums with your own money, they may be considered gifts to the trust and subject to gift taxes. (If your estate is large enough, premiums may also be subject to generation-skipping taxes.) As you can see, a trust must be properly drawn to avoid these problems. If a competent attorney writes the trust agreement, the value of the policies and other assets put in the trust should be out of your estate and pass to beneficiaries free of estate and inheritance taxes.

Uses of Insurance Trusts

Two circumstances might call for an insurance trust. Suppose you are married to your second wife and have two teenage children from your first marriage. Your wife will need most of your estate to live on. You can create an irrevocable insurance trust that owns a policy on your life. When you die, the proceeds from the policy are held in the trust for your children and are free from estate taxes.

Suppose you want to consolidate assets to simplify probate

proceedings. You create a revocable living trust and fund it with cash and securities. You retain ownership of the policy but name the trust as the beneficiary of both the policy and your pension benefits. The person you name as trustee can now manage all your assets and avoid delay at probate. But keep in mind that a revocable trust won't save any taxes.

ADMINISTRATION AND RECORD KEEPING

If you set up a trust, revocable or irrevocable, good record keeping is essential. To achieve savings on taxes and probate costs, the trust must have a separate identity. Comingling trust assets with nontrust property could render the trust ineffective for accomplishing your goals.

WHO SHOULD BE THE TRUSTEE?

You may act as a trustee of a revocable trust or an irrevocable trust in which you retain no interest and control. Depending on your state law, you may be able to act as the sole trustee. If you cannot be the only trustee, you usually can share the trustee's duties with someone else. If you cannot or do not want to be a trustee, here are some possible choices:

- *An adult child or other relative.* Guard against potential conflicts of interest. Someone who stands to benefit from your estate may have different objectives from you.
- *A lawyer, accountant, or other professional.*
- *A bank or trust company.* If you plan to transfer a substantial amount of money to a trust, choosing a bank makes a lot of sense. However, most banks charge a minimum fee, so it's usually not economical to appoint a bank as trustee of a modest trust. Nor is a bank the best choice if you anticipate complications in administering the assets held in trust. Business or real estate

interests can complicate a trust. Some banks also have trouble exercising discretion over a trust with more than one beneficiary. If you decide on a bank, check its investment track record. If the investments it has managed have performed poorly, you may want a different bank or someone else to act as trustee.

Appendixes

APPENDIX A

WORKSHEETS

WORKSHEET 1 *Preretirement Income and Expenses*

Monthly Income		Monthly Expenses	
Wages or self-employment income	______	Housing	______
Interest	______	Utilities	______
Dividends	______	Real estate taxes	______
Rental income	______	Repairs, upkeep	______
Annuity income	______	Food	______
Trust income	______	Clothing	______
Other income	______	Laundry, cleaning	______
		Personal care	______
		Commuting	______
		Entertainment	______
		Vacation, travel	______
		Hobbies, sports	______
		Other travel	______
		Health insurance	______
		Auto insurance	______
		Life insurance	______
		Homeowner's insurance	______
		Newspapers, magazines, books	______
		Education expenses	______
		Contributions	______
		Credit cards, other debts	______
		Income taxes (federal and state)	______
		Savings, investments	______
		Miscellaneous	______
Total monthly income	______	Total monthly expenses	______
× 12		× 12	
Total annual income	______	Total annual expenses	______

WORKSHEET 2 *Your Savings and Investments*

Type of Account	Where Held	Account Number	Amount in Account	Interest Rate or Rate of Return	When Account Matures (If Applicable)	Are Interest Earnings Tax-Exempt?	Are Interest Earnings Tax-Deferred?
Regular checking							
NOW account checking							
Bank money-market deposit account							
Bank savings account							
Certificates of deposit							
6-month							
1-year							
1½-year							
3-year							
5-year							
other							
Credit union savings accounts							

U.S. Treasury bills							
U.S. savings bonds (series EE)							
Money-market mutual fund							
Tax-exempt money-market fund							
Bond mutual funds							
Stock mutual funds							
Other mutual funds							
Cash-value life insurance							
Deferred annuities							
Defined contribution plan vested balance (other than 401[k])							
401(k) plan							
Expected monthly benefit from defined benefit pension plan							
Stocks (list separately)							
Bonds (list separately)							

WORKSHEET 3 *Postretirement Expenses*

Monthly Expenses

Housing	________
Utilities	________
Real estate taxes	________
Repairs, upkeep	________
Food	________
Clothing	________
Laundry, cleaning	________
Personal care	________
Entertainment	________
Vacation, travel	________
Hobbies, sports	________
Other travel	________
Health insurance	________
Auto insurance	________
Life insurance	________
Homeowner's insurance	________
Newspapers, magazines, books	________
Contributions	________
Credit cards, other debts	________
Savings, investments	________
Miscellaneous	________
Total monthly expenses	________
× 12	
Total annual expenses	________

WORKSHEET 4 *Will You Have Enough Money?*

Make extra copies of blank worksheets so you can revise and update them later.

Date worksheet completed: ____________.

A. WHEN WILL YOU RETIRE?

1. Retirement date: ________
2. Years from now: ________

B. NEEDS IN RETIREMENT

1. Estimated total monthly expense (including health-insurance premiums, but excluding income tax payments). Use Worksheets 1 and 3 to help figure these expenses.

Pre-19	19 –19	Post-19
________	________	________

2. Additional one-time expenses on retirement date
   a. Moving ________
   b. Home ________
   c. Other ________
   d. Total: (a) + (b) + (c) = ________

C. RESOURCES

	Pre-19	19 –19	Post-19
1. Monthly Social Security benefit	________	________	________
2. Monthly pensions	________	________	________
3. Monthly employment earnings	________	________	________

4. Other assets to provide retirement income
   a. Sale of home (current market value less selling costs) ________

b. Mortgage balance at date of sale ________

c. (b) × Factor A (pages 290–91) = ________

d. Net value of home: (a) − (c) = ________

e. Other current savings, including employer savings plan ________

f. Projected value of (e): (e) × Factor B (pages 290–91) = ________

g. Future annual savings, including employer and employee contributions to employer savings plan ________

h. Future savings: (g) × Factor C (pages 290–91) = ________

i. Total accumulation: (d) + (f) + (h) = ________

j. Net accumulation: (i) − (B2d) = ________

k. Monthly income from (j): $\frac{1}{12}$ × .04 × (j) = ________

5. Total income after retirement: (1) + (2) + (3) + (4k)

	Pre-19	**19 -19**	**Post-19**
6. Estimated federal and state income tax: .20 × (5) =	________	________	________
7. Net income: (5) − (6)	________	________	________

D. COMPARE RESOURCES AND NEEDS

1. Resources	________	________	________
2. Needs	________	________	________
3. Shortfall or surplus	________	________	________

INSTRUCTIONS AND EXPLANATION FOR WORKSHEET 4

A.1. You may want to consider several possible retirement dates. If so, duplicate the worksheet and complete a set for each retirement date you consider.

A.2. Enter the nearest whole number of years until your retirement date.

B.1. Make up a budget, in today's dollars, of your needs for income in retirement. Use Worksheet 3. Include your costs for health insurance after retirement, but do not include income tax you will pay, since you will deduct income taxes from your income in section C of this worksheet.

Your needs may change during various periods of retirement. Your health-insurance costs certainly will change. In addition, your resources may also change. Social Security can start at age 62, or at a later age with higher benefits. You or your spouse may be eligible for a pension beginning at some date after you retire. Complete a column of the worksheet for each period after retirement when you expect a significant change in either your needs or your resources. You may not need all three columns. If you need more than three columns, duplicate the worksheet and add more.

The years are shown as "19__," but, of course, some of them may be in the next century and should be "20__."

B.2.b. If you plan to purchase a new home when you retire, enter its cost, in today's dollars, including closing costs (estimate 4 percent of the price). Ignore any proceeds from selling your present home; this will be reflected in section C.

C.1. You and your spouse should each ask the Social Security Administration for an estimate of your benefits.

Alternatively, you can make a rough estimate of your benefit. If your 1991 salary was $51,300 or higher, your estimated monthly benefit beginning at age 65 will be $1,023. If your 1991 salary was less than $51,300, estimate your benefit at age 65 as $380 plus 1.25 percent of your 1991 annual salary. In either case, if you plan to have your benefit begin before age 65, subtract 7 percent for each year you take a benefit before age 65, or subtract 20 percent if your benefit will start at age 62. If you were covered under Social Security for fewer than 35 years, your benefit will also be reduced. Your spouse will receive a benefit based on his or her own earnings record or a benefit that equals 50 percent of yours, whichever is higher.

C.2. You or your spouse may be entitled to a deferred vested pension from a prior employer. In addition, you may each be entitled to a pension from your present employer. Ask your personnel department for an estimate of what your pension will be if you retire or terminate employment on your expected retirement date. Ask them to estimate your pension both as a single-life annuity and as a 100 percent joint-and-survivor annuity (if that option is provided).

C.3. If either you or your spouse plans to work part-time or full-time after the retirement date shown in A.1., enter the estimated monthly earnings.

C.4.a. If you plan to sell your present home when you retire, enter the present market value, less any costs to fix up the house before sale, broker's fees (8 percent in some areas), legal and other fees, and taxes (estimate 2 percent). Typically, you will realize approximately 90 percent of the proceeds. You should also deduct any tax on the profit (net proceeds less your cost, except that there is no tax on profits you reinvest in a new home within two years of the sale of your old home). If you are at least age 55 (or if either you or your spouse is at least age 55 and you are joint owners), and if you have lived in your house at least three of the five years prior to the sale, the first $125,000 of the gain is not taxable. If you have to pay a tax on the gain, estimate the combined federal and state income tax as 35 percent of the gain.

C.4.b. If you plan to sell your present home when you retire, enter the estimated balance of your mortgage at that time, if any. You may have a schedule showing your mortgage balance at various dates. If not, you can ask the bank that holds your mortgage, or you can estimate the balance by subtracting from your present mortgage balance the product of the number of years until your retirement date (item A.2.) times the amount your mortgage balance decreased last year.

C.4.c. Multiply the amount (if any) on line C.4.b. by Factor A (pages 290–91) for your number of years to retirement. This adjusts your expected mortgage balance to today's dollars to take account of expected 5 percent future inflation.

C.4.e. Include here the balance that you and your spouse now have in any employer profit-sharing plan, savings plan, thrift plan, 401(k) plan, and ESOP or similar program, as well as IRAs, savings accounts, and other investments.

C.4.f. Multiply the amount on line C.4.e. by Factor B (pages 290–91) for your number of years to retirement. This adjusts your present savings to reflect expected investment income between now and your retirement date in excess of the rate of inflation. It adds only 4 percent per year because it assumes that you can earn 4 percent more than inflation (9 percent if inflation is 5 percent).

C.4.g. Enter the amount that you and your employer will add to your savings each year between now and your retirement, through employer programs and your individual savings.

C.4.h. Multiply the amount on line C.4.g. by Factor C (pages 290–91) for your number of years to retirement. This accumulates your future savings to reflect expected investment income between now and your retirement date in excess of the rate of inflation. It adds only 4 percent per year, as noted above.

C.4.j. Subtract your additional one-time needs at retirement (B.2.d.) from your total accumulation at retirement (C.4.i.) to arrive at your net accumulation.

C.4.k. If you want your accumulated savings to provide a flow of income that will keep up with inflation, you should draw only 4 percent the first year. To determine your monthly income from your accumulated savings, determine 1/12 of 4 percent of C.4.j.

C.5. Add C.4.k. to the amounts of C.1., C.2., and C.3. in each column.

C.6. If you are a tax expert or can get the assistance of one, you can estimate your federal and state income tax on the taxable portion of the amount shown on C.5. plus the taxable portion of the annual amounts you expect to withdraw from tax-deferred savings plans. For a rough estimate, assume that your taxes will be 20 percent of the amount on C.5.

C.7. This is the estimated amount, in today's dollars, that you will have available to spend after retirement.

D. Is B.1. larger than C.7.? For many people it will be. If B.1. is larger than C.7., go back and see what you can change. Some of the items you can change may be your retirement date, your monthly budget, your plans for selling your home or buying a new one, your preretirement savings plan, and your plans for possible part-time work after retirement. If you have more than enough money for one period but not enough for another, you can move some money from one period to another by using less than 4 percent of your investments in one period and by using more than 4 percent in another. You may plan to use your investments at a faster rate than the 4 percent, knowing that if your income later becomes inadequate you can get a mortgage on your house or sell it to provide funds for living expenses.

FACTORS FOR WORKSHEET 4

Years to Retirement	Factor A[1]	Factor B[2]	Factor C[3]
1	0.952	1.040	1.020
2	0.907	1.082	2.081
3	0.864	1.125	3.184
4	0.823	1.170	4.331
5	0.784	1.217	5.525
6	0.746	1.265	6.766
7	0.711	1.316	8.056
8	0.677	1.369	9.399
9	0.645	1.423	10.794
10	0.614	1.480	12.246
11	0.585	1.539	13.756
12	0.557	1.601	15.326
13	0.530	1.665	16.959
14	0.505	1.732	18.658
15	0.481	1.801	20.424

Years to Retirement	Factor A[1]	Factor B[2]	Factor C[3]
16	0.458	1.873	22.261
17	0.436	1.948	24.171
18	0.416	2.026	26.158
19	0.396	2.107	28.225
20	0.377	2.191	30.374
21	0.359	2.279	32.609
22	0.342	2.370	34.933
23	0.326	2.465	37.350
24	0.310	2.563	39.864
25	0.205	2.666	42.479
26	0.281	2.772	45.198
27	0.268	2.883	48.026
28	0.255	2.999	50.967
29	0.243	3.119	54.026
30	0.231	3.243	57.207
31	0.220	3.373	60.515
32	0.210	3.508	63.955
33	0.200	3.648	67.534
34	0.190	3.794	71.255
35	0.181	3.946	75.125
36	0.173	4.104	79.150
37	0.164	4.268	83.336
38	0.157	4.439	87.690
39	0.149	4.616	92.217
40	0.142	4.801	96.926

[1]The present worth of $1 payable at the future retirement date, discounted at 5 percent per year as an estimate of inflation.
[2]The amount $1 invested today will grow to at the future retirement date, compounded at 4 percent to reflect the expected investment return in excess of the rate of inflation.
[3]The amount $1 invested each year until your retirement date will grow to at that date, compounded at 4 percent to reflect the expected investment return in excess of the rate of inflation.

WORKSHEET 5 *Life Insurance Versus a Joint-and-Survivor Annuity*

This worksheet helps you determine whether you are better off taking an insurance policy or a joint-and-survivor annuity from your pension. The example provided will guide you through the calculations.

	Example		Your Situation	
	Monthly	Annual	Monthly	Annual
Amount of monthly pension to employee (life annuity)	$1,000	$12,000	$_____	$_____
Amount of monthly pension to employee (50 percent joint-and-survivor)	$900	$10,800	$_____	$_____
Amount of monthly pension to spouse (50 percent joint-and-survivor)	$450	$5,400	$_____	$_____

STEP 1. Find the difference between your annual pension if you take a life annuity or if you take a joint-and-survivor annuity. In our example, the difference is $1,200 ($12,000 – $10,800 = $1,200).

STEP 2. Ask your insurance agent how large a policy you can buy with the difference. (You should compare several companies.) Enter the amounts below. (The agent will probably try to sell you whole life or universal life, arguing that term insurance premiums are too expensive at your age. Note, however, that whole life premiums aren't exactly low cost.) In our example, we have assumed the $1,200 buys a $20,000 whole life policy.

Example	Company A	Company B	Company C
$20,000	$______	$______	$______

STEP 3. How large an annuity guaranteed for your spouse's life does the face amount of the policy buy? Ask the agent. (You are converting the policy into monthly payments for your spouse.) Use the annuity rates for your spouse's sex and age at retirement and enter the amounts below. In our example, the $20,000 death benefit could be converted into a life annuity paying $200 a month.

Example	Company A	Company B	Company C
$200	$______	$______	$______

STEP 4. Compare these amounts to the amount of monthly income your spouse receives if you take the joint-and-survivor annuity. In this example, the joint-and-survivor annuity pays $450 a month. Obviously, if the insurance buys less monthly income than the joint-and-survivor annuity, which often is the case, the joint-and-survivor option is the better buy.

WORKSHEET 6 *Medicare-Supplement Policy Checklist*

Use this worksheet to compare Medicare-supplement policies.

Plan Type	Company	Annual Premium	Preexisting Conditions: Look-Back	Preexisting Conditions: Waiting Period	Automatic Claims Handling	Underwriting Requirements
PLAN A						
PLAN A						
PLAN A						
PLAN B						
PLAN B						
PLAN B						
PLAN C						
PLAN C						
PLAN C						
PLAN D						
PLAN D						
PLAN D						

PLAN E
PLAN E
PLAN E

PLAN F
PLAN F
PLAN F

PLAN G
PLAN G
PLAN G

PLAN H
PLAN H
PLAN H

PLAN I
PLAN I
PLAN I

PLAN J
PLAN J
PLAN J

WORKSHEET 7 *Long-Term-Care Policy Checklist*

Use this worksheet to help compare features of a long-term-care policy. The example shows what kinds of information should be included.

	Example	Policy 1	Policy 2	Policy 3
COMPANY	Equitable Life and Casualty			
POLICY NAME	Equicare			
DAILY BENEFITS FOR				
Skilled-nursing care	actual expense up to $75/day			
Intermediate care	same			
Custodial care	same			
Percentage of eligible charges paid	100			
Home care	$75			
Other noninstitutional care	none			
MAXIMUM BENEFITS				
Number of years for nursing home benefits	4 years			

Number of years for home-care benefits	2 years			
Total lifetime benefits	$300,000			
ELIMINATION PERIOD	0 days			
GATEKEEPER (BENEFIT TRIGGER)				
Medical necessity	no			
Doctor certification	yes			
Activities of daily living	no			
Number of ADLs needed	N/A			
Are ADLs specifically defined?	N/A			
Prior hospital confinement required	no			
RESTRICTIONS ON FACILITIES	must be state licensed			
PREEXISTING CONDITIONS				
Look-back period	none			
Months before coverage starts	none			

WORKSHEET 7 *Long-Term-Care Policy Checklist* (continued)

	Example	Policy 1	Policy 2	Policy 3
INFLATION PROTECTION				
Amount of increase	5% per year based on initial age			
Compound or simple	simple			
Maximum benefit for nursing care	$150			
Maximum benefit for home care	$150			
Additional premium required each year	yes			
HOME-CARE BENEFITS				
Skilled care	yes			
Intermediate care	yes			
Custodial care	yes			
Homemaker, chore worker, or companion	yes			

Is care allowed in places other than your home?	yes			
OTHER FEATURES				
Nonforfeiture benefit	no			
Waiver of premium	after 90 days			
ANNUAL PREMIUM				
Without inflation protection	$675*			
With inflation protection	$775 1st year*† $813.75 2d year			

*1991 annual premium for a person age 65.
†Premium increases annually—ask for a 10-year premium schedule.

WORKSHEET 8 *What You'll Pay Annually for Health Insurance*

In this worksheet, fill in your annual premiums for a Medicare-supplement policy, any coverage from your former employer, and coverage from a long-term-care policy. Then total how much you spend on these items. If you are paying premiums for a spouse, make a copy of the worksheet and fill in the same information for him or her. Take these totals into consideration as you plan your postretirement budget.

	1992	1993	1994	1995
Medicare Part A	0*	0	0	0
Medicare Part B	$381.60	$439.20	$493.20	$553.20
Medicare-supplement policy	______	______	______	______
Employer-provided coverage	______	______	______	______
Long-term-care policy	______	______	______	______
Total	______	______	______	______

*Assumes you are not required to pay Part A premiums.

WORKSHEET 9 *Taking Stock of Your Assets and Liabilities*

Date: ________

Use this worksheet as you begin to do your estate planning.

		YOU	YOUR SPOUSE	JOINTLY
A. Real estate and residential property	1. Residence	________	________	________
	(Less mortgage, including home equity loans)	________	________	________
	Net equity	________	________	________
	Other	________	________	________
	(Less mortgage)	________	________	________
	Net equity	________	________	________
B. Investments	2. Stocks and bonds	________	________	________
	3. Closely held or controlled companies	________	________	________
	4. Other business interests and investments	________	________	________
C. Cash	5.	________	________	________
D. Life insurance	6.	________	________	________
E. Personal and household goods	7. Jewelry and furs	________	________	________
	8. Paintings and antiques	________	________	________
	9. Automobiles	________	________	________
	10. Other	________	________	________

WORKSHEET 9 *Taking Stock of Your Assets and Liabilities* (Continued)

		YOU	YOUR SPOUSE	JOINTLY
F. Amounts owed to you	11.	______	______	______
G. Inheritance and trusts	12. Potential inheritance	______	______	______
	13. Interests in trust	______	______	______
H. Retirement benefits	14. Pension	______	______	______
	15. Profit-sharing	______	______	______
	16. IRA	______	______	______
	17. Keogh	______	______	______
	18. 401(k)	______	______	______
	19. Other	______	______	______
I. Miscellaneous	20.	______	______	______
J. Total assets	21.	______	______	______
K. Liabilities (excluding mortgages listed in A)	22.	______	______	______
L. Value of your estate (assets minus liabilities)	23.	______	______	______

INSTRUCTIONS AND EXPLANATION FOR WORKSHEET 9

To begin your estate planning, first estimate its current value and what will be left for your beneficiaries after liabilities and taxes.

For many of the categories, such as investments and life insurance, you may need to assemble the figures on a separate sheet or on Worksheet 2 and transfer the totals to this worksheet.

Although the worksheet is generally self-explanatory, note the points that follow. Each item should be put in the proper column, depending on whether it is owned by you or your spouse or jointly.

A.1. For each residence or other real property, note the current fair market value (generally the price a willing buyer would pay a willing seller), the approximate amount due on your mortgage, and your net equity (value less mortgage).

B.2. List the approximate total value of publicly traded stocks, bonds, and mutual funds. You can obtain the values from your brokerage statement or the stock pages of a newspaper.

B.3. If you are a stockholder or partner in a family business or other company that is not publicly traded, indicate the value of your interest here. Although the value of your interest may be hard to determine precisely, you probably have some notion of what the company could be sold for. If not, you can most likely arrive at an appropriate value by referring to the company's book value (generally the net worth shown on your business's books or balance sheet), by using a multiple of earnings appropriate for the type of business, or by comparing your company with similar businesses.

Your interest in a closely held business may be the largest asset in your estate.

B.4. List your investments in partnerships, limited partnerships, joint ventures, and the like. Such investments, too, may be difficult to value, since there is generally no market for them. Your cost may be the only realistic value.

C.5. List the amount of your cash and other liquid assets, including items such as money-market accounts, Treasury securities, certificates of deposit, and checking accounts.

D.6. List the total amount of life insurance that you own or control. On a separate schedule, list each policy, showing the company name, policy number, owner, name of beneficiary, face value, and amount of loans against the policy. A policy owned by your spouse, your child, or some other person is not considered part of your estate for tax purposes but will be among your liquid assets available to the person who collects the proceeds.

E.7–10. List the approximate total value of your personal and household possessions. Note that since personal and household possessions of a married couple are not registered in anyone's name, their ownership may be difficult to establish if one spouse dies. Ownership may ultimately be determined by establishing who originally paid for a particular item or who insured it.

F.11. Enter the value of any notes or other amounts that are payable to you. Do not include loans that are uncollectible.

G.12–13. If you expect to inherit from your parents or anyone else, or if you have an interest in a trust that will become part of your taxable estate, indicate the figures here. If your only trust interest is the right to receive income for life, and if principal may be invaded only by a trustee but not by you, the trust assets are probably not taxable in your estate.

H.14–19. List the benefits that would be payable upon your death from pension, profit-sharing, or other qualified plans, IRAs, Keogh accounts, 401(k) plans, or other types of deferred compensation or employment benefits. It may be necessary to obtain this information from the plan administrator where you work. Retirement benefits are one type of asset that may be subject to both estate *and* income taxes.

I.20. List any assets not shown above.

J.21. Total the figures in each column.

K.22. List any substantial amounts you owe. You might include balances due on personal loans and substantial credit card balances.

L.23. Subtract your liabilities from your assets to arrive at the approximate value of your estate.

WORKSHEET 10 *List of Probate and Nonprobate Assets*

Use this worksheet to help with your estate planning.

PROBATE ASSETS	NONPROBATE ASSETS

APPENDIX B

STATE AGENCIES ON AGING

ALABAMA
Commission on Aging
136 Catoma Street
Montgomery, AL 36130
(205) 261-5743
(800) 243-5463
(toll-free in Alabama)

ALASKA
Older Alaskans Commission
P.O. Box C
Juneau, AK 99811-0209
(907) 465-3250

AMERICAN SAMOA
Territorial Administration on Aging
Government of American Samoa
Pago Pago, AS 96799
011 (684) 633-1251

ARIZONA
Aging and Adult Administration
1400 West Washington, 950A
Phoenix, AZ 85007
(602) 255-4446
(602) 255-3323 (TDD)

ARKANSAS
Office of Aging and Adult Services
Department of Human Services
P.O. Box 1437
Little Rock, AR 72203-1437
(501) 682-2441

CALIFORNIA
Department of Aging
1600 K Street
Sacramento, CA 95814
(916) 322-5290
(916) 323-8913 (TDD)

COLORADO
Aging and Adult Services Division
Department of Social Services
1575 Sherman Street
10th Floor
Denver, CO 80203-1714
(303) 294-5912

CONNECTICUT
Department of Aging
175 Main Street
Hartford, CT 06106
(203) 566-3238
(800) 443-9946
(toll-free voice/TDD in CT)

DELAWARE
Department of Health and Social Services
Division of Aging
1901 North DuPont Highway
New Castle, DE 19720
(302) 421-6791
(800) 223-9074
(toll-free in DE)

DISTRICT OF COLUMBIA
D.C. Office on Aging
1424 K Street, N.W.
2d Floor
Washington, DC 20005
(202) 724-5623

FLORIDA
Aging and Adult Services
1321 Winewood Boulevard

Room 323
Tallahassee, FL 32399-0700
(904) 488-2650

GEORGIA
Office of Aging
878 Peachtree Street, N.E.
Suite 632
Atlanta, GA 30309
(404) 894-5333

GUAM
Office of Aging
Government of Guam
P.O. Box 2816
Agana, GU 96910
011 (671) 734-2942

HAWAII
Executive Office on Aging
335 Merchant Street
Room 241
Honolulu, HI 96813
(808) 548-2593

IDAHO
Idaho Office on Aging
Statehouse, Room 108
Boise, ID 83720
(208) 334-3833

ILLINOIS
Department on Aging
421 East Capitol Avenue
Springfield, IL 62701
(217) 785-2870
(800) 252-8966
(toll-free voice/TDD nationwide)

INDIANA
Aging Division
Department of Human Services
P.O. Box 7083
Indianapolis, IN 46207-7083
(317) 232-7020
(800) 622-4972
(toll-free in IN)

IOWA
Department of Elder Affairs
914 Grand Avenue, Suite 236
Des Moines, IA 50319
(515) 281-5187
(800) 532-3213
(toll-free in IA)

KANSAS
Department on Aging
Docking State Office Building
122 South
915 Southwest Harrison Street
Topeka, KS 66612-1500
(913) 296-4986
(800) 432-3535
(toll-free in KS)

KENTUCKY
Division for Aging Services
Department for Social Services
275 East Main Street
6th Floor West
Frankfort, KY 40621
(502) 564-6930
(502) 564-5497 (TDD)
(800) 372-2991
(toll-free in KY)
(800) 372-2973
(toll-free TDD in KY)

LOUISIANA
Governor's Office of Elder Affairs
P.O. Box 80374
Baton Rouge, LA 70898
(504) 925-1700

MAINE
Bureau of Maine's Elderly
Statehouse, Station 11
Augusta, ME 04333-0011
(207) 289-2561

MARYLAND
Office on Aging
301 West Preston Street
10th Floor
Baltimore, MD 21201
(301) 225-1100
(301) 383-7555 (TDD)
(800) 243-3425
(toll-free in MD)

MASSACHUSETTS
Executive Office of Elder Affairs
38 Chauncy Street, 2d Floor
Boston, MA 02111
(617) 727-7750
(800) 882-2003
(toll-free in MA)
(800) 872-0166
(toll-free TDD in MA)

MICHIGAN
Office of Services to the Aging
P.O. Box 30026
Lansing, MI 48909
(517) 373-8230

MINNESOTA
Minnesota Board on Aging
444 Lafayette Road
St. Paul, MN 55155-3843
(800) 652-9747
(toll-free in MN)

MISSISSIPPI
Division of Aging and Adult Services
421 West Pascagoula Street
Jackson, MS 39201
(601) 949-2070
(800) 222-7622
(toll-free in MS)

MISSOURI
Division of Aging
P.O. Box 1337
Jefferson City, MO 65102
(314) 751-3082
(800) 392-0210
(toll-free in MO)

MONTANA
Aging Services Bureau
Department of Family Services
P.O. Box 8005
Helena, MT 59604
(406) 444-5900
(800) 332-2272
(toll-free in MT)

NEBRASKA
Nebraska Department on Aging
State Office Building
P.O. Box 95044
Lincoln, NE 68509
(402) 471-2306

NEVADA
Division of Aging Services
Department for Human Resources
505 East King Street, Room 101
Carson City, NV 89710
(702) 885-4210 (voice/TDD)

NEW HAMPSHIRE
Division of Elderly and Adult Services
6 Hazen Drive
Concord, NH 03301
(603) 271-4680
(800) 351-1888
(toll-free in NH)

NEW JERSEY
Division on Aging
Department of Community Affairs
101 South Broad Street, CN 807
Trenton, NJ 08625
(609) 292-4833

(800) 792-8820
(toll-free in NJ)

NEW MEXICO
State Agency on Aging
224 East Palace Avenue
4th Floor
Santa Fe, NM 87501
(505) 827-7640 (voice/TDD)
(800) 432-2080
(toll-free in NM)

NEW YORK
New York State Office for the Aging
Agency Building 2, ESP
Albany, NY 12223
(518) 474-5731
(800) 342-9871
(toll-free in NY)

NORTH CAROLINA
Division of Aging
Department of Human Resources
1985 Umstead Drive
Raleigh, NC 27603
(919) 733-3983
(800) 662-7030
(toll-free voice/TDD in NC)

NORTH DAKOTA
Aging Services
Department of Human Services
600 East Boulevard
Bismarck, ND 58505
(701) 224-2310
(701) 224-2699 (TDD)
(800) 472-2622
(toll-free in ND)

OHIO
Ohio Department of Aging
50 West Broad Street, 9th Floor
Columbus, OH 43266-0501
(614) 466-5500
(614) 466-6191 (TDD)

OKLAHOMA
Special Unit on Aging
P.O. Box 25352
Oklahoma City, OK 73125
(405) 521-2281
(405) 521-2827 (TDD)

OREGON
Senior Services Division
Department of Human Resources
State of Oregon
313 Public Service Building
Salem, OR 97310
(503) 378-4728
(800) 232-3020
(toll-free voice/TDD in OR)

PENNSYLVANIA
Department of Aging
231 State Street
Harrisburg, PA 17101
(717) 783-1549

PUERTO RICO
Office of Elder Affairs
Call Box 50063
Old San Juan Station
San Juan, PR 00902
(809) 721-0753

RHODE ISLAND
Department of Elderly Affairs
160 Pine Street
Providence, RI 02903
(401) 277-2880 (voice/TDD)
(800) 322-2880
(toll-free in RI)

SOUTH CAROLINA
Commission on Aging
915 Main Street
Columbia, SC 29201
(803) 734-3203

SOUTH DAKOTA
Office of Adult Services and Aging
700 Governors Drive
Pierre, SD 57501
(605) 773-3656

TENNESSEE
Commission on Aging
706 Church Street
Suite 201
Nashville, TN 37219
(615) 741-2056

TEXAS
Texas Department on Aging
P.O. Box 12786, Capitol Station
Austin, TX 78711
(512) 444-2727 (voice/TDD)
(800) 252-9240
(toll-free in TX)

UTAH
Division of Aging and Adult Services
P.O. Box 45500
Salt Lake City, UT 84145-0500
(801) 538-3910

VERMONT
Department of Rehabilitation and Aging
103 South Main Street
Waterbury, VT 05676
(802) 241-2400

VIRGIN ISLANDS
Department of Human Services
Barbel Plaza South
Charlotte Amalie
St. Thomas, VI 00802
(809) 774-0930

VIRGINIA
Department for the Aging
700 East Franklin Street
10th Floor
Richmond, VA 23219
(804) 225-2271 (voice/TDD)
(800) 552-4464
(toll-free in VA)

WASHINGTON
Aging and Adult Services Administration
OB-44A
Olympia, WA 98504
(206) 753-2502
(206) 753-4927 (TDD)
(800) 422-3263
(toll-free in WA)

WEST VIRGINIA
Commission on Aging
State Capitol
Charleston, WV 25305
(304) 348-3317
(800) 642-3671
(toll-free in WV)

WISCONSIN
Bureau on Aging
P.O. Box 7851
Madison, WI 53707
(608) 266-2536

WYOMING
Commission on Aging
Hathaway Building
Cheyenne, WY 82002
(307) 777-7986
(800) 442-2766
(toll-free in WY)

APPENDIX C

STATES WITH HIGH-RISK HEALTH INSURANCE POOLS

CALIFORNIA
Executive Director
Major Risk Medical Insurance Program
744 P Street, Room 1077
Sacramento, CA 95814
(916) 324-4695

COLORADO
Colorado Uninsurable Health Insurance Plan (CUHIP)
Division of Insurance
303 West Colfax, Suite 500
Denver, CO 80204
(303) 866-6425

CONNECTICUT
Health Reinsurance Association
One Tower Square
4 NB
Hartford, CT 06183-6130
(203) 527-5369

FLORIDA
Administrator—SCHA
Mutual of Omaha Insurance Co.
P.O. Box 31276
Omaha, NE 68131
(800) 422-8559

GEORGIA
Georgia High-Risk Health Insurance Plan
State of Georgia
708 West Tower
Floyd Memorial Building
Atlanta, GA 30334
(404) 656-6054

ILLINOIS
Illinois Comprehensive Health Insurance Program
400 West Monroe Street
Suite 202
Springfield, IL 62704
(217) 456-0224

INDIANA
Blue Cross/Blue Shield of Indiana
Associated Insurance Companies, Inc.
P.O. Box 40438
Indianapolis, IN 46240
(317) 581-1005
(800) 552-7921

IOWA
Administrator—ICHIA
Mutual of Omaha Insurance Co.
P.O. Box 31746
Omaha, NE 68131
(800) 445-8603

LOUISIANA
Louisiana Health Insurance Association
7904 Wrenwood Blvd., Suite D
Baton Rouge, LA 70809
(504) 926-6245

MAINE
Mutual of Omaha Insurance Co.
P.O. Box 31276
Omaha, NE 68131
(800) 456-0224

MINNESOTA
Minnesota Comprehensive Health Association
P.O. Box 64566
St. Paul, MN 55164
(612) 456-5290

MISSOURI
Missouri Health Insurance Plan (MHIP)
Missouri Health Insurance Pool
4444 Forest Park Boulevard
Suite 642
St. Louis, MO 63108
(314) 658-4818

MONTANA
Montana Comprehensive Health Association
Blue Cross/Blue Shield of Montana
404 Fuller Avenue
P.O. Box 4309
Helena, MT 59604
(406) 444-8200

NEBRASKA
Blue Cross/Blue Shield of Nebraska
P.O. Box 3248
Omaha, NE 68180-0001
(402) 390-1814

NEW MEXICO
Vice President, Claims
Blue Cross/Blue Shield of New Mexico
12800 Indian School Road, N.E.
Albuquerque, NM 87112
(505) 292-2600

NORTH DAKOTA
Blue Cross/Blue Shield of North Dakota
4510 13th Avenue, S.W.
Fargo, ND 58121-0001
(701) 282-1100
(800) 342-4718

OREGON
Blue Cross/Blue Shield of Oregon
P.O. Box 1271
Portland, OR 97207
(503) 220-6363
(800) 777-3168

SOUTH CAROLINA
Blue Cross/Blue Shield of South Carolina
P.O. Box 61173
Columbia, SC 29260
(803) 736-0043
(800) 868-2503

TENNESSEE
Blue Cross/Blue Shield of Tennessee
P.O. Box 6249
Chattanooga, TN 37401-6249
(615) 755-6210

TEXAS
Blue Cross/Blue Shield of Texas
P.O. Box 655082
Dallas, TX 75265-5082
(800) 338-2227
(214) 669-3926

UTAH
Utah Comprehensive Health Insurance Pool (CHIP)
2265 South 1300 West
Suite B
Salt Lake City, UT 84119
(801) 973-9741

WASHINGTON
Mutual of Omaha Insurance Co.

P.O. Box 31726
Omaha, NE 68131
(800) 456-0224

WISCONSIN
Administrator—HIRSP
Mutual of Omaha Insurance Co.
P.O. Box 31746
Omaha, NE 68131-0746
(800) 228-7044

WYOMING
Blue Cross/Blue Shield of Wyoming
Box 2266
Cheyenne, WY 82001
(307) 634-1393

APPENDIX D

STATE INSURANCE COUNSELING PROGRAMS

CALIFORNIA
Health Insurance Counseling & Advocacy Programs (HICAP)
1600 K Street
Sacramento, CA 95814
(916) 323-7315

IDAHO
Senior Health Insurance Benefits Advisors (SHIBA)
Idaho Department of Insurance
500 South 10th Street
Boise, ID 83720
(208) 334-2250

ILLINOIS
Senior Health Insurance Program (SHIP)
Illinois Department of Insurance
320 West Washington Street
Springfield, IL 62767
(217) 782-0004

IOWA
PACT: Protection and Advocacy Through Community Training
Iowa Insurance Division
Lucas State Office Building
Sixth Floor
Des Moines, IA 50319
(515) 242-5190

MARYLAND
Maryland Office on Aging
301 West Preston Street
Baltimore, MD 21201
(301) 225-1270

MASSACHUSETTS
Serving Health Information Needs of Elders (SHINE)
Executive Office of Elder Affairs
38 Chauncey Street
Boston, MA 02111
(617) 727-7750

NEW JERSEY
Senior Health Insurance Program (SHIP)
Department of Community Affairs
Division on Aging
CN 807
Trenton, NJ 08625
(609) 292-4303

NEW MEXICO
Health Insurance Benefits Assistance Program (HIBAC)
New Mexico Agency on Aging
224 East Palace Avenue
Fourth Floor
Santa Fe, NM 87501
(505) 827-7640

NORTH CAROLINA
Senior Health Insurance Information Program (SHIIP)
Department of Insurance
P.O. Box 26387
Raleigh, NC 27611
(919) 733-0433

OHIO (Pilot Program)
Office of Attorney General
Health, Education and Human Services Section
State Office Tower

30 East Broad Street
Columbus, OH 43215
(614) 466-8600

WASHINGTON
Senior Health Insurance Benefits Advisors (SHIBA)
Department of Insurance
Building AQ
Olympia, WA 98504
(206) 753-2408

WISCONSIN
Wisconsin Bureau on Aging
1 West Wilson Street
P.O. Box 7851
Madison, WI 53707
(608) 266-2568

APPENDIX E

STATE INSURANCE REGULATORS

ALABAMA
135 S. Union Street, #181
Montgomery, AL 36104-3401
(205) 269-3550

ALASKA
P.O. Box D
Juneau, AK 99811-0800
(907) 465-2515

ARIZONA
3030 North Third Street
Suite 100
Phoenix, AZ 85012
(602) 255-5400

ARKANSAS
400 University Tower Building
12th and University Street
Little Rock, AR 72204
(501) 686-2900

CALIFORNIA
3450 Wilshire Boulevard, #201
Los Angeles, CA 90010
(213) 736-2572

COLORADO
303 W. Colfax Avenue, Suite 500
Denver, CO 80204
(303) 866-6400

CONNECTICUT
P.O. Box 816
Hartford, CT 06142-0816
(203) 297-3800

DELAWARE
841 Silver Lake Boulevard
Dover, DE 19901
(302) 739-4251

DISTRICT OF COLUMBIA
613 G Street, N.W.
6th Floor
Washington, DC 20001
(202) 727-7424

FLORIDA
State Capitol
Plaza Level Eleven
Tallahassee, FL 32399-0300
(904) 822-3100

GEORGIA
2 Martin L. King Jr. Drive
Floyd Memorial Building
704 W. Tower
Atlanta, GA 30334
(404) 656-2056

HAWAII
1010 Richards Street
Honolulu, HI 96813
(808) 586-2790

IDAHO
500 South 10th Street
Boise, ID 83720
(208) 334-2250

ILLINOIS
320 W. Washington Street
4th Floor
Springfield, IL 62767
(217) 782-4515

INDIANA
311 W. Washington Street
Suite 300

Indianapolis, IN 46204-2787
(317) 232-2385

IOWA
Lucas State Office Building
6th Floor
Des Moines, IA 50319
(515) 281-5705

KANSAS
420 S.W. 9th Street
Topeka, KS 66612
(913) 296-7801

KENTUCKY
229 W. Main Street
Frankfort, KY 40602
(502) 564-3630

LOUISIANA
P.O. Box 44214
Baton Rouge, LA 70804
(504) 342-5900
or
950 North 5th Street
Baton Rouge, LA 70801-9214

MAINE
State Office Building
State House, Station 34
Augusta, ME 04333
(207) 582-8707

MARYLAND
501 St. Paul Place
Stanbalt Building
6th Floor South
Baltimore, MD 21202
(301) 333-6300

MASSACHUSETTS
280 Friend Street
Boston, MA 02114
(617) 727-7189

MICHIGAN
611 W. Ottawa Street
2nd Floor North
Lansing, MI 48933
(517) 373-9273

MINNESOTA
133 East 7th Street
St. Paul, MN 55101
(612) 296-6848

MISSISSIPPI
1804 Walter Sillers Building
P.O. Box 79
Jackson, MS 39205
(601) 359-3569

MISSOURI
301 W. High Street, Room 630
P.O. Box 690
Jefferson City, MO 65102-0690
(314) 751-4126

MONTANA
126 N. Sanders
Mitchell Building, Room 270
P.O. Box 4009
Helena, MT 59601
(406) 444-2040

NEBRASKA
Terminal Building
941 O Street, Suite 400
Lincoln, NE 68508
(402) 471-2201

NEVADA
1665 Hot Springs Road
Carson City, NV 89710
(702) 687-4270

NEW HAMPSHIRE
169 Manchester Street
P.O. Box 2005

Concord, NH 03301
(603) 271-2261

NEW JERSEY
20 West State Street, CN 325
Trenton, NJ 08625
(609) 292-5363

NEW MEXICO
PERA Building
P.O. Box Drawer 1269
Santa Fe, NM 87504-1269
(505) 827-4500

NEW YORK
160 W. Broadway
New York, NY 10013
(212) 602-0429

NORTH CAROLINA
Dobbs Building
430 N. Salisbury Street
P.O. Box 26387
Raleigh, NC 27611
(919) 733-7343

NORTH DAKOTA
Capitol Building, 5th Floor
600 E. Boulevard Avenue
Bismarck, ND 58505
(701) 224-2440

OHIO
2100 Stella Court
Columbus, OH 43266-0566
(614) 644-2658

OKLAHOMA
P.O. Box 53408
Oklahoma City, OK 73152-3408
(405) 521-2828
or
1901 North Walnut
Oklahoma City, OK 73105

OREGON
440 Labor and Industries Building
Salem, OR 97310
(503) 378-4271

PENNSYLVANIA
Strawberry Square
13th Floor
Harrisburg, PA 17120
(717) 787-5173

RHODE ISLAND
233 Richmond Street
Suite 237
Providence, RI 02903
(401) 277-2223

SOUTH CAROLINA
1612 Marion Street
P.O. Box 100105
Columbia, SC 29202-3105
(803) 737-6160

SOUTH DAKOTA
Insurance Building
910 E. Sioux Avenue
Pierre, SD 57501-3940
(605) 773-3563

TENNESSEE
500 James Robertson Parkway
Volunteer Plaza
Nashville, TN 37243-0565
(615) 741-2241

TEXAS
333 Guadalupe Street
Austin, TX 78714-9104
(512) 463-6468

UTAH
State Office Building, Room 3110
Salt Lake City, UT 84114-1201
(801) 538-3803

VERMONT
State Office Building
120 State Street
Montpelier, VT 05602
(802) 828-3301

VIRGINIA
1200 Jefferson Building
1220 Bank Street
P.O. Box 1157
Richmond, VA 23209
(804) 786-7691

WASHINGTON
Insurance Building AQ21
Olympia, WA 98504
(206) 753-7301

WEST VIRGINIA
2019 Washington Street, E
Charleston, WV 25305
(304) 348-3394

WISCONSIN
P.O. Box 7873
Madison, WI 53707-7873
(608) 266-3585

WYOMING
Herschler Building
122 West 25th Street
Cheyenne, WY 82002
(307) 777-7401

APPENDIX F

STATES THAT ALLOW LIVING WILLS AND HEALTH-CARE PROXIES

	LIVING WILL			HEALTH-CARE PROXY		
State	Statute	Form	Suggested Form	Statute	Form	Suggested Form
Alabama	X	X				
Alaska	X	X		X		X
Arizona	X	X		X		X
Arkansas	X		X	X		X
California	X	X		X		X
Colorado	X	X				
Connecticut	X	X		X		
Delaware	X			X		
D.C.	X	X		X		X
Florida	X		X	X		
Georgia	X	X		X	X	
Hawaii	X		X			
Idaho	X		X	X	X	
Illinois	X		X	X	X	
Indiana	X	X				
Iowa	X		X	X		X
Kansas	X	X		X	X	
Kentucky	X	*				
Louisiana	X		X	X		
Maine	X		X			
Maryland	X	X				
Massachusetts	X			X		
Michigan	X			X	*	
Minnesota	X		X	X		X
Mississippi	X	X		X	X	
Missouri	X		X	X		
Montana	X		X	X		
Nebraska						
Nevada	X	X		X	X	
New Hampshire	X		X	X	X	

State	LIVING WILL			HEALTH-CARE PROXY		
	Statute	Form	Suggested Form	Statute	Form	Suggested Form
New Jersey	X			X		
New Mexico	X					
New York	X		X	X		X
North Carolina	X	X		X		X
North Dakota	X			X	*	
Ohio	X			X		
Oklahoma	X	X				
Oregon	X	X		X	X	
Pennsylvania	X			X	X	
Rhode Island	X			X	X	
South Carolina	X	X				
South Dakota	X	*		X		
Tennessee	X		X	X		
Texas	X		X	X	X	
Utah	X	X		X	X	
Vermont	X		X	X	X	
Virginia	X		X	X	*	
Washington	X	X		X		
West Virginia	X	X		X	X	
Wisconsin	X	X		X	X	
Wyoming	X		X	X		

*Because this state's law was passed so recently, it is not yet clear whether there is a required form.

APPENDIX G

ORGAN DONOR ORGANIZATIONS

Kidney Foundation of New York, Inc.
1250 Broadway, Suite 2001
New York, NY 10001
(212) 629-9770

Eye Bank for Sight Restoration, Inc.
210 E. 64 Street
New York, NY 10021
(212) 980-6700

Living Bank
4545 Post Oak Place, Suite 315
Houston, TX 77027
(713) 528-2971
Mailing address:
P.O. Box 6725
Houston, TX 77265

Medic Alert
2323 Colorado Avenue
Turlock, CA 95380
(209) 668-3333

National Kidney Foundation
30 E. 33 Street
New York, NY 10016
(212) 889-2210

You can also obtain a donor card from the Consumer Information Center, Pueblo, CO 81009, (719) 948-3334.

The following organizations accept donations of temporal (ear) bones:

Massachusetts Eye & Ear Infirmary
243 Charles Street
Boston, MA 02114
(617) 573-3700

National Temporal Bone Bank Center
University of Minnesota Medical Center
Harvard Street at E. River Road
Minneapolis, MN 55455
(612) 626-3000

APPENDIX H

DEPARTMENT OF HOUSING AND URBAN DEVELOPMENT (HUD) FIELD OFFICES

REGION I (Boston)

Boston Regional Office
Room 375
Thomas P. O'Neill, Jr. Federal Building
10 Causeway Street
Boston, MA 02222-1092

Commercial No. (617) 565-5234
FTS No. 835-5234

FIELD OFFICES

Bangor Office
First Floor
Casco Northern Bank Building
23 Main Street
Bangor, ME 04401-6394

Commercial No. (207) 945-0467
FTS No. 833-7427

Burlington Office
Room B-28
Federal Building
11 Elmwood Avenue
P.O. Box 879
Burlington, VT 05402-0879

Commercial No. (802) 951-6290
FTS No. 832-6290

Hartford Office
First Floor
330 Main Street
Hartford, CT 06106-1860

Commercial No. (203) 240-4523
FTS No. 244-4523

Manchester Office
Norris Cotton Federal Building
275 Chestnut Street
Manchester, NH 03101-2487

Commercial No. (603) 666-7681
FTS No. 834-7681

Providence Office
330 John O. Pastore Federal Building and U.S. Post Office—Kennedy Plaza
Providence, RI 02903-1785

Commercial No. (401) 528-5351
FTS No. 838-5351

REGION II (New York)

New York Regional Office
26 Federal Plaza
New York, NY 10278-0068

Commercial No. (212) 264-6500
FTS No. 264-6500

FIELD OFFICES

Albany Office
Leo W. O'Brien Federal Building
N. Pearl Street and Clinton Avenue
Albany, NY 12207-2395

Commercial No. (518) 472-3567
FTS No. 562-3567

Buffalo Office
Fifth Floor
Lafayette Court
465 Main Street
Buffalo, NY 14203-1780

Commercial No. (716) 846-5755
FTS No. 437-5755

Camden Office
The Parkade Building
519 Federal Street
Camden, NJ 08103-9998

Commercial No. (609) 757-5081
FTS No. 488-5081

Newark Office
Military Park Building
60 Park Place
Newark, NJ 07102-5504

Commercial No. (201) 877-1662
FTS No. 349-1808

REGION III (Philadelphia)

Philadelphia Regional Office
Liberty Square Building
105 S. Seventh Street
Philadelphia, PA 19106-3392

Commercial No. (215) 597-2560
FTS No. 597-2560

FIELD OFFICES

Baltimore Office
Third Floor
The Equitable Building
10 N. Calvert Street
Baltimore, MD 21202-1865

Commercial No. (301) 962-2520
FTS No. 922-3047

Charleston Office
Suite 708
405 Capitol Street
Charleston, WV 25301-1795

Commercial No. (304) 347-7000
FTS No. 930-7036

Pittsburgh Office
412 Old Post Office Courthouse
7th Avenue and Grant Street
Pittsburgh, PA 15219-1906

Commercial No. (412) 644-6428
FTS No. 722-6388

Richmond Office
First Floor
The Federal Building
400 N. 8th Street
P.O. Box 10170
Richmond, VA 23240-0170

Commercial No. (804) 771-2721
FTS No. 925-2721

Washington, D.C., Office
820 First Street, N.E.
Washington, DC 20002-4205

Commercial No. (202) 275-8185
FTS No. 275-9206

Wilmington Office
Suite 850
824 Market Street
Wilmington, DE 19801-3016

Commercial No. (302) 573-6300
FTS No. 487-6300

REGION IV (Atlanta)

Atlanta Regional Office
Richard B. Russell Federal Building

75 Spring Street, S.W.
Atlanta, GA 30303-3388

Commercial No. (404) 331-5136
FTS No. 841-5136

FIELD OFFICES

Birmingham Office
Suite 300
Beacon Ridge Tower
600 Beacon Parkway, West
Birmingham, AL 35209-3144

Commercial No. (205) 731-1617
FTS No. 229-1617

Caribbean Office
New San Juan Office Building
159 Carlos Chardon Avenue
San Juan, PR 00918-1804

Commercial No. (809) 766-6121
FTS No. 498-5201

Columbia Office
Strom Thurmond Federal Building
1835-45 Assembly Street
Columbia, SC 29201-2480

Commercial No. (803) 765-5592
FTS No. 677-5592

Coral Gables Office
Gables 1 Tower
1320 S. Dixie Highway
Coral Gables, FL 33146-2911

Commercial No. (305) 662-4500
FTS No. 822-4510

Greensboro Office
415 N. Edgeworth Street
Greensboro, NC 27401-2107

Commercial No. (919) 333-5363
FTS No. 699-5363

Jackson Office
Suite 910
Doctor A. H. McCoy Federal Building
100 W. Capitol Street
Jackson, MS 39269-1096

Commercial No. (601) 965-5308
FTS No. 490-4738

Jacksonville Office
325 W. Adams Street
Jacksonville, FL 32202-4303

Commercial No. (904) 791-2626
FTS No. 946-2626

Knoxville Office
Third Floor
John J. Duncan Federal Building
710 Locust Street
Knoxville, TN 37902-2526

Commercial No. (615) 549-9384
FTS No. 854-9384

Louisville Office
601 West Broadway
P.O. Box 1044
Louisville, KY 40201-1044

Commercial No. (502) 582-5251
FTS No. 352-5251

Memphis Office
Suite 1200
One Memphis Place
200 Jefferson Avenue
Memphis, TN 38103-2335

Commercial No. (901) 544-3367
FTS No. 222-3367

Nashville Office
Suite 200
251 Cumberland Bend Drive
Nashville, TN 37228-1803

Commercial No. (615) 736-5213
FTS No. 852-5213

Orlando Office
Suite 270
Langley Building
3751 Maguire Boulevard
Orlando, FL 32803-3032

Commercial No. (407) 648-6441
FTS No. 820-6441

Tampa Office
Suite 700
Timberlake Federal Building Annex
501 E. Polk Street
Tampa, FL 33602-3945

Commercial No. (813) 228-2501
FTS No. 826-2504

REGION V (Chicago)

Chicago Regional Office
626 W. Jackson Boulevard
Chicago, IL 60606-5601

Commercial No. (312) 353-5680
FTS No. 353-5680

and

547 W. Jackson Boulevard
Chicago, IL 60606-5760

Commercial No. (312) 353-6236
FTS No. 353-6236

FIELD OFFICES

Cincinnati Office
Room 9002
Federal Office Building
550 Main Street
Cincinnati, OH 45202-3253

Commercial No. (513) 684-2884
FTS No. 684-2884

Cleveland Office
Room 420
One Playhouse Square
1375 Euclid Avenue
Cleveland, OH 44114-1670

Commercial No. (216) 522-4058
FTS No. 942-4065

Columbus Office
200 N. High Street
Columbus, OH 43215-2499

Commercial No. (614) 469-5737
FTS No. 943-7345

Detroit Office
Patrick V. McNamara Federal Building
477 Michigan Avenue
Detroit, MI 48226-2592

Commercial No. (313) 226-7900
FTS No. 226-7900

Flint Office
Room 200
605 N. Saginaw Street
Flint, MI 48502-1953

Commercial No. (313) 766-5112
FTS No. 378-5112

Grand Rapids Office
2922 Fuller Avenue, N.E.
Grand Rapids, MI 49505-3499

Commercial No. (616) 456-2100
FTS No. 372-2182

Indianapolis Office
151 N. Delaware Street
Indianapolis, IN 46204-2526

Commercial No. (317) 226-6303
FTS No. 331-6303

Milwaukee Office
Suite 1380
Henry S. Reuss Federal Plaza
310 W. Wisconsin Avenue
Milwaukee, WI 53203-2289

Commercial No. (414) 297-3214
FTS No. 362-1493

Minneapolis–St. Paul Office
220 Second Street, South
Minneapolis, MN 55401-2195

Commercial No. (612) 370-3000
FTS No. 333-3002

Springfield Office
Suite 206
509 W. Capitol Street
Springfield, IL 62704-1906

Commercial No. (217) 492-4085
FTS No. 955-4085

REGION VI (Fort Worth)

Fort Worth Regional Office
1600 Throckmorton
P.O. Box 2905
Fort Worth, TX 76113-2905

Commercial No. (817) 885-5401
FTS No. 728-5401

FIELD OFFICES

Albuquerque Office
625 Truman Street, N.E.
Albuquerque, NM 87110-6443

Commercial No. (505) 262-6463
FTS No. 474-6463

Dallas Office
Room 860
525 Griffin Street
Dallas, TX 75202-5007

Commercial No. (214) 767-8359
FTS No. 729-8300

Houston Office
Suite 200
Norfolk Tower
2211 Norfolk
Houston, TX 77098-4096

Commercial No. (713) 653-3274
FTS No. 522-3271

Little Rock Office
Suite 200
Lafayette Building
523 Louisiana Street
Little Rock, AR 72201-3707

Commercial No. (501) 378-5931
FTS No. 740-5401

Lubbock Office
Federal Office Building
1205 Texas Avenue
Lubbock, TX 79401-4093

Commercial No. (806) 743-7265
FTS No. 738-7265

New Orleans Office
Fisk Federal Building
1661 Canal Street
New Orleans, LA 70112-2887

Commercial No. (504) 589-7200
FTS No. 682-7200

Oklahoma City Office
Murrah Federal Building
200 N.W. Fifth Street
Oklahoma City, OK 73102-3202

Commercial No. (405) 231-4181
FTS No. 736-4891

San Antonio Office
Washington Square
800 Dolorosa
San Antonio, TX 78207-4563

Commercial No. (512) 229-6800
FTS No. 730-6806

Shreveport Office
Joe D. Waggoner Federal Building
500 Fannin Street
Shreveport, LA 71101-3077

Commercial No. (318) 226-5385
FTS No. 493-5385

Tulsa Office
Suite 110
Boston Place
1516 S. Boston Street
Tulsa, OK 74119-4032

Commercial No. (918) 581-7435
FTS No. 745-7435

REGION VII (Kansas City)

Kansas City Regional Office
Room 200
Gateway Tower II
400 State Avenue
Kansas City, KS 66101-2406

Commercial No. (913) 236-2162
FTS No. 757-2162

FIELD OFFICES

Des Moines Office
Room 239
Federal Building
210 Walnut Street
Des Moines, IA 50309-2155

Commercial No. (515) 284-4512
FTS No. 862-4512

Omaha Office
Braiker/Brandeis Building
210 S. 16 Street
Omaha, NE 68102-1622

Commercial No. (402) 221-3703
FTS No. 864-3703

St. Louis Office
Robert A. Young Federal Building
Third Floor
1222 Spruce Street
St. Louis, MO 63103-2836

Commercial No. (314) 539-6560
FTS No. 262-6560

REGION VIII (Denver)

Denver Regional Office
Executive Tower Building
1405 Curtis Street
Denver, CO 80202-2349

Commercial No. (303) 844-4513
FTS No. 564-4513

FIELD OFFICES

Casper Office
4225 Federal Office Building

100 East B Street
P.O. Box 580
Casper, WY 82602-1918

Commercial No. (307) 261-5252
FTS No. 328-5252

Fargo Office
Federal Building
653 Second Avenue North
P.O. Box 2483
Fargo, ND 58108-2483

Commercial No. (701) 239-5136
FTS No. 783-5136

Helena Office
Room 340
Federal Office Building, Drawer 10095
301 S. Park
Helena, MT 59626-0095

Commercial No. (406) 449-5205
FTS No. 585-5205

Salt Lake City Office
Suite 220
324 S. State Street
Salt Lake City, UT 84111-2321

Commercial No. (801) 524-5379
FTS No. 588-5241

Sioux Falls Office
Suite 116
"300" Building
300 N. Dakota Avenue
Sioux Falls, SD 57102-0311

Commercial No. (605) 330-4223
FTS No. 782-4223

REGION IX (San Francisco)

San Francisco Regional Office
Phillip Burton Federal Building and U.S. Courthouse
450 Golden Gate Avenue
P.O. Box 36003
San Francisco, CA 94102-3448

Commercial No. (415) 556-4752
FTS No. 556-4752

Indian Programs Office, Region IX
Suite 1650
2 Arizona Center
400 N. Fifth Street
Phoenix, AZ 85004-2361

Commercial No. (602) 379-4156
FTS No. 261-4156

FIELD OFFICES

Fresno Office
Suite 138
1630 E. Shaw Avenue
Fresno, CA 93710-8193

Commercial No. (209) 487-5033
FTS No. 467-5034

Honolulu Office
Prince Jonah Federal Building
300 Ala Moana Boulevard
P.O. Box 50007
Honolulu, HI 96850-4991

Commercial No. (808) 541-1323
FTS No. 551-1343

Las Vegas Office
Suite 205
1500 E. Tropicana Avenue
Las Vegas, NV 89119-6516

Commercial No. (702) 388-6500
FTS No. 598-6500

Los Angeles Office
1615 W. Olympic Boulevard
Los Angeles, CA 90015-3801

Commercial No. (213) 251-7122
FTS No. 983-7122

Phoenix Office
Suite 1600
2 Arizona Center
400 N. Fifth Street
P.O. Box 13468
Phoenix, AZ 85004-2361

Commercial No. (602) 379-4434
FTS No. 261-4434

Reno Office
1050 Bible Way
P.O. Box 4700
Reno, NV 89505-4700

Commercial No. (702) 784-5356
FTS No. 470-5356

Sacramento Office
Suite 200
777 Twelfth Street
Sacramento, CA 95814-1997

Commercial No. (916) 551-1351
FTS No. 460-1351

San Diego Office
Room 5-S-3
Federal Office Building
880 Front Street
San Diego, CA 92188-0100

Commercial No. (619) 557-5310
FTS No. 895-5310

Santa Ana Office
Box 12850
34 Civic Center Plaza
Santa Ana, CA 92712-2850

Commercial No. (714) 836-2451
FTS No. 799-2451

Tucson Office
Suite 410
100 N. Stone Avenue
Tucson, AZ 85701-1467

Commercial No. (602) 670-6237
FTS No. 762-5220

REGION X (Seattle)

Seattle Regional Office
Arcade Plaza Building
1321 Second Avenue
Seattle, WA 98101-2058

Commercial No. (206) 553-5414
FTS No. 399-5414

FIELD OFFICES

Anchorage Office
Federal Building—U.S. Courthouse
222 W. Eighth Avenue
#64
Anchorage, AK 99513-7537

Commercial No. (907) 271-4170
FTS No. 868-4170

Boise Office
Suite 220
Plaza IV
800 Park Boulevard
Boise, ID 83712-7743

Commercial No. (208) 334-1990
FTS No. 554-1990

Portland Office
520 Southwest Sixth Avenue
Portland, OR 97204-1596

Commercial No. (503) 326-2561
FTS No. 423-2561

Spokane Office
Eighth Floor East
Farm Credit Bank Building
West 601 First Avenue
Spokane, WA 99204-0317

Commercial No. (509) 353-2510
FTS No. 439-2510

APPENDIX I

STATES WITH PROPERTY TAX RELIEF PROGRAMS

State	Homestead Exemption or Credit	Deferral Program
Alabama	X	
Alaska	X	
Arizona	X	
Arkansas		
California	X	X
Colorado	X	X
Connecticut		
Delaware	X	
District of Columbia	X	X
Florida	X	X
Georgia	X	X
Hawaii	X	
Idaho	X	
Illinois	X	X
Indiana	X	
Iowa	X	X
Kansas		
Kentucky	X	
Louisiana	X	
Maine		X
Maryland		
Massachusetts	X	X
Michigan		X
Minnesota	X	
Mississippi	X	
Missouri		
Montana	X	
Nebraska	X	
Nevada		
New Hampshire	X	X
New Jersey	X	

State	Homestead Exemption or Credit	Deferral Program
New Mexico	X	
New York	X	
North Carolina	X	
North Dakota	X	X
Ohio	X	
Oklahoma	X	
Oregon		X
Pennsylvania		
Rhode Island		
South Carolina	X	
South Dakota		
Tennessee		X
Texas	X	X
Utah	X	X
Vermont		
Virginia		X
Washington	X	X
West Virginia	X	
Wisconsin	X	X
Wyoming	X	

APPENDIX J

NATIONAL SENIOR CITIZENS ORGANIZATIONS

A number of organizations represent senior citizens' interests in state legislatures and in Congress. Some of them also sell insurance and prescription drugs, and offer discounts on a variety of services. Look carefully at these organizations and decide which ones you want to represent you. If you consider buying insurance from any, be sure to compare their policies with those offered by regular insurance companies.

American Association of Retired Persons (AARP)
601 E Street, N.W.
Washington, DC 20049
(202) 434-2277

The AARP is a nonprofit membership organization dedicated to addressing the needs and interests of persons 50 and over. The organization aims to enhance the quality of life for all by promoting independence, dignity, and purpose.

The organization sponsors seminars and offers publications on a variety of topics of interest to seniors. The AARP also sells insurance, investments, and prescription drugs through the mail and through its walk-in pharmacy in Washington.

Gray Panthers
1424 16th Street, N.W., Suite 601
Washington, DC 20036
(202) 387-3111

The Gray Panthers is an activist organization involved in issues such as health care, age discrimination, and problems of the disabled. Local chapters conduct letter-writing campaigns, collect signatures for petitions, and contact elected representatives to discuss issues of concern to the organization. Members receive a quarterly journal.

National Alliance of Senior Citizens
1700 18th Street, N.W., Suite 401
Washington, DC 20009
(202) 986-0117

The National Alliance of Senior Citizens is a nonprofit lobbying organization that deals with such issues as Social Security, pensions, and health care. The organization aims to find private sector alternatives. It offers members benefits and services such as discounts on moving services, telephone services, and prescription drugs.

National Council of Senior Citizens
1331 F Street, N.W.
Washington, DC 20004
(202) 347-8800

The National Council of Senior Citizens is a nonprofit membership group that lobbies on behalf of senior citizens. It also offers a benefit package that includes various health-insurance policies, prescription drugs, and discounts from hotels, motels, and car-rental agencies. The organization also has a job-assistance program that helps seniors find jobs and offers training. Members receive a newspaper.

Older Women's League
730 11th Street, N.W., Suite 300
Washington, DC 20001
(202) 783-6686

The Older Women's League is an advocacy organization that works on behalf of middle-age and older women. It is concerned with such issues as health care, Social Security, housing, and workplace discrimination. Local chapters write letters, pay visits to elected officials, and sponsor workshops on topics of interest to older women. Members receive a monthly newsletter.

Index